# TEACHING IN THE POP CULTURE ZONE
## USING POPULAR CULTURE IN THE COMPOSITION CLASSROOM

ALLISON D. SMITH

TRIXIE G. SMITH

REBECCA BOBBITT

Editors

WADSWORTH
CENGAGE Learning

Australia • Brazil • Japan • Korea • Mexico • Singapore • Spain • United Kingdom • United States

**WADSWORTH**
CENGAGE Learning

For product information and technology assistance, contact us at **Cengage Learning Customer & Sales Support, 1-800-354-9706**

For permission to use material from this text or product, submit all requests online at **www.cengage.com/permissions** Further permissions questions can be emailed to **permissionrequest@cengage.com**

ISBN-13: 978-1-428-23101-6
ISBN-10: 1-428-23101-3

**Wadsworth**
25 Thomson Place
Boston, MA 02210
USA

Cengage Learning is a leading provider of customized learning solutions with office locations around the globe, including Singapore, the United Kingdom, Australia, Mexico, Brazil, and Japan. Locate your local office at: **international.cengage.com/region**

Cengage Learning products are represented in Canada by Nelson Education, Ltd.

For your course and learning solutions, visit **academic.cengage.com**

Purchase any of our products at your local college store or at our preferred online store **www.ichapters.com**

Cover images, left to right: (c) Michael Ochs Archive/Getty Images, (c) Yui Mok/PA Photos/Landov, (c) Adam Radosavljevic/Shutterstock, Inc., (c) Universal/The Kobal Collection/The Picture Desk, (c) ImageDJ/Index Open

Printed in the United States of America
1 2 3 4 5 6 7 11 10 09 08

# Contents

# Preface

## The Pop Culture Zone in the Composition Classroom

*Teaching in the Pop Culture Zone: Using Popular Culture in the Composition Classroom* is designed to be a resource for new teachers and for those newly interested in incorporating popular culture into their writing courses. Picking up on Mary Louise Pratt's pedagogical idea of the contact zone, we see popular culture as an effective way to create contact zones, as well as safe house communities, within the writing classroom.

We have diverse students who have experienced popular culture in myriad ways, providing the framework for a contact zone. Our students listen to different styles of music, enjoy a variety of television shows and films, and belong to various subcultures and familial groups. Even when they have watched or listened to the same pieces, they have experienced and analyzed them in unique ways. Their own experiences with popular culture allow them to "meet, clash, and grapple" with the texts and with each other—in class and in their writing. The sense of authority created in the safe house gives them the confidence to move into the contact zone and truly question each other as well as established authorities, even their own perceptions and interpretations of various events and/or media.

Popular culture is ubiquitous within American culture; it is something our students know, enjoy, and already critique. *Teaching in the Pop Culture Zone* enables us to address topics and interests that are not only familiar and relevant to our students, but also pleasurable for them. When students are given the opportunity to discuss and write about their own interests, and when their knowledge and opinions are given weight in assignments, students feel more comfortable with writing instruction and more confident in their own writing ability.

## The Essay Collection

Because popular culture encompasses a variety of media—including film, television, music, popular literature, folklore, and technology—using popular culture in composition courses allows us to explore multiple forms of literacy that are significant in students' lives. The authors in this book address the necessity of developing these multiple literacies to prepare students for the media-driven world in which we live, and they challenge us as teachers to try new genres and technologies. If you read the contributor biographies at the end of the book, you will notice that some of the authors in this collection are either graduate students or those new to their roles as instructors, and some are more experienced teachers and published popular culture scholars. The Call for Papers for this project specifically targeted graduate students and new instructors, along with those more experienced in the art of bringing popular culture into the writing classroom. We are pleased to be able to include contributors who are at various stages in their careers.

The essays cover a wide variety of pop culture topics, ranging from the Oscar-winning film *Shakespeare in Love* to the widely-popular hip-hop song "My Humps" by the Black-Eyed Peas to the obituary as popular reading. The authors also discuss a variety of pedagogical methods and types of assignments, including traditional essays, group discussions, and multimedia projects. We hope you will try some (or all) of the assignments presented in this book as you bring popular culture into your classroom. Remember, you do not have to start with a semester-long class devoted to popular culture; you can ease your way in with just one assignment. Once that project is successful, you will be looking for other ways to incorporate pop culture. As you do, listen to your students, pay attention to the chatter before and after class, look at their MySpace and Facebook pages, learn what pop culture media and themes are important to them, and then use those in your classes to build bridges with your students.

To help you get started using popular culture in the composition classroom, we have provided an extensive For Further Reading section at the end of the book. Entries include general sources on popular culture, cultural studies, or pedagogy; more specific works that focus on analyzing elements of popular culture; and other works that discuss the connections between popular culture and the writing class.

## Acknowledgments

From all of us, we thank the following people who helped us at various times throughout this project: Allison's English 6/7570 students in spring 2007, Dianna Baldwin, Buffy the Vampire Slayer, Star McKenzie Burruto, Katrina Byrd, Jimmie Cain, Jaime Espil, Mark Francisco, Kevin Haworth, Jessica McKee, the Graduate College at MTSU, Dickson Musselwhite, our families and friends, Rachel Robinson Strickland, Michael Rosenberg, Tom Strawman, Keri Mayes Tidwell, Holly Tipton, and Stacia Watkins. We also give our thanks to all those who assisted us with the editorial, production, and marketing process: Lyn Uhl, Publisher; Laurie Runion, Development Editor; Megan Power, Editorial Assistant; Jessica Rasile, Content Production Manager; and the people at Newgen.

Finally, we give our appreciation to our reviewers. Your insights helped us initially narrow the number of essays down to these that represent a cross-section of pop culture in the writing classroom, and your additional reviews helped us refine the content. We truly appreciate your assistance.

Earnest Cox, *University of Arkansas at Little Rock*
Carolyn Embree, *University of Akron*
John Levine, *University of California, Berkeley*
Jacquelyn Lyman, *Anne Arundel Community College*
Leanne Maunu, *Palomar College*
Stacia Watkins, *Middle Tennessee State University*

# Assigning the Obituary: Using Figures from Popular Culture to Help Students Argue from Research

*Stephanie Roach*

## Why Obituaries

In "Lives after Death," a writer for *The Economist* observes: "In earlier times, British newspapers' obituary pages were as solemn as the classified death notices that accompanied them. But since the mid-1980s they have become a source of daily fascination and delight" (64). Essentially, the article argues that since the mid-1980s, the obituary has become something of a pop culture phenomenon: "the obituary as entertainment" (64). Marilyn Johnson's recent book, *The Dead Beat: Lost Souls, Lucky Stiffs and the Perverse Pleasures of Obituaries*, not only confirms that the trend of obituaries as entertainment continues, but also confirms how entrenched obituaries have become in the popular culture.

Johnson's study of famed obituarists from "the big three" papers in the United States—the *New York Times*, the *Washington Post*, and the *Los Angeles Times*—and "the big four" in London—the *Daily Telegraph*, the *Guardian*, the *Independent*, and *The Times* (7)—explores the history and art of obituary writing, exposing the sub-culture of the obituary obsessed and investigating the pull of the genre for the casual reader. After all, Johnson reminds us, "[t]he obituary pages, it turns out, are some of the best-read pages in the newspaper" (7). "[B]ooming as literature and folk art across the English-speaking world" (17), obituaries draw us in because, Johnson posits, "the emotion is there, the tension, the entertainment, the tragedy, the comic relief" (7).

Johnson's treatment of the obituary does "the obituary as entertainment" one better: *The Dead Beat* presents the obituary as the consummate pop culture pleasure. To read an obituary is, Johnson argues, to consider an iconic departure, to "stand in the back of the old theater, feeling that warm and special glow that comes from contemplating and appreciating what has just left the building" (5). Johnson does not gloss the reference, though the strength of the catch phrase "Elvis has left the building" clearly resonates. In the popular imagination, "Elvis has left the building" has become a stock, sometimes comic stock replacement for "someone has exited" or "something is finished." But as made famous by Elvis' announcer Al Dvorin at stage shows and on recordings of live performances, "Elvis has left the building" was not just a sign that the music was over ("Elvis"): "Elvis has left the building" was a call to pay attention, to mark the fact of Elvis' absence as something significant[1].

---

[1] Dvorin picked up the phrase from announcer Horace Logan's spontaneous utterance at a December 1956 concert. The phrase "Elvis has left the building" was a call to attention. Logan, the Louisiana Hayride's announcer, attempted to get the crowd back in their seats after an early performance by Elvis, but his popularity at the time of the show had risen far past opening act status. The crowd, many of whom were teenage Elvis fans, began to disperse after his set. Logan got on the mike to try to turn the tide: "Please, young people . . . Elvis has left the building. He has gotten in his car and driven away . . . Please take your seats" ("Elvis"). Logan's announcement was a call to action, a call, to rephrase Johnson, to contemplate and appreciate what was still in the building.

Certainly the obituary as a genre is at heart about calling attention to the importance of absence by helping readers consider the significance of what was once present. As such, the obituary is, to draw again from Johnson, a contemplative and appreciative act of writing and reading. That the obituary as rhetoric is so reflective is what has made the obituary, at least the write-your-own-obituary assignment, something of a composition classroom staple. That the obituary as a source of "fascination and delight" is a ready popular culture enjoyment, artifact, and model text is what makes the write-another's-obituary assignment a potential pedagogical powerhouse. What follows is a look at previous uses of the obituary in the classroom, a current popular culture approach to the obituary assignment, and an argument for how an obituary assignment sitting squarely in the delights of popular culture can draw from and contribute to those delights while helping students practice what Gerald Graff and Cathy Birkenstein call "the moves that matter in academic writing" (*x*).

## Early Obituary Assignments in the Classroom

In a late issue of the *Exercise Exchange* in 1969, Richard D. Kepes offered a simple and, as he describes it, effective writing assignment: ask students to write their own obituary. In 1972, Chet Corey expounded on the significance of the obituary assignment "as an exercise in living": "Through the obituary assignment you will gain an insight into their ability to follow directions, a grasp of their present writing skills, a glimpse into their imaginations, something of their backgrounds, and a vision of their dreams" (198). By studying the obituary genre ("Simply send your students home to the evening's newspaper") and trying to practice its conventions, Corey argues that students "must struggle with chronology and order of importance as they contemplate education, occupations, and family relationships," and that ultimately, the write-your-own-obituary assignment helps students and instructors see the "intrinsic worth" of each student (198-99).

In 1974, the personal obituary assignment and Corey's version of it in particular came under fire by Lynn Z. Bloom in a response piece to Corey's original *College Composition and Communication* article. In "The Personal Obituary: A Biography of Values," Bloom argues that the obituary genre causes difficulty for freshman writers particularly when students must take a personal tack: "some students (like some of the rest of us) are terrified of death, particularly their own. Because they don't want to discuss it, these students have extreme difficulty in writing even the most perfunctory of obituaries" (210). Moreover, Bloom believes that the type of obituary described by Corey is too formulaic: "You should include your name; place of birth; date of birth; names of parents; business experiences, include military service; what you want to become in life (should appear as your occupation if you feel you might achieve this goal); place of death, date of death; and place of burial" (Corey 198). Bloom argues that there is more value in the assignment if one frames the assignment to aim for what Alden Whitman, then chief obituarist of the *New York Times,* called the "'new style' obituaries," obituaries that provide more of a dynamic portrait and are therefore less formulaic.

The "new style" obituary is "constructed as a whole and written with grace, capturing the subject's unique flavor" (Whitman qtd. in Bloom 211). As Bloom describes it, the new style obituaries

>emphasize the central and significant aspects of the subject's life, more often arranged in order of prominence or to give an impression of the subject's dominant characteristics

than according to the chronology of his activities; they quote from his typical and
memorable speeches, writing, and conversations; they are . . . candid, including revealing
details. (211)

To meet the spirit of this new style, Bloom offers her own write-your-own-obituary assignment.
Actually, she offers two alternatives. The first, however, still reads a bit like Corey's formula:

If you think you (or some significant attributes of yourself—emotional, spiritual,
intellectual, vocational, or whatever) are currently 'dead' or at a 'dead end,' then give
the obituary the date on which your 'death' occurred and provide an explanation of it.
Consider what you were like when 'alive,' what caused the 'death,' and what the
consequences are of your demise. (210)

Bloom's other alternative is more "prospective and projective" and moves the assignment
somewhat away from the obituary genre: "If you consider yourself currently alive, then project
your life into the future as far as you think likely, and discuss the potential fulfillment—or
defeat—of your hopes and goals" (210-11). Nevertheless, Bloom's modified "exercise in living"
draws a student through a process of "defining and arranging his values and his past, present, and
future modes of existence into a meaningful whole," thus creating a "biography of values" similar
to Corey's catalog of "intrinsic worth" (Bloom 211; Corey 199).

In 1984, Dennis Chase contributes to the ongoing conversation about and use of the obituary
assignment, reminding us in "Death in Freshman Composition" that the value of the assignment
is in how writing one's own obituary combines values clarification with skill development in
composition. Though fewer composition teacher scholars write about the write-your-own-
obituary assignment after the late 1980s[2], the assignment seems to maintain traction in the
classroom. Later, however, as popular culture themes and texts gain status in the writing
classroom, the personal values clarification aspect of the write-your-own-obituary assignment
suggests an important cultural analysis role that the obituaries of others might play. Elizabeth
Penfield's *Point Taken: A Brief Thematic Reader* is an example of a contemporary application of
an obituary assignment in the context of cultural analysis.

## A Current Popular Culture Obituary Assignment

Within the theme section "Pop Culture," Penfield includes essays on country music, fried
chicken, the television show *Seinfeld*, gender age inequalities in Hollywood, and violence in
movies, as well as the *Guardian*'s obituary of George Harrison. Penfield's frame for the section
argues: "Popular culture encompasses all the forms of enjoyment that exist within a given
society" (117). Studying these diverse enjoyments helps us, she suggests, define popular culture
and understand cultural taste (117-18). Like the other essays in the section, the Harrison obituary
is presented as a commentary on pop culture enjoyment as well as a source of enjoyment itself.

Given the apparatus accompanying Harrison's obituary such as a "Before You Read"
assignment and suggestions for "Discussing the Text" and "Brief Response," Penfield intends the
obituary reading to help students understand something about the obituary form, the "thoroughly

---

[2] Journalism instructors more than compositionists take up the obituary assignment in their scholarship,
focusing on writing others' obituaries as a way to practice an important news-writing genre and use the
occasion of sudden "death" to simulate newsroom practices. See, for example, Denis M. Murley's 1986
*Journalism Educator* article "Rewrite Day Class is Demanding Test of Student Abilities."

British" nature of the text, the non-chronological approach of the text, the popularity of the Beatles, the obituary's attempt to separate Harrison from the Beatles, and the interesting facts of Harrison's biography (123, 128). The "Extended Response" assignments move beyond the reading: one assignment asks students to research a current music sensation in order to "analyze the reasons behind the person or group's appeal"; the other asks students to "Choose a figure from popular culture, and then research that person's life so that you can write his or her obituary" (128).

Both assignments ask students to draw from research, yet the assignment that focuses on a cultural study of popularity seems to encourage more argument from research than the obituary assignment. Penfield's obituary assignment states that one must research the person's life, yet previous questions draw attention to "fact" in the obituary reading and declare "obituaries are often straight factual pieces" (128). In context, then, Penfield seems to be encouraging the obituary as a fact-finding and fact-assembling assignment, a way to come to and report the fascinating details of a figure in popular culture.

## What the Obituary Assignment Can Do

In contrast to Penfield's approach, however, the "new style" obituaries Bloom once suggested we turn our assignments toward and the celebrity obituaries that Johnson touts encourage not just reporting facts of research but using research to "communicate the significance of a person. . . . to write well, to capture a person with economy and grace" (117). In fact, Johnson insists that the best celebrity obituaries develop "what the world would lose when it lost each of them" (130). For Johnson, then, what it takes to write a good obituary "that weighs and measures the life," starts with but goes beyond "reporting skills" (60, 117). Ultimately, Johnson suggests that the point of an obituary is the "heroic act" of crafting a story about someone else's story: "There goes *one*, the only one, the last of his kind" (223). The implication is that, as a "tight little coil of biography" (10), the obituary is wound by acts of scrupulous selection, by a writer's choices in telling a story about the whole.

Because what starts with research ends with careful research writing, the obituary can become a great classroom tool. An obituary assignment can help present important concepts of information literacy and provide the occasion for practicing research writing strategies. As students think about how to build a legacy, how to wind the spring and give action to the details of biography of someone who delights and fascinates them, they engage in research and practice integrating research into their text. "You don't," as the *New York Times* obituary editor Chuck Strum argues, "have to say 'the police said' after every paragraph, but you have to gracefully say how you know this" (qtd. in Johnson 59). Strum's comment is especially useful here because he is making a case not just for author accountability in obituaries (and therefore publication credibility), but also for the importance of a repertoire of writing strategies that allow for the smooth integration of research. As Graff and Birkenstein argue in *They Say I Say: The Moves that Matter in Academic Writing*, "people don't just make claims, but *work* those claims in various

# THE OBITUARY/LEGACY ESSAY:
## USING RESEARCH TO ARGUE FROM BIOGRAPHY

Your task is to choose a living, well-known person and then research that person's life so that you can write an obituary/legacy essay about him or her. An obituary in its simplest form is a notice of death including a short biography. When the person is famous locally, nationally, or internationally, magazines and newspapers often write a longer obituary, sometimes referred to as a legacy. An obituary/legacy essay includes the standard notice of death and a short biographical account, but also makes an argument about what made this person so special.

In the obituary essay you write, you will not simply be reporting the details of a life, but you will be interpreting biographical events and using them as evidence for your claims. You will be making an argument about a person from the facts of his or her biography.

- You may choose any living, well-known person (an actor, musician, radio personality, politician, world leader, scientist, architect, inventor, athlete, etc.)—anyone who has made a name for him or herself in the world and who is alive (published obituaries on this person won't yet exist). Your obituary essay will be about a living person, yet to suit the context of the obituary/legacy essay, you will write about the person as if s/he were dead. We will discuss this textual requirement and other recognizable obituary features in class.

- Once you have chosen a figure, you will have to do research. Research is a significant component of this essay assignment. We will have a class Library Orientation to help you get started on searching the internet for credible information about this person and using the library databases and holdings to find and select print articles.

- As you research, ask yourself: What is significant about who this person is or what s/he has done? Why is this person important? What would s/he leave behind? Why should s/he be remembered? How should s/he be remembered? You should discuss your answers with your peers.

- You should consult several sources as well as several kinds of sources about your chosen person before selecting the best sources to use in your essay. You must use at least three sources in your final essay, including one newspaper source and one article from a magazine or journal. All sources—your required newspaper source, your required magazine or journal sources, and your minimum third source (newspaper, magazine, journal, internet or other)—should be judiciously selected for credibility. Don't just settle on the first sites/articles you find. We will discuss strategies for evaluating sources in class.

- The sources you use should provide that you can use in arguing about a legacy. As you select passages to paraphrase and quote consider: What argument am I making? What evidence best supports my claims? How can I present the relevance and significance of the evidence to my readers? Our class activities will help you make arguments from biography and practice the techniques writers use to integrate (introduce, identify, interpret, investigate, and incorporate) sources.

- Your essay will include a properly formatted Works Cited page listing in correct MLA style all sources used in your essay. You will also include MLA in-text citations every time you quote from, paraphrase, summarize, or otherwise use a source, and your in-text citations will be properly formatted to directly correspond to your Works Cited entries. You can avoid plagiarism by indicating clearly what thoughts and/or words are yours and what thoughts and/or words belong to others. Strategies for avoiding plagiarism will be discussed in class. You will also work with me in your conference on your sources.

- Ultimately, your job is to write an interesting, thoughtful, well-researched, and well-crafted obituary essay. You'll be analyzing your selected figure's life and work, coming to some conclusion about what makes this person uniquely important. Remember, you are not simply writing a report. Instead, you are crafting an obituary that has something to say about the person beyond the facts of his or her biography. Be sure to develop an argument about this person's legacy and skillfully integrate your research to support claims about the legacy.

ways" (131). An obituary assignment can help students consider how and why strong writers work their claims.

I've been using this obituary assignment at the end of the first semester of a two-semester writing sequence. Our sequence begins by introducing students to techniques of argumentation and narrative in College Rhetoric that students expand on in our research intensive second semester course in Critical Writing and Reading. The second semester aim is to bring students to longer, sustained arguments that are more complex and more thoroughly researched. It is the expectation that by the time they enter Critical Writing and Reading students have had at least one library experience. The obituary assignment has been a useful way for me to bring students into the library and have them practice critical research and research writing strategies in a shorter argument. I should say up front that there is little groundbreaking in my version of the assignment, but in framing the function of research in writing an obituary as more than a fact-finding mission, this obituary assignment has created significant instructional opportunities in my classroom.

It is worth nothing that while I only require three full pages or about 900 words (not including the Works Cited) for this assignment, students, even those who have struggled throughout the semester to meet longer assignments, typically write five or more pages. Indeed, the students' interest in the rock star, actress, religious leader, head of state, newscaster, architect, inventor, computer genius, etc. that they oftentimes surprisingly select to write about and the great delight they take in this person encourage students to want others to share in the fascination. Thus, lessons previously offered about clearly stating one's position and summarizing other sources in terms of one's focus, supporting arguments with reason and evidence, making the relevance and meaning of quotations and evidence clear to readers, creating overall coherence by explicitly connecting ideas, and helping readers understand the so what and the who cares suddenly have more resonance. Moreover, the assignment opens up the possibility for in-depth and nuanced discussions of genre writing, academic integrity, information literacy, and academic documentation. Meanwhile, students are also investigating concepts of fame, importance, taste, and delight as they read about and debate the merits of their figures of interest, and students are dealing with cultural assumptions and implications in the work and lives of their popular figure that they must explain (or smooth over on occasion) in trying to get others to see the value they themselves see in the figure. The result is engaged and successful student writing. For example, consider the following introductory, body, and concluding selections from three student essays[3]:

---

**Destined for Stardom**

When Kirsten Dunst made her feature film debut in 1989, it was obvious that she would become a star. Filming television commercials at age three was just the beginning (*Internet Movie Database*). She shined as a child star and grew to be loved and respected by many. At age 22, Kirsten had made 33 movies, just as many as Nicole Kidman, 15 years Kirsten's senior (Woods 124). While Kirsten was a superb actress, she remained a down-to-earth, normal, humble person. She said "I don't really feel like I've proven myself. I feel like I have so much to learn and growing to do" (Strauss). Without a doubt, Kirsten would have become one of Hollywood's greatest actresses. . . .

---

[3] Student authors of the essays used here gave their express permission to the author to quote from their writing.

---

**Lived Strong**

. . . Lance Armstrong had to overcome more than any other athlete in the world and not just because he beat cancer. Lance was the hardest working athlete in all of sport; but because he was so superior, his talent seemed too good to be true. He was also the least trusted having been test for numerous drugs including steroids more than any other athlete. Yes, that is more than Barry Bonds, more than Michael Johnson, and even more than Mark McGuire. His hotel is constantly being searched for anything really, but mostly for drugs. In 2002 Lance was tested 24 times, that's twice a month ("Tour"). There were constant rumors about performance enhancing drugs and even an accusatory book about Lance, none of which were true. He had to rise above cursing, spitting and even beer throwing fans every year at the Tour de France. He also had to race against the top competitors in the world, such as cyclists Jan Ullrich, Iban Mayo, Ivan Basso and Tyler Hamilton. As if that wasn't enough, Lance also had to face the *Sports Illustrated* cover jinx having appeared on it before the Tour De France. Usually people that appear on the cover of *Sports Illustrated* have an occurrence of bad luck when they are tested the most. Luckily, he never believed in superstitions. . . .

---

**A Passion for Women and Children**

. . . Hillary Rodham Clinton, all throughout her life, continuously made moves to improve the lives of her fellow citizens. She saw opportunity in her profession and eventually in her marriage where she could put her passions to work to benefit the lives of so many people. Through Single Parent Scholarships and heading the Task Force for the National Health Care she touched the lives of many underprivileged Americans. While her efforts for remodeling legislation for rating systems and abortion may have been unfinished due to her unexpected death, she still fought to the very end of her life to help women and children. Hillary could have used her profession and opportunity to increase tax cuts or fund international relations; instead, all her efforts were directed towards benefiting others. Aside from being First Lady and the first women Senator, Hillary Rodham Clinton should especially be remembered for her passion to help women and children and the work she did to fulfill this passion.

---

## Why the Obituary Assignment

The preceding excerpts represent some of the typical successes of the average (and below average) student in responding to this assignment: success with purpose, relevant evidence, drawing the pieces together. Many students are also willing to dig deeper for evidence and revise more for this assignment. The obituary assignment focused on the use of research and accompanied by significant classroom work on information literacy, academic integrity, and source integration, as well as ongoing classroom discussion of the importance and delights of these figures of popular culture, formal peer review of drafts, and an extended one-on-one conference that allows for further feedback, intervention, and investigation has led to some of my more satisfying moments as a teacher.

Moreover, many of the pedagogical approaches I use with this assignment, such as peer review, conferencing, discussions of source integration, and encouraging analysis of the significance of some aspect of our culture, have fallen flat in other contexts. One possible reason is that with other assignments students struggle more to absorb this lesson of Graff and Birkenstein: when you explain why your text matters, "you are urging your audience to keep reading, pay attention, and care" (96). With other assignments, students do not often see why they themselves should care. But with the obituary assignment, because the figures of popular culture students write about matter to them, they are driven to urge their audiences to care. They are interested in using the conventions of the obituary that ask readers to pay attention and in learning more about the moves in academic writing that in this and other contexts do the same. The results of students focusing on asking their readers to "keep reading, pay attention, and care," are rich, interesting essays that draw from the delights of popular culture and are delightful to read. Even more exciting is the fact that students report that their work on the obituary has given them more confidence and authority as writers.

James Ferguson, who marshaled the era of the "new style" obituary at the *Independent*, says that he came to love the obituary as a student:

> They were terrific—you didn't know what you would read next, which is the exciting thing about the obits page. It could be about anything, and all sorts of subject areas that people never read about in the newspapers. You can write learned disquisitions through the life of one person. It's great plowmen, or champion bagpipers—the great tapestry of human life. It's wonderful, that opportunity! (qtd. in Johnson 176-77)

For almost the same reasons—never knowing what I'll read next, encountering successful disquisitions, seeing students engage deeply in the tapestry of life and rhetoric, finding great pedagogical opportunity and wonderful result in the delights of popular culture—I love the obituary assignment.

In "The Obituary as an Exercise in Living" Chet Corey muses that "English teachers are a morbid bunch of caretakers!": "Who else," he points out, "would linger with Shakespeare over a freshly dug grave, wander with Gray through a country churchyard, contemplate approaching death with Bryant, or listen to Dickenson from beyond the grave" (198). Or, of course, who else would find delight in an obituary assignment? He may be right about some oddities of the profession, but the possibilities in the obituary assignment for engaging popular culture and advancing writing instruction would be sinister to ignore.

## Works Cited

Bloom, Lynn Z. "The Personal Obituary: A Biography of Values." *CCC* 25 (1974): 209-11.

Chase, Dennis. "Death in Freshman Composition." *Texas Tech Journal of Education* 11 (1984): 269-73.

Corey, Chet. "The Obituary as an Exercise in Living." *CCC* 23 (1972): 198-99.

"Elvis has left the building." *The Phrase Finder*. 2007. Gary Martin. 10 Apr. 2007 <http://www.phrases.org.uk/meanings/elvis-has-left-the-building.html>.

Graff, Gerald, and Cathy Birkenstein. *They Say I Say: The Moves that Matter in Academic Writing*. New York: Norton, 2006.

Johnson, Marilyn. *The Dead Beat: Lost Souls, Lucky Stiffs, and the Perverse Pleasures of Obituaries*. New York: Harper Collins, 2006.

Kepes, Richard D. "Write Your Own Obituary." *Exercise Exchange* 16.3-4 (1969): 2.

"Lives after Death." *The Economist* 24 Dec. 1994: 64-67.

Murley, Denis M. "Rewrite Day Class is Demanding Test of Student Abilities." *Journalism Educator* 41.3 (1986): 30-31.

Penfield, Elizabeth. *Point Taken: A Brief Thematic Reader*. New York: Pearson, 2004.

# Beyond the Boob Tube: Using Television Fandom to Create Community

## *Hillary Robson*

Early in my teaching career, I can remember sitting at a Mexican restaurant in a small college town waiting for a colleague of mine to join me for dinner. She had invited me to teach a workshop in her Expository Writing class: a three hour, once-a-week, Saturday morning course comprised of nine students often hesitant to engage in conversation and group work. I looked forward to the experience but was filled with trepidation. Friends and colleagues struggling to engage their students were often the focus of conversation throughout graduate school. As a result, finding common ground had become the focus of my personal pedagogy.

While deep in discussion about our students' general lack of enthusiasm, my colleagues posed a groundbreaking question: "What if our problems stem from the lack of community our students feel? We talk in class. . . . We *love* discussion and sharing our views. But maybe that's because we have so much in common. We've been in school a lot longer than our students; we're part of the academic community. Our students don't have the same wealth of experience that we do."

Lack of community may be just the cause of the rift between students and teachers. Students do not feel comfortable having in-depth conversations with relative strangers (their classmates) about bizarre subjects like rhetorical modes, personal narratives, and peer review. So the question is, how do we build community among our students in the expository writing classroom?

Seeking a diversion from this seemingly impossible question, I turned my eyes to the television set overhead. A muted screen featured the promotional ad for that night's new episode of *Grey's Anatomy,* the popular ABC network drama about a host of too-pretty surgical interns and their weekly trials and tribulations. I, like 22 million other Americans, was an avid viewer and hoped I had remembered to set my TiVo to record. The conversation among a group of women sitting opposite me suddenly sprang to life, and I unabashedly eavesdropped with interest.

"What do you think Meredith is going to do? Who is she going to choose?" One woman asked her companions while taking a healthy sip of margarita.

"I think it's going to be the vet. I would pick the vet."

"Not me, I'd pick McDreamy. He's so cute."

The women dissolved into schoolgirl giggles as a man close to their age turned around from the booth in front of them. "I think she shouldn't pick either one of them. George is still in love with her; I'm sure of it."

Their conversation inspired me. I had my instant community facilitator—not *Grey's Anatomy*, but television, the great equalizer.

Most of our students watch television; 96 percent of Americans and Europeans watch at least one hour of television each week (Lime). Composition specialist Bronwyn Williams is an avid supporter of integrating television into the writing classroom, citing our students' ability to read postmodern visual texts more "easily and competently than many of their teachers,"(3) and the fact that television "incorporates all forms of public discourse" (9). Describing the power of the medium in *Tuned In: Television and the Teaching of Writing,* Williams discusses his students' reactions when he opens the cabinet containing the TV set in the center of the class: "I notice a small wave of alertness rippling through the class. They quit slouching, lean forward just slightly, and all eyes . . . are now directed at the TV set" (1).

Television can prove a very useful tool in writing classroom curriculum as a means of introducing the *value* of reading to our students. Reading inspires explorations in new areas of study, as "students' lack of experience with and lack of interest in print texts makes it more difficult for them to explore the extended analysis that is vital for certain kinds of intellectual work" (Williams 20). As teachers of composition, we are charged with the important duty of providing students with tools for engaging in intellectual work that requires careful reading and informed writing. Television can provide text for our students to critically analyze and contextualize both the worlds inside and outside the composition classroom.

A quality educational experience hinges on allowing our students to cultivate their unique identities as well as the development of critical thinking, analysis, and discourse skills that prove necessary for other courses in the academy as well as the "real world" job market. In "Delivering College Composition," Kathleen Blake Yancey describes composition as a *socializing* experience: "We, as teachers, are charged with 'normalizing' our student's behaviors to become 'acceptable' society members" (2) and "composition as a universal requirement has a long history in this country, one directly connected to the formation of identity" (4). The nature of the composition classroom—what to teach, how to teach it—is in perpetual debate. Joseph Harris provides a succinct description for the problem: "the whole argument over whether we should teach 'personal essays' or 'academic discourse' . . . tends quickly to dissolve into a stand-off . . . and thus turns both into something students I have met show little interest in either reading and writing" (qtd in Blake-Yancey 6). The question, then, becomes why *can't* we teach *both*?

Gerald Graff warns what can happen if teachers attempt to merely create miniaturized academics out of their students: "schooling takes students who are perfectly street smart and exposes them to the life of the mind in ways that make them feel dumb. Why is this? Why in many cases do street smarts not only fail to evolve naturally into academic smarts, but end up seeming opposed to academic smarts, as if the two can't coexist in the same head" (2). Our students enter our classrooms with a world of information based on interests sprung from their favorite novels, films, television shows, and musical artists; often they have built a kind of scholarly knowledge about those areas of independent study. That unique knowledge and understanding based on student interest is *fandom*.

So, why fandom? Why television? As Herbert Blau proposes: "In all forms of society, there is one specific kind of production which predominates over the rest, whose relations thus assign rank and influence to the others" (121). In American society, that production is television. There is an excellent chance that we, like our students, are intimately familiar with at least one show, series, actor, or character from the medium. To quote Philip Auslander, "television can no longer be seen just as an element in our cultural environment, one discourse among many, but must be seen as an environment within itself" (2). Our identities, both at the personal and social levels, are influenced by what, when, and where we watch—and of equal importance, what we choose not to watch.

In *Fan Cultures*, Matt Hills proposes that "everybody knows what a 'fan' is. It's somebody who is obsessed with a particular star, celebrity, film, TV programme, band; somebody who can produce reams of information on their object of fandom, and can quote their favorite lines or lyrics, chapter and verse" (ix). Fans and fandoms generate fan *communities*, individual societies based "[u]pon and] around the reception and remediation of cultural texts, [with a developed] complex system of belonging" (Jaynemanne). Fandom, then, is an ideal tool for getting students to open up within their classrooms. And television is a medium that most of our students can readily access at home, in their dorm rooms, or even on the internet, making it an ideal media format for bringing a community based upon shared interests into the expository writing classroom.

What follows is a discussion of my use of television and fandom in the expository writing classroom, along with tips and tools for its facilitation. As I use television throughout the course of the semester, each section is divided into five specific content areas. My primary goal is taking my students from an individual comfort zone, to a group contact zone, to a class-wide community zone. Each activity and worksheet helps cultivate essay ideas; however, these are merely models to inspire your ideas about what will work best in your own classroom.

## Groundbreaker #1:
## Who Are You? Using Definition to Create Audience

The first week of class is daunting for both students and teachers: students are unfamiliar with the world of composition, from the discourse on your syllabus to the expectations for "polished, xxx word-length essays." As their teacher, you might also be uneasy, wondering who your students are, where they have come from, and what their expectations are for the course. Television can be an icebreaker that takes advantage of shared anxieties to build common ground from day one, creating a precedent for classroom discussion. Instead of the standard first-day-of-class line of questioning— "What's your name, major, and who do you want to be when you grow up,"— I use Icebreaker One: "I Like to Watch" to diffuse the tensions in my classroom and allow my students to get to know each other based on their shared interests:

| Icebreaker #1: I Like to Watch. . . | | |
|---|---|---|
| **Individual** | **Small Group** | **Class** |
| On a piece of paper, ask students to write down three TV shows they watch every week. | Break new classmates into groups of 3-5, and have them introduce themselves by what they watch. | Have each group list series they share in common; use this list to come up with a top ten for the class. |

I find that this exercise allows students to have in-depth discussions that can easily bridge to writing assignments. I use the top ten television show list generated in class to allow students to rate and evaluate the shows that they have seen or would like to see in the future. Worksheet 1 "Top Ten Television Shows" is one I use in my class to provide ideas for later brainstorming activities, journal prompts, or a means for generating participation points:

| Worksheet 1: Top Ten Television Shows |
|---|
| 1. List the Class Top Ten. CIRCLE the shows you have seen. Put a STAR next to shows you watch on a regular basis, and a TRIANGLE next to shows you do not watch. <br><br> 2. What television show are you a fan of? <br><br> 3. How often do you watch this show? <br><br> 4. Is it on the top 10 list?      YES    NO <br><br> 5. What show from the top ten could you commit to watch at least 2 episodes of? <br><br> 6. Do you think you will like this show?  YES    NO |

After discussing what shows students like, I transition the classroom discussion to fandom. Providing examples of fan activities, behaviors or popular fan groups induces some interesting discussions about my students' understanding of what it means to be a fan. I use Icebreaker Number Two, "What it Means to be a Fan," to begin a conversation about culture.

| Icebreaker #2: What it Means to Be a Fan | | |
|---|---|---|
| Individual | Small Group | Class |
| Journal or in-class writing prompt "I think being a fan means…" | Have students discuss what it means to be a fan, and then come up with a group definition | Have each group designate their definitions, make connections between shared understandings and differences, and form a class-wide definition. |

Teresa McKenna discusses the importance of engaging in cultural discourse in the classroom, where if we can "understand difference as the common cultural reference point it becomes the basis for unity" (432). I have found that something as seemingly innocuous as defining fans and fan culture can reflect stereotypical understandings my students have that are incorrect and often hurtful. Opening avenues for embracing diversity and difference can evolve into a semester-long project. I use a web-supported environment, such as WebCT or Desire2Learn, so groups can post their definitions on the classroom message boards for outside class discussion. The common threads reflected in these discussion posts provide a wealth of inspiration for a process-oriented essay topic about creating definitions about fans and fandom.

After our in-class discussion, I show students a clip from the movie *Trekkers* that documents Star Trek fandom and shows how these fans are conceptualized in culture. The clip helps us to understand what stereotypes are associated with specific fan cultures. The clips allow students to begin to experience and understand culture and create an appreciation early in the semester for listening to and respecting the "audience of their peers"—a phrase that comes up often on our assignment sheets, but one our students do not understand unless they *know* that audience.

# Groundbreaker #2:
# The Descriptive Essay: Describing the Object of Fandom

Once my class as a collective defines what we understand fandom to be, we move to other topics, such as talking about what, specifically, we identify with as fans. This conversation builds upon previous discussions and incorporates some of those first-day stories about what our students are watching on television. I use Icebreaker 3, "Why You Watch What You Watch," as an in-class writing prompt that provides ideas for small group discussion:

| Icebreaker 3: Why You Watch What You Watch ||
|---|---|
| **Individual** | **Small Group** |
| Journal or in-class writing prompt "My favorite show is _____ because…." | In pairs or groups of three, have students tell each group member what they watch and why; give response reports on their classroom discussions |

When students share information about their favorite show, it produces a wealth of classroom discussion that can directly inspire brainstorming, journaling, and discussion. I allow my students to spend a full class period on this subject because I find that it acts as an instant topic generator for the descriptive essay. At the conclusion of the class period, I have students write informal "response reports" outlined in worksheet two, "Your Favorite Show."

| Worksheet 2: Your Favorite Show |
|---|
| 1. What show was described to you? |
| 2. Have you watched this show before?  YES     NO |
| 3. When does this show air: |
| 4. What, according to your partner's description, is the show about? |
| 5. Does the show sound interesting?   YES     NO |
| 6. Why or why not? |

A main theme of my class is active listening, as it is an important part of building audience. Worksheet 2 allows students to see how well they have described their favorite show through solicited feedback from their peers. I use these classroom exercises to fuel idea generation for a detailed descriptive essay about their favorite television series.

# Groundbreaker #3:
# How Did I Get Here? The Personal Narrative Assignment

The personal narrative is a way for students to creatively tell a story with deep personal significance, but many new teachers fear the content of these essays, worried they may be too emotional or laden with heavy personal significance. In *Tuned In,* Williams offers inspired ideas for navigating the personal narrative to a less emotional place: "our students have long histories of television viewing that they can, and if given the opportunity, will discuss in detail and with authority" (37). In my classes, I base my personal narrative assignment on my students' television viewing histories since it provides a safe space for my students to discuss their own histories, interests, and important memories, using Icebreaker Number Four, "Making Memories" to generate in-class discussion.

| Icebreaker 4: Making Memories | | |
|---|---|---|
| **Individual** | **Small Group** | **Class** |
| Journal or in-class writing prompt "When I first watched my favorite show, I felt...'" | In pairs, students tell their personal stories to their classmates, and generate "similar experience" lists | Each pair gives brief presentations about what they share in common about their memorable viewing experiences |

The personal narrative is in concert with the views of Wendy Bishop, who encourages creative nonfiction in the composition classroom. Like Bishop, I believe that when writing is on the personal level, students are far more invested in the process and product of their writing. Because the subject is more personal in nature, it is ideal for the midpoint of the semester because my students are starting to feel as though they are a part of a community, and that camaraderie helps them feel comfortable to open up and share their personal viewing experiences. I follow up in-class exercises with an essay building worksheet, Worksheet 3, "Remembering When," to help students further reflect on audience and how they can strengthen their own narrative essays. The goal of the third worksheet is to provide a self-reflective space for my students so that they may evaluate their own memories and compare them to others in the class.

| Worksheet 3: Remembering When |
|---|
| 1. Did anyone have the same favorite show as you?      YES      NO |
| 2. How did that make you feel? |
| 3. What similarities do your memories have with others in the class? |
| 4. What differences do your memories have from others in the class? |
| 5. Do you think your memories seemed believable when compared with others? |

In the course of this unit on personal narrative, I show clips from popular series of television past, many of which my students watched as small children and remember fondly. Most students have at least viewed re-runs of series like *Friends, Scrubs*, and *Lost* that incorporate flashbacks as part of the continuing narrative. These clips help us to reflect on nostalgia and how certain shows help to shape who we are as adults. My students really enjoy this portion of the semester, as it allows a break from standard "academic" writing, and provides a chance for self-reflection.

## Groundbreaker #4:
## But My Show Is Better than Yours: The Argumentative Essay

At this point in the semester, my students have shared their favorite programs and narrative viewing histories. They have generated top ten lists and defined what it means to be a fan. They have engaged in argumentation at least once in the course of the semester and have evaluated the effectiveness of their classmates' argumentation and their own. As the calendar reaches the final part of the semester, students have been unwittingly preparing themselves for the argumentative essay.

Argument is a central component of effective language and communication skills for both teachers and students. Coincidentally, argument is also one of the most dreaded subject matters within the composition classroom. Despite this hesitation, "argumentation need not be a joyless, bloodless activity" (Graff 7) nor should it be relegated to the worlds of academics and upper management. Argument writing can be fun, and this next exercise can prove why.

Before we begin, we watch an episode of the courtroom drama *Law & Order* or selected clips from an actual trial case (courtesy of Court TV). The courtroom—real or scripted—is the inspiration for the structure of the argumentative essay. We focus on opening and closing arguments and see how lawyers present evidence for or against the defendant. After viewing the clips, my class divides into pairs of two who do not share the same favorite series, and one full class period is devoted to formulating their cases for a class-wide presentation during the following week of classes. I use Icebreaker 5, "Ladies and Gentlemen of the Jury," as a foundation for this exercise.

| Icebreaker 5: Ladies and Gentlemen of the Jury…. | | |
|---|---|---|
| **Individual** | **Small Groups** | **Class** |
| Journal or in-class writing prompt "You should watch this show because…" and enumerate 5 reasons their classmates should watch | Each pair has three tasks to complete: 1. Presenting their argument 2. Providing rationale/defense for their argument 3. Arguing against their partner | Each pair presents their "Evidence" to a jury of their peers, taking time to present their best prosecution and defense arguments. |

Prior to the presentation, I assign students by pair groups to evaluate each of their classmates' arguments. Evaluating arguments based on the balance of provided information, the effectiveness of persuasion, and presentation of ideas can provide an ideal blueprint for student essays based on argument or evaluation. Worksheet 4, "Evaluating Argument" is used for student evaluation.

---

**Worksheet 4: Evaluating Argument**

_____ VS _____

On a scale from 1-10, where 1 is "poor" and 10 is "excellent," evaluate:

_____ The Defendant's Opening Argument
_____ The Defendant's Closing Argument
_____ The Defendant's Supporting Evidence

_____ The Prosecutor's Opening Argument
_____ The Prosecutor's Closing Argument
_____ The Prosecutor's Supporting Evidence

Who won the case?

Why?

---

# Groundbreaker #5:
# Where Do We Go From Here? Using Fandom, Television, and Community to Inspire the Research Essay

By the end of my expository writing class, my students are well-prepared for the research essay. They have engaged in thoughtful discussion with their peers, defined and described their object of fandom, written a personal history, and articulated their argumentative points. They have received and made evaluations about their ideas, and have composed at least three essays on a variety of topics inspired by personal research. The next logical step is putting these skills to action in a research essay.

I structure the final research essay a bit differently than previous assignments. As my main focus is on building community, I require at least one source in the research paper to be from a fellow student's essay. I facilitate this by hosting the essay files on an in-class website, WebCT, Desire2Learn, or other internet based platform and bringing printed copies of essays for an in-class "Research Day." Students go through each other's papers and choose the ones they might want to use, and then request that the writer digitally send or give them a printed a copy.

I have five required sources that include a classmate's essay, a book, journal, and internet source. The final source is a student-choice source. By using multiple sources, students can develop citation skills and learn how to properly integrate cited materials into their paper. I use a worksheet for the final essay that helps to set up proper documentation, and another evaluation worksheet that I let students use to rate the effectiveness of incorporated citations during peer review. To help with generating sources for research, we spend a week in class discussing and using proper research skills, visiting the campus library and a computer lab to go over book, journal, and internet sources.

Students spend the last few sessions of class presenting their papers. On the last class meeting, I show a brief, ten-minute clip from a "goodbye" clip show of a television series, one that documents the important milestones and memories through the years of the series. *M*A*S*H, Friends,* and *Will & Grace* are examples of some wonderful series that provide clips. There's a wealth of series to choose from, and I often end up with an amalgamation of my own from many series. I show this clip to fuel a self-reflection exercise, an in-class writing assignment where students write a letter to themselves about what they have learned about their own writing process, about their classmates, and how they feel that they have grown as a writer. We then discuss those responses and see what areas they all felt they experienced growth in, and what differences they have in their own processes. This last class session helps students to reflect on where they have come and who they are as a group of individuals, and gives them confidence about the abilities and skills they have learned in the course of the semester.

## Conclusion

This method of using television and fandom in the composition classroom might not work for every teacher and student, but it can prove successful for those naturally interested and engaged with television. If your students share your enthusiasm, then television may be an ideal fit for exploring identity and inspiring writing. I first used fandom and television and witnessed the students come alive as they told me about their favorite shows and what it meant to be a fan. From that day on, I was convinced that fandom was an ideal teaching tool for me, as I found it brought life to classroom discussions and made nervousness virtually nonexistent for both me and my students.

I have entered several classrooms with a fandom-based pedagogy, using television, music, film, and literature, and have had positive results every time. My students become engaged with the discussion and material and are eager to share that enthusiasm with their classmates. The awkwardness of first time introductions disappears when standing on common ground discussing what we love. Students' trepidations about peer review, classroom critique, and group work dissipate when they feel as though they are part of a community with shared interest. Throughout my teaching experiences, I have found that television has proven the most effective tool for utilizing fandom and creating this community. I encourage you to find your own tool and with it, to forge ahead into uncharted territories with your students—and build communities of your own.

## Works Cited

Auslander, Philip. *Liveness: Performance in a Mediated Culture*. London: Routledge, 1999.
Blake-Yancey, Kathleen. "Delivering College Composition: A Vocabulary for Discussion."
    *Delivering College Composition: The Fifth Canon*. Ed. Kathleen Blake-Yancey. Portsmouth,
    NH: Boynton-Cook. 2006. 1-16.
Blau, Herbert. *To All Appearances: Ideology and Performance*. New York: Routledge, 1992.
CCCC. "Statement of Principles and Standards for the Postsecondary Teaching of Writing."
    1989. *NCTE*. 12 Apr. 2007 <http://www.ncte. org/cccc/resources/positions123790.htm>.

Graff, Gerald. *Clueless in Academe: How Schooling Obscures the Life of the Mind*. New Haven: Yale UP, 2003.

Hills, Matt. *Fan Cultures*. London: Routledge, 2000.

Jaynemanne, Darshana. "Microstatecraft: Belonging and Difference in Imagined Communities." *Refractory* 3.1. (2004) 12 Feb. 2006 <http://www.refractory/unimelb.edu.au.Journalissues/vol3/ jayemanne.html>.

Lime Marmalade. "Dealing with TV Licensing" 2007. *Marmalade.net*. 22 May 2007 <http://www.marmalade.net/lime/>.

McKenna, Teresa. "Borderness and Pedagogy: Exposing Culture in the Classroom." *The Critical Pedagogy Reader*. Ed. Antonia Darder, Marta Baltodanto, and Rodolfo D. Torres. New York: Routledge Falmer, 2003. 430-39.

Williams, Bronwyn. *Tuned In: Television and the Teaching of Writing*. Portsmouth, NH: Boynton-Cook, 2002.

# Bringing Social Networking Sites into the Writing Classroom Using MySpace and Facebook

## *Stephanie Vie*

Chances are, if you have not already heard about MySpace.com or Facebook.com, you soon will. College students in the United States comprise the majority of the population of these and similar online social networking sites used to socialize with friends and family. Whether they are searching for contacts from the past or looking to meet new friends, these individuals have eagerly joined online social networking sites in record numbers, hundreds of which are available, each with a slightly different look and feel. Many boast millions of users, prompting researchers to take notice of the potential of these Web 2.0 technologies to fundamentally change our communication behaviors.

MySpace is arguably the most popular of all of the currently available online social networking sites with approximately 173 million members as of April 2007. The site, which debuted in 2003, offers many communicative features: an instant messaging client; an in-house e-mail system, MySpace Mail; music videos and song downloads; and photo galleries and slideshows, among others. Facebook, introduced in 2004, has only 19 million members and is also more restrictive than MySpace in its feature offerings. There are no instant messaging clients, music videos, streaming profile songs, or photo slideshows in Facebook, though the site does offer unlimited photo storage and an in-house e-mail system. Though Facebook and MySpace differ significantly, both of these online social networking sites specifically target college students.

As social networking sites become more familiar to our students, writing instructors should consider the ways in which they could—and already do—impact the writing classroom and our pedagogical frameworks for approaching the teaching of writing. Indeed, students engage in a multitude of composing processes online, including in online social networking sites. They produce a great deal of writing in these spaces through their blogs, comments, the personal profile, and messages to each other. Thus, the immense popularity of online social networking sites coupled with the sheer amount of writing produced by students in these sites illustrates the potential for these spaces to impact composition teachers' understandings of student writing.

In this essay, then, I provide specific classroom assignments that can be adapted for a variety of writing courses, from first-year composition to professional writing to advanced composition as well as others. These assignments showcase how MySpace and Facebook, two popular culture sites fashionable with college students, can be used to teach rhetorical awareness and technological literacy skills in the writing classroom. For the purposes of this project, I draw on Cynthia L. Selfe's dual-level definition of technological literacy outlined in *Technology and Literacy in the Twenty-First Century*. At the level of literacy activities or events, technological literacy refers to "events that involve reading, writing, and communicating within computer-based environments," such as researching, organizing, and using technological tools (Selfe 11-12). At another, more complex level are literacy practices: understanding the complex sets of cultural beliefs and values that influence our understandings of what it means to read, write, and communicate with computers (12). The following assignments ask students to engage with technological literacy on both levels as well as consider issues of rhetorical awareness as applied to their own virtual personas.

## Classroom Activities

As noted in the previous section, online social networking sites can be brought into the writing classroom in various ways to teach technological literacy and rhetorical awareness. What follows are some pedagogical suggestions for how to use MySpace and Facebook in writing courses that can be employed by instructors who are interested in using such sites in the classroom. In some cases, I have offered suggested readings to assign to students prior to beginning the activity; these readings serve as springboards for the activities and the discussions to follow.

### "About Me": An Online Social Networking Autobiography

Online social networking sites like MySpace and Facebook that privilege the construction of an individual user profile can be used to teach aspects of rhetorical awareness. These sites can spur students to become aware of the power differentials, the discourse conventions, and the different audience members—both anticipated and unanticipated—that any writer must engage with when putting words on a page. The following assignment invites students to think critically about how their personal profile in an online social networking site might be viewed by different audience members. It also asks them to contemplate how public and private profiles may result in different assumptions about the individual profiled by particular audiences.

Students are asked to choose a public MySpace or Facebook user profile to analyze. They can analyze a user profile they have already created or create a new profile for the purposes of this assignment, or choose someone famous (a film star, musician, politician, or similar) who has a public profile. (If the student chooses to analyze another individual's profile, such as a politician, then obviously the assignment will shift slightly to an online social networking biography.) Throughout the autobiography, students should focus on a phrase shared by both MySpace and Facebook: "About me."

In this assignment, students should respond to the following questions (though these are certainly not exhaustive):

- MySpace and Facebook user profiles include an "about me" section for individuals to fill out. Construct an autobiographical narrative about how you chose to fill out your "about me" section. If you change the information in this section regularly, how do you change it and why?

- If you have included a photograph, listed favorites (movies, music, television, books, or activities), and joined groups, how do these profile features add to the construction of your individual identity detailed in the "about me" section? In other words, how does your default photo reflect what you see as your online identity? How might others view you based on what your favorites, your photos, or your groups say about you?

- Examine your audience: Who are you writing or talking to in your profile? (Think of this as your intended audience.) When you set up your profile, who did you imagine might take a look at it? Who did you intend to see this profile? How well do you think that your "about me" reflects the assumptions members of this intended audience may make about you? Now think about your unintended audience—people who may come across your profile that you didn't expect. (Members in this group might include parents, teachers, employers, and so on.) Again, how do you think your construction of "about me" reflects the assumptions members of your unintended audience may make about you? How might members of your unintended audience view you based on your MySpace or Facebook profile?

- Finally, think about how switching your profile from public to private would impact the ability for others to gather information about you. In what ways are you limited by keeping your profile public—for example, you may not post particular pictures or blogs because your profile is public. Similarly, in what ways would you be limited by making your profile private?

As the majority of college students participate in MySpace and Facebook, this assignment can ask students to think carefully and critically about their own identity construction online while carefully considering issues of audience. As well, students may also make connections between identity, audience, and power as they reflect on how their profiles might be viewed differently by individuals in their inner circle—their intended audience—and by members of their unintended audience. By considering how their profile picture, "about me" text, groups, and favorites all come together to paint a picture of the individual profiled, students can gain a stronger awareness of how their online identities may overlap and even clash with how others see them.

To extend the previous assignment and encourage students to analyze not only textual but also visual and auditory composition, instructors can ask students to re-envision their own "about me" page in different ways. One possibility involves reframing the personal profile as a multimedia collage. This works particularly well when translating a Facebook profile into a MySpace profile (since Facebook does not allow HTML, CSS, or JavaScript in the personal profile). Thus, students could consider how their profile might change if they had to move from Facebook to MySpace or vice versa: What multimedia elements might they add or delete and why? How would the addition or deletion of multimedia elements like music videos, songs, or graphics influence the student's ability to define his or her personality through the "about me" section?

Similarly, instructors might require students to re-envision their MySpace profile so that it features only images and sounds—no text. Students would still have to fill out the different sections of "about me" (favorite movies, favorite books, heroes, activities, and so on) but rely on only images and sounds for their composition. Essentially, the student's personal profile would rely on multimedia elements to make a visual argument of sorts about him or herself. After constructing their visual argument, students would write a reflective essay justifying the use of the particular multimedia elements they chose: For example, why did they choose these pictures, videos, and songs? How do they work together to build an argument that persuades the reader to see the individual profiled in a specific way? What difficulties did they encounter when attempting to create an about me page without relying on any text? Next, students could exchange

MySpace profiles (but not read the reflective essays yet) and in pairs describe what they see as the visual argument of the other's personal profile. This peer review helps students see some of the different ways their personal profile can be read by a classmate. From here, students could revise their multimedia "about me" in response to the in-class reading by a peer. Throughout this assignment, students reflect on the role of multimedia elements in online composing and how these elements influence their ability to construct a virtual identity in MySpace.

Finally, students could be required to re-envision their MySpace or Facebook profile for an entirely new audience and, after doing so, evaluate what they changed about their previous profile and why. The majority of students create their online social networking profiles for themselves and their friends. By asking them to add to and delete information from their profile for a prescribed audience, students would be required to carefully weigh the appropriateness of the textual and multimedia elements featured on their profile based on their perceptions of that audience. For example, students could be asked to recreate their Facebook profile as an online portfolio for future employers or to redo their MySpace page for inclusion in a classroom montage that would be shown on an overhead screen in class.

These redesign activities ask students to analyze their audience and select appropriate discourse conventions for that audience as well as consider the power differentials between the students and their intended audience members. In the first example, students would need to consider what sort of information "about me" an employer would value, what language and tone would be suitable to use for addressing future employers, and what photographs or other multimedia elements would reflect appropriately on the students' profiles. One important factor for students to reflect on is examining what information they deleted in making the switch from the original personal profile to the revised profile. Students would write a justification of what information they deleted and why they made that choice based on their assumption of how that information would be received by their audience (the future employer). Students are apt to see connections among the power differentials between themselves and future employers and the virtual personas they project in online social networking sites.

In the second example, students would have to think about how their profiles would appear to other students and the instructor when shown as part of a classroom montage during class. Again, students would need to consider what information, language, tone, and visuals would be appropriate for such a mixed audience. They would need to justify based on their analysis of their intended audience what changes in the layout, text, and visual and auditory elements would be most effective for that audience. As in the previous example, students would need to justify the deletion of particular information based on the knowledge that their peers and instructor would be viewing the profile. (An interesting extension of this portion of the assignment might ask students to create a hierarchical map of the power relationships between the different individuals in the class as well as themselves; students would then detail what profile information they believe appropriate to reveal to individuals on different levels of the map and why.)

## I'll be Seeing You: Critiquing Profiles as an Employer

The previous assignment asks students to focus on their own rhetorical choices made when constructing (and refining) the user profile in MySpace and Facebook. This assignment extends the mission of the prior task by asking students to assume a different position from which to write, that of an employer concerned with the proliferation of online social networking profiles and their effect on the workplace. In doing so, students must consider how a member of their chosen discourse community (in this assignment, an upper-level employee of a particular company) would write as well as what perspective this individual would have on social networking in the workplace. In this assignment, students should first read several media articles about employers' concerns regarding social networking and the workplace and discuss them in class; an online search in a publication like *The New York Times*, *Time*, *Newsweek*, or similar should turn up many suitable pieces. Students then choose an upper-level employee of one of the companies described in the news articles to portray. Alternatively, they can write from the perspective of the president or chancellor of their institution.

Assuming the persona—including the diction, style, and tone they think this individual would use—of their chosen employer, students write a critique of a MySpace or Facebook profile. Ideally a student would choose to analyze the same profile used in the "About Me" assignment, but he or she may opt to look up a user who works for the chosen employer and analyze that profile instead. Writing from the perspective of the employer, the student should compose an advisory letter critiquing the individual's profile and how it reflects on the employer. Throughout the letter, students should integrate facts culled from the news articles discussed in previous class periods. Finally, the letter should end with at least one suggestion of how to present a more professional profile befitting an individual who works for this employer. This assignment allows students to build on what they have learned about audience in the previous assignment by pushing them to consider how professional online social networking site profiles look to current and prospective employers.

As well, issues of power will undoubtedly come up in conversation and in the advisory letters as students consider whether employers have the right to demand that their employees portray themselves in certain ways online or surveil employees' profile pages. To have students respond specifically to issues of power, the following writing prompts can be used to follow-up on the critique of a personal profile by an employer.

- You have recently received a critique of your MySpace or Facebook profile by an employer. Write a letter of response in which you address the critique and revisions suggested by the employer and justify why you will or will not be taking the employer's advice. In your letter of response, take a stand on the issue of employers viewing employees' social networking profiles without the employee's knowledge. Do you think it is appropriate for employers to keep track of their employees' actions outside of the workplace? Why or why not?

- Imagine that the critique of your MySpace or Facebook profile from an employer had ended with the words, "You're fired." Write a researched argument detailing your stance on the issue of employees being fired for their actions and words online. In your response, draw on the examples of real-life employees who have been fired for their online writing. Be sure to focus on whether or not you believe online social networking profiles can be cause for firings and why.

- Imagine instead that your critique came not from an employer but the president of your university. The president of your school has sent you a letter informing you that, based on things you've said about a teacher or fellow students at your school, you will be expelled from classes for this semester and forced to apologize to your classmates. Write a response outlining your legal rights as a student (having students research or debate First Amendment rights prior to this assignment could be helpful) and describe what you think is the appropriate response by the school in this situation.

These writing prompts can be used either as standalone assignments or as extensions of the previous "about me" projects that extend the discussion of rhetorical awareness into legal and ethical arenas as well.

## Let's be "Friends": The Social Dynamics of the Top 8

This assignment asks students to consider how issues of audience impact the construction of their MySpace Top 8. The concept of the MySpace Top 8 is familiar to most students, even those who do not participate in online social networking sites. The MySpace Top 8 is a section of the user profile where an individual can showcase eight friends' profiles; their pictures and user names then are associated with the individual's user profile. While MySpace has since changed the Top 8 feature to allow users to highlight four, eight, twelve, sixteen, twenty, or twenty-four friends, the concept of the Top 8 has entered the popular culture lexicon. In contrast, Facebook features a randomized set of six user profiles from an individual's main network (usually a school) rather than allowing the user to choose which profiles to feature. Finally, both sites describe all connections among individuals with the term friend. No other descriptive terms are used aside from friend, so a user may be friends with his or her parents, teachers, employers, significant other, classmates, siblings, and others.

All of these individuals essentially hold the same weight in terms of importance in Facebook because of the randomization of the top six friends in a network. However, in MySpace, users must carefully consider who to include in the Top 8 friends list. In this assignment, therefore, students are asked to discuss how they decided to populate their top friends list as well as how they chose the order of the friends within the Top 8. For example, the number one friend space is often reserved for someone particularly special to the user. Who is featured in their MySpace top friends list? (If the student does not have a MySpace account, ask them to think of how they would populate an imaginary MySpace account.) Why did they choose those particular friends? How often do they change their MySpace Top 8 and why? They can also investigate how the population and placement of the Top 8 friends reflects their offline friendships; for example, some individuals place bands or films in their Top 8 to avoid disappointing any of their friends. Returning to the idea of audience, how did the student make choices about the placement of the Top 8 friends based on who he or she assumed would view this profile page? To conclude this assignment, a student might write a letter to one of their friends in the Top 8 justifying their removal from this section. Using appropriate language and tone for the situation, the student should explain why he or she is removing their friend from the Top 8 and outline what he or she thinks might be the intended outcome of the situation. If students in the class are friends with each other on MySpace, they could even write letters of response to persuade the individual to keep them in the Top 8. Throughout, students must be aware of their audience and use suitable rhetorical strategies to persuade their reader(s) of the suitability of removing a top friend—or of keeping him or her in the Top 8.

## The Electronic Cottage Revisited: Technology, Time, and Romanticism

While the previous assignments impel students to consider online identity construction and rhetorical awareness, this assignment asks them to think about how technology has been assimilated into U.S. culture and, as a result, how technology impacts time and their daily lives. First, students should read Langdon Winner's "Mythinformation" and "Whatever Happened to the Electronic Cottage?" After discussing these two readings in class, students then keep a daily "tech diary" of their use of various technologies, including online social networking activities (if applicable), for one week.

When the week is over, students share their tech diaries with each other in small groups and compare how much time different individuals spend with technology. Students may additionally begin to consider how to define technology and what constitutes "using technology." In particular, ask students to highlight how much time they spend in online social networking sites: checking messages, updating profiles, posting comments, writing blogs, and so on. Now, using either Winner's metaphor of a "technology-saturated future" from "Whatever Happened" or "computer romantics" from "Mythinformation," have students write a response to Winner using details from their tech diaries and quotes from one or both of his texts that discusses how their own experiences using technology reflect on his ideas. For example, students can assess whether they consider themselves to be "computer romantics" and how their technology use and time spent in MySpace and Facebook reflect that identity. Do they believe that social networking sites, for example, might provide new avenues for participatory democracy and, if so, how? Or, students can discuss why they do or do not believe that we live in Winner's "technology-saturated future" or electronic cottage and how the recent explosion of online social networking sites contributes to their view.

One possible follow-up assignment that would help students make connections between their attitudes toward online social networking sites and technological literacy is a technology literacy autobiography. This assignment helps students continue to see the impact of technology on society, their school, and themselves. Chapters from Selfe and Gail E. Hawisher's *Literate Lives in the Information Age* can be provided as models, while typical writing prompts might include the following:

- What are some of your earliest associations with computers? What kinds of technologies did you grow up with?

- How have others (parents, siblings, friends, teachers) helped shape your attitudes toward technology? What roles did some of these individuals play in your growth as a user of technology?

- How has technology influenced your composing processes? Your reading habits? What values do you see reflected in your interactions with technology as you read and write?

- You have already characterized your own relationship with technology earlier in this course. How do you think others view your relationship to technology? How might you like to portray yourself to others and how might you do so?

Students can be encouraged to include visuals in their autobiography.

## User-generated or User-stolen Intellectual Property?

Online social networking sites also provide rich moments to talk about intellectual property issues with students. The following writing prompts ask students to research intellectual property law (including the Digital Millennium Copyright Act, or DMCA) and its application to online social networking sites. First, have students read (in part or in full) Universal Music Corporation's lawsuit against MySpace (UMG Recordings, et al. *v.* MySpace, Inc., Nov. 17, 2006) as well as Danielle Nicole DeVoss and James E. Porter's *Computers and Composition* article "Why Napster Matters to Writing: Filesharing as a New Ethic of Digital Delivery." Next, have students write a response to the following portion of the Universal lawsuit against MySpace:

> Defendant MySpace.com ("MySpace") is one of the world's largest and best known "social networking sites." The foundation of MySpace is its so-called "user-generated content." However, much of that content is not "user-generated" at all. Rather, it is the "user-stolen" intellectual property of others, and MySpace is a willing partner in that theft. No intellectual property is safe in the MySpace world of infringement . . .

In this response, students should draw both on DeVoss and Porter's article as well as legal documents regarding the DMCA and the Universal lawsuit to defend either MySpace or Universal Music Corporation. (A variation on this assignment would be to have students mimic the style of the Universal lawsuit and write a response in the style of a legal brief from MySpace's perspective responding to the lawsuit.) In particular, how might Universal and MySpace reach an agreement that respects others' work while at the same time respects users' interests in access, Fair Use, and works in the public domain (DeVoss and Porter 202)?[4]

To extend this assignment further, students could create a video response (or "video blog") regarding the MySpace/Universal controversy appropriate for posting to YouTube (a video-sharing site that was also sued by Universal in 2005).[5] In class, show the trailer for the film *Alternative Freedom*, a documentary about copyright law and digital rights that features interviews with digital activists like Lawrence Lessig.[6] Analyze the visual argument presented in

---

[4] Both YouTube and MySpace reached agreements with Universal in 2006 to use filtering software to block unlicensed material from appearing in these sites. Instructors may wish to have students consider whether this was an appropriate measure to take; alternatively, they may have students rhetorically analyze the language and tone of the original Universal lawsuit against MySpace and contrast it with Universal's press release in February 2006, "Universal Music Group Joins With MySpace.com for Video-on-Demand," available online at http://new.umusic.com/News.aspx?NewsId=360.

[5] One caution for instructors who may want to have students post their finished videos on YouTube or look at other video blogs on YouTube as examples: Comments on YouTube are uncensored and sometimes contain a great deal of profanity. Instructors may want to download a local copy of a video file and show it sans comments or prescreen the page the video appears on to ensure it is appropriate for class.

[6] The trailer is available online at <http://alternativefreedom.org/?page_id=7>.

this approximately three-minute trailer and discuss how the filmmakers used text, visuals, and sound to attempt to persuade the viewer. In particular, what associations do they derive from some of the images in the video and why might those images have been chosen (for example, the Statue of Liberty, bombs dropping from planes, the cover of DJ Danger Mouse's *The Grey Album*). Finally, students use video equipment to create their own response in the style of the *Alternative Freedom* trailer by juxtaposing words, pictures, and music that responds to the MySpace/Universal lawsuit. They should provide their stance on the issue, support their stance with appropriate evidence, and create an aesthetically pleasing video montage. Such an assignment also provides an opportunity to teach what DeVoss and Porter refer to as a "positive ethic of sharing" regarding intellectual property, fair use guidelines, and Creative Commons materials as students work with music and images for their project (202).

How can the previous assignments help students strengthen their technological literacy and learn more about rhetorical awareness in online spaces? Harnessing students' prior engagement with online social networking sites teaches students that what they learn in their composition classes is applicable not only to the classroom but outside of it as well. Students learn to employ rhetorical techniques and tools such as audience analysis, diction, tone, and evidence not only in print-based texts like the academic essay but also in spaces that can make use of multimedia elements like sound, video, and images. Assignments such as these teach students that rhetorical awareness is not only a classroom-based skill but something that can be applied to nearly all aspects of their lives, including in spaces perhaps dismissed as popular and therefore nonacademic. As rhetorical awareness is valuable not just in the classroom but in everyday life, students have the opportunity to think about their interactions with others in online social networking sites in ways that will help them extend their classroom knowledge to their lives outside the classroom as well. Finally, as students already participate in online social networking sites—and in particular, they are already *writing* in these spaces—harnessing students' interest in social networking can bring a new level of engagement to the writing classroom.

## Works Cited

DeVoss, Dànielle Nicole, and James E. Porter. "Why Napster Matters to Writing: Filesharing as a New Ethic of Digital Delivery." *Computers and Composition* 23 (2006): 178-210.

Selfe, Cynthia L. *Technology and Literacy in the Twenty-First Century*: *The Importance of Paying Attention*. Carbondale, IL: Southern Illinois UP, 1999.

Selfe, Cynthia L., and Gail E. Hawisher. *Literate Lives in the Information Age*: *Narratives of Literacy from the United States*. Mahwah, NJ: Erlbaum, 2004.

Winner, Langdon. "Mythinformation." *Composing Cyberspace: Identity, Community, and Knowledge in the Electronic Age*. Ed. Richard Holeton. Boston: McGraw Hill, 1995. 226-39.

---. "Whatever Happened to the Electronic Cottage?" *Tech Knowledge Revue* 27 July 2001 <http://netfuture. org/2001/Jul2701_121.html>.

# Composition Fellows: The Pop-culturation of J.R.R. Tolkien's *The Fellowship of the Ring*

## *Karen Wright*

I have been a fan of J.R.R. Tolkien's *The Lord of the Rings* for decades, but the 21st century has seen an increased interest in Middle-earth thanks to film director Peter Jackson. Inspired by the availability of the DVD, I decided that *Part One: The Fellowship of the Ring* would make an exciting theme for my composition class. If my students had not read the book, it was likely that many had seen the highly regarded film adaptation. I would use both. However, since this was an expository writing class, my goal was not to focus exclusively on literary analysis, but rather to use *The Fellowship of the Ring* as course content to engage students and to generate good writing. I will describe how my students embraced this popular literature, transformed it into imaginative multimedia projects, and became agents of their own and each other's success.

I set out to introduce my students to Tolkien and *The Lord of the Rings*, hoping for an acculturation to Middle-earth as we followed the Fellowship together. I began the semester as a zealous guide on our journey, borrowing from foreign language studies and adopting a type of immersion technique—all Tolkien, all the time. I designed Tolkien-themed handouts for such issues as grammar and incorporating quotations. My WebCT course homepage was full of photos from the film and links to Tolkien fan sites. Daily journaling prompts elicited reactions to characters and storylines. Essay assignments used *The Fellowship* as a jumping-off point for possible plot deviations, and students were encouraged to write in character. The DVD allowed us to compare scenes from the book to the same scenes in the film. Students led discussions of the reading with chapter handouts and quizzes that they designed. By semester's end, the hoped-for acculturation had taken place as Middle-earth had enchanted students, and it had evolved into a pop-culturation of sorts as students enthusiastically produced such creative projects as skits, videos, and music.

In designing the course, I sought to create a community of enthusiastic co-learners who would embrace *The Fellowship of the Ring* and help each other to connect to it as well. The first challenge was to ensure that students would actually read the novel. Many of today's students balk at the idea of reading a novel as lengthy as *The Lord of the Rings*, but my class would only be dealing with the first third, *The Fellowship of the Ring*. To make the reading more manageable, I divided the book into three sections, which would correspond to essay assignments as well as discussion group activities. Next, I determined what type of essays to assign and matched them with the reading sections. Finally, I wanted to use the film adaptation but felt that it should come after the reading was complete, so I scheduled it toward the end of the semester and followed it with a related essay assignment.

Before we began to read the novel, the first essay assignment kicked off our journey through Middle-earth by asking students to either identify with a character in *The Lord of the Rings* or to describe a journey that they themselves had experienced. This brief essay revealed students' familiarity with the story and previewed their writing ability. While students revised and edited their in-class drafts over the next few days, I introduced them to J.R.R. Tolkien and the marvelous world he had created in *The Lord of the Rings*.

When we began the novel, the last thing that I wanted to do was to give daily lectures on the assigned reading, so I formed discussion groups comprised of three or four students each. Each group was required to present to the class one chapter per reading section (three chapters total). Although I presented the leftover chapters, which provided an opportunity to model basic presentation components, I tried to give the students adequate freedom in presenting their chapters. With each chapter discussion, students would rely less on me and more on themselves and each other.

## Section One: The Journey Begins

The first reading section covered the first eight chapters of the novel, which introduced Middle-earth (and the Shire specifically), the protagonist Frodo, the other hobbits, and the crisis to be overcome. Our class discussions focused primarily on summary—entering this fictional world that Tolkien had imagined and grasping the problem of the One Ring. Discussion guidelines for the first section called for: 1) A 10-question quiz to give to the class; 2) Questions to generate class discussion; and 3) A handout that included a synopsis (summary) of the chapter, a list of major characters in that chapter—include background information if it has not been provided previously, and a list of key concepts that emerge in the chapter. For example, themes in Chapter 1 include social class and Bilbo's sense of humor.

I presented the first chapter complete with a handout and a quiz to demonstrate what I expected from this assignment. The quiz, designed to hold students accountable for the assigned reading, also elicited several groans from the class. Although I was not willing to dismiss the quiz requirement, I made a deal: I would take the quizzes along with the students, and any question I missed would not count against them. However, if they answered it correctly, then they would earn bonus points for that question. This compromise worked great because the student discussion groups wrote the quizzes for their assigned chapters and, therefore, kept each other accountable for the reading homework. Occasionally, a super-easy quiz would be offered, but it was more common for students to delight in trying to stump the instructor.

Likewise, the second essay was based on the first reading section, and I assigned a literary analysis of a character, setting, or theme that we had encountered thus far. Although the entire course would not be devoted to literary analysis, I did want to encourage an investment in the story early on, and because we were not too far into the story, it would be easier for students to narrow the focus of their subjects, which always improves the writing despite students' resistance to doing so. For this essay, I also wanted to introduce incorporating quotations and MLA style. Just for fun, I developed a *Fellowship*-based handout about incorporating quotations that I reviewed in class and posted on my WebCT course homepage

**ASSIGNMENT: Literary Analysis.** Write an essay for the purpose of developing an interpretation of a character, setting, or theme in *The Lord of the Rings, Part One: The Fellowship of the Ring* that is insightful and interesting to readers. You can assume that your audience is as familiar with the text as you are. They are already engaged in the story and have their own interpretations of it, but your job is to present your own thoughtful reading of it. **Use your own brain; do not use secondary sources**. Your interpretation is neither right nor wrong—it is simply *yours*.

**TOPICS:**

1.  You may **analyze** anything that we have encountered in *The Fellowship of the Ring* through Book 1, Chapter 8 that falls into one of the following three categories: Any character other than Frodo (I don't want to read 25 essays about Frodo.) What motivates the character? Does he/she have conflicts to resolve? How does the character fit into the story? What kind of language does the character use? How does he/she interact with other characters?

2.  Setting (Shire, Bree, Old Forest, Buckland, Tom Bombadil's house, etc.) How does the setting influence the mood of the story? The mood of the characters? What kind of language does Tolkien use to describe the setting?

3.  Theme (nature, social class, ethnicity, music, chance, etc.)

## Section Two: A Plan Emerges

The second reading section saw the hobbits encounter the mysterious ranger Strider, flee from the Black Riders, and eventually arrive at Rivendell where the fate of the One Ring would be determined. Because our next essay assignment would be argumentative, I encouraged students to develop more analytical skills. The presentation guidelines instructed the groups to help the class explore key concepts or events through insightful discussion questions and interesting handouts. I encouraged more creative handouts, making them informative and visually appealing, and modeled this assignment by leading another chapter discussion. Creativity was emphasized to help prepare students for the next presentation.

The third essay was a lot of fun. Although we all knew the outcome of the Council of Elrond, I thought it would be interesting to see what other creative solutions my students could imagine. I assigned an argumentative essay to encourage their creativity.

**ASSIGNMENT: Argument/Persuasion.** Write an essay for the purpose of swaying your audience's point of view. Under no circumstances should you combine any of the three topics given. Do not use quotes from the text or from secondary sources; you are essentially writing in character.

**TOPICS:**

1. The Council of Elrond is in full swing. You have heard the history and evidence confirming that Frodo's ring is the One Ring. You cannot believe that your fellow Council members are actually discussing some hare-brained scheme to take the Ring to Mount Doom to try to destroy it. Have they lost their minds?! Why not just hand-deliver it to Sauron himself? *You* have a much better idea. Present your alternative solution to the Council.

2. The Council of Elrond has just concluded, and the plan of action has been determined: Frodo will attempt to destroy the Ring in the fires of Mount Doom. As the head of the Fellowship Recruiting Team, it is your job to evaluate candidates to accompany Frodo on his quest and forward your recommendations to Elrond. The scouts have returned from their surveillance, so time is up. Present your top three choices to Elrond. Just for fun, assume that Gandalf can use his magic to transport anyone we have met so far to Rivendell to go on the Quest.

3. The Council of Elrond has just concluded, and the plan of action has been determined: Frodo will attempt to destroy the Ring in the fires of Mount Doom. As the head of the Troubleshooting Committee, it is your job to anticipate problems and try to prevent them; your responsibilities extend to the area of Frodo on his quest and forward your recommendations to Elrond. The scouts have returned from their surveillance, so time is up. Present your top three choices to Elrond. Just for fun, assume that Gandalf can use his magic to transport anyone we have met so far to Rivendell to go on the Quest.

The argumentative/persuasive essay was my favorite assignment from this semester. To help students get started and to encourage them to consider some minor characters as well, I provided a sample paragraph for option #2, in which I argue for the inclusion of Barliman Butterbur in the Fellowship. Some of my students truly rose to the challenge on this assignment and came up with imaginative, well-constructed arguments for using, hiding, or disposing of the Ring. Students who chose to recommend or oppose Fellowship team members largely stuck with the major players, such as Aragorn, Legolas, and Gandalf, but even those popular characters inspired some creative arguments for their inclusion.

**Student Example:**

The last necessary addition to the Fellowship may seem less qualified than the previous two; nevertheless, Samwise Gamgee shows the strongest commitment to his fellow comrades on the quest. He values these individuals more than anything else in the world and will do anything for them and for the success of the mission. Without completely understanding the importance of the quest, his naïveté will permit him to enter even the most perilous of situations without fear. No, he does not have any unique skills as far as fighting evil is concerned, and he may attract attention when none is wanted and otherwise get in the way, but without Sam's constant encouragement the quest would be futile. A less important, yet undoubtedly relevant quality Sam possesses is his esteemed skill in the culinary arts. While this may not prove enough to ward off his enemies, it may provide just enough mental and physical sustenance to keep the Fellowship alive. Moreover, including Sam in the journey also reminds Frodo of what he must protect – the Shire and the Hobbits he loves – which are also at stake in this struggle between good and evil. As Frodo's closest companion and confidant when he feels he can trust no other, Sam will be invaluable on this perilous trek.

## Section Three: The Fellowship Ends

The third reading section followed the Fellowship on their journey south, through Moria and Lothlórien, and along the Great River Anduin, until Frodo and Sam part with the rest of the Company and head off to Mordor on their own. Because many exciting events happen in this section to elicit an emotional response, I invited students to explore a personal connection to the story for their next presentation. I dismissed the handout and quiz requirements and instead asked the students to apply their own talents and experiences to a creative project. My suggestions included:

- Convert a particular scene into a comedy sketch
- Create an original piece of artwork
- Set one of Tolkien's poems to music
- Prepare some "authentic" recipes
- Write a poem "a la Bilbo" that describes a particular event
- Share the diary entries of a member of the Fellowship
- Do a dramatic reading
- Report on the life and career of J.R.R. Tolkien
- Use your imagination and HAVE FUN!

The students' response to my invitation was overwhelmingly positive. I was amazed at the time and effort that some groups invested. One group created a video modeled after TBS's "Dinner and a Movie" program in which the hosts prepare a meal and conduct informal interviews relevant to the featured film of the evening. Several groups performed skits in front of the class; a particularly good one mimicked a news program, including live interviews with Frodo and Sam "from the field." Three young women sang one of Tolkien's poems set to rap music, and they choreographed dance moves as well. A few groups researched and prepared recipes of food described in the book—the Elven *lembas* were especially popular. One young man who had struggled throughout much of the semester surprised me with a diary entry written from Gimli's perspective upon finding his murdered kinfolk in the mines of Moria. By encouraging my students to tap their own interests and abilities, I freed them to produce some of their most thoughtful work all semester.

It seemed natural that the third essay should also highlight a personal connection, so I assigned a response to literature.

---

**ASSIGNMENT: Response to Literature.** Write an essay for the purpose of examining your reaction to a scene in *The Fellowship of the Ring*. This essay varies from a standard literary analysis in that you must draw on your own experiences to help you explain to your reader why you view the scene as you do. Questions to ask yourself include: "What did I find interesting in the reading? Why? What part of the reading best relates to my life? How so?"

**TIPS:**

- **Use your own brain; do NOT use any sources other than** *The Fellowship of the Ring*.

- **Limit your topic** to one scene. For example, do not write about the Fellowship's entire journey through Moria; instead, write about getting into Moria *or* the discovery of Balin's Tomb *or* Gandalf's confrontation with the Balrog.

- **Clearly articulate your reaction** to the scene. Use language that is understandable and precise. For example, don't say, "Frodo's flight to the Ford of Bruinen was awesome!" Instead, say, "My heart raced along with Frodo's as he fled to the Ford of Bruinen—would he escape the Black Riders?"

- **Explain the link** between the text and your response. For example, don't just say, "I thought the scene was scary." Instead, say, "I got chills when Frodo was stabbed by the Black Rider because I flashed back to the time I was mugged."

---

Unfortunately, these essays were not nearly as ambitious as the presentations. The students did not seem to know what to say. In hindsight, swapping the order of Essay 2 (Literary Analysis) and Essay 4 (Response to Literature) might have been more effective.

# The Film

After we finished reading *The Fellowship of the Ring*, we watched the DVD of the film adaptation. This took a few days, but I used the shorter version to save time. The video led naturally to a comparison/contrast essay about the book and the film.

**ASSIGNMENT: Comparison/Contrast.** Write an essay for the purpose of comparing and contrasting a scene in *The Fellowship of the Ring* with its corresponding film adaptation. For this essay, you will draw on your knowledge of description, plot awareness, and critical thinking.

**TIPS:**

**Use your own brain**; do NOT use any sources other than the print and film versions of *The Fellowship of the Ring*. [I will allow artists' interpretations (drawings/paintings) if necessary, but of course, these must also be properly documented.]

Select one scene from the text of *The Fellowship of the Ring* and compare and contrast this scene with the presentation of the same scene in the film. In your comparison, you should consider what, if any, detail is left out of the movie version and whether or not new detail or information is added to the movie scene that appears elsewhere in the book presentation.

Remember that details are the heart and soul of this essay because the comparison of details forms the foundation of your opinion about how closely the film matches the book.

You should arrive at some conclusion as to **why** the scene differs from the book or **why** it is true to the book. You must remember that your ultimate purpose is to make a judgment about the scene—either it is essentially the same as Tolkien wrote it in the book or it is essentially different from how he wrote it in the book.

This essay was particularly effective in promoting in-depth reading. Because writers had to describe scenes in great detail and support their analyses with quotations, they read and re-read textual passages to refer to in their writing. Nevertheless, because we had enjoyed a fun and collegial atmosphere, students infused their writing with that same jovial spirit.

**Student Example**

Conversely, in the film adaptation, Jackson has taken the liberty of removing the unnecessary thoughtful gifts and replacing them with fluffier, pointless-but-cool-looking items. Hardest hit in this flawed representation is Samwise Gamgee. The movie completely skips Sam's G-Dirt and further demeans him by not giving him one the daggers the others receive. Sam is so flustered by the situation that he boldly inquires whether or not the Lady Galadriel might "happen to have any more of those nice shiny daggers?" (*Lord*). Eventually, Sam does receive a gift although it is merely rope, which in the book, the entire Company receives in addition to their individual items. Meanwhile, Legolas still comes out with his admirable bow, and likewise, Frodo receives his phial of the "Light of Galadriel" (*Lord*). Merry and Pippin do not receive belts but instead receive the daggers mentioned above which have, according to the movie, battled against Sauron before. However, according to the text, these daggers were actually forged by "The Men of the Westernesse," and all four hobbits received them months beforehand from Tom Bombadil (Tolkien142). Scandalously, the film omits Tom's character altogether. Furthermore, Gimli's crush-inspired antics are watered down in the film and only alluded to briefly later. The two scenes are similar in that all the characters do receive some sort of parting gift, but this is about the only thing they have in common.

## Middle-earth and More

The semester that I borrowed J. R. R. Tolkien's *The Lord of the Rings* for my course content theme was one of the most enjoyable semesters I have ever taught. Not only did I have extensive knowledge of Tolkien and his work, but also I could not help but infuse my class with my own passion for them. Even students who resisted the theme in the beginning caught my excitement and produced quality work in the process. This level of knowledge and enthusiasm is what makes using pop culture in the writing classroom work. Any instructor could tap into his or her own passion and develop an engaging composition theme around it.

Conversely, the lack of a clearly-defined course theme can be detrimental. Since my *Fellowship*-themed semester, I have tried numerous other course themes, including one I call "Passions and Pursuits." While this theme was promising because it allowed students to explore their own interests all semester through various writing assignments, it presented some unforeseen problems. Students with clear goals and declared majors typically succeeded. However, less-focused students struggled a bit more despite my encouragement to write about their hobbies if they had not yet chosen a career field. I also noted that more female students than male students floundered with such freedom of choice.

Determining that students really wanted more clearly defined parameters, I returned to narrowing my content theme to such topics as politics and society. Although these topics were more serious, I still relied on pop culture media for writing prompts and assignments. For example, if I were lucky enough to teach in a high-tech classroom, I would show television clips from *The Daily Show* found at www.comedycentral.com and have students do in-class journaling afterward, which prompted that day's discussion. During the 2004 presidential campaign, students imagined working on a College Voter Task Force and evaluated the effectiveness of 30-second advertising spots of the two major candidates, John Kerry and George W. Bush, found on their respective websites. And one of my favorite essay assignments asked students to analyze an editorial cartoon, which works great for this and many other content themes, including *The Lord of the Rings*. (Besides newspapers, a good source for editorial cartoons is www.slate.com.)

For my most recent composition course, I chose the theme "The Academic Gourmet." My students wrote all of their essays about food in various contexts (family, society, literature, and popular culture). We read the short novel *Like Water for Chocolate* by Laura Esquivel before watching the film adaptation, which is remarkably faithful to the book. Because I enjoyed the discussion groups so much during the *Fellowship*-themed semester, I used the same idea for the food theme with nearly equal success. Students also did presentations about the food-related pop culture phenomenon of their choice; two that were particularly memorable involved the role of food in the science fiction television shows *Star Trek* (replicated freely by machines) and *Firefly* (used as currency) and the Endless characters' relationships with food in the graphic novels of Neil Gaiman. I also borrowed a terrific essay assignment from a colleague in which students collaborated in small groups to construct a 20-question interview (with corresponding answers) of a character in the novel. This assignment required an in-depth understanding of the character as well as audience awareness and would have been terrific for my Tolkien semester.

These examples show that pop culture can add a fun and timely component to any instructor's interests and composition classes. Not only can instructors draw upon a wide array of topics and media to engage their students, but also students can enrich class discussions and their writing by bringing their own knowledge and experience of pop culture into the classroom.

Finding such common ground promotes a more student-centered classroom, which helps both students and instructors to succeed.

## Works Cited

*The Lord of the Rings: The Fellowship of the Ring.* Dir. Peter Jackson. DVD. New Line Home Entertainment, 2002.

Tolkien, J.R.R. *The Fellowship of the Ring: Being the First Part of The Lord of the Rings.* New York: Ballantine, 1994.

# Conflict in the Borderlands: Using Multiculturalism in the Writing Classroom to Help Students Articulate Cultural Identity

*Keri Mayes Tidwell*

*Every student brings to class a picture of the world in his or her mind that is constructed out of his or her cultural background and unique and complex experience. As writing teachers, we can help students articulate and understand that experience, but we also have the important job of helping every writer to understand that each of us sees the world through our own particular lens, one shaped by unique experiences. In order to communicate with others, we must learn to see through their lenses as well as try to explain to them what we see through ours. In an interactive classroom where students collaborate with other writers, this process of decentering so one can understand the 'other' can foster genuine multicultural growth.*

Maxine Hairston (190)

The above quote, taken from Maxine Hairston's controversial article "Diversity, Ideology, and Teaching Writing," illustrates my goals as a writing instructor and provides the basic structure for this paper. First, students need to understand that their identities are a direct result of the cultural influences and experiences in their lives. Second, by using a foreign film as the class "text," students will look through the lens of another—a Mexican woman—and examine how culture determines who a person is and will become. Finally, students will compare what they have learned about their own cultural identities with what they have learned about the influence another culture can have on that identity, as well as how one's cultural identity affects and influences the cultural identities of others.

Conflict in the writing classroom may arise from the cultural differences among students. According to Min-Zhan Lu in "Professing Multiculturalism: The Politics of Style in the Contact Zone," "a multicultural approach to student writing…views the classroom as a potential 'contact zone'" (447). Mary Louise Pratt calls the "contact zone" the "social spaces where cultures meet, clash, and grapple with each other, often in contexts of highly asymmetrical relations of power" (34). Every student is unique and brings with him/her to the classroom his/her own experiences, values, and beliefs about life based on the culture both in which s/he has been raised and where s/he lives today. As a result, students often occupy multiple subject positions simultaneously. Sometimes these subject positions clash and conflict, causing the individual to suppress one as s/he articulates another. Lu says that students must "negotiate a position in response to these colliding voices" ("Professing" 440). While this personal negotiation of positions might *appear* easy, asking students to choose positions "in the context of the socio-political power relationships within and among diverse discourses and in the context of their personal life, history, culture, and society," may be difficult for them to do (448). Thus, using a multicultural approach in the writing classroom may frustrate students as they struggle to locate their cultural identities by forcing them to make choices and take action. Lu would insist, however, that with the pain comes the inevitable reward of "a new consciousness" ("Conflict" 888). This new consciousness will empower students, providing them with an awareness of different cultural perspectives.

## I. First, students need to understand that their identities are a direct result of the cultural influences and experiences in their lives.

In her essay, "One Person, Many Worlds: A Multi-Cultural Composition Curriculum," Delores Schriner states that "there is no such thing as a singular 'Anglo-American experience'" (97). Even if every student in the classroom is from the United States, this does not mean that every student is the same; the wide variety of subject positions that make up every student contribute to the heterogeneity of the classroom. Maxine Hairston would contend that because students "are our greatest multicultural resource, one that is authentic, rich, and truly diverse," they should be the "content" of the writing class (190). For the first few weeks of class, I follow Hairston's advice, keeping the students and their experiences as the source of and material for the writing assignments, but, then, I bring in an entirely different culture—the culture of the Mexican woman—as a means of comparison so that students can examine how this culture affects their cultural identities.

In the first class, students deconstruct and examine their individual cultural identities first through freewriting and then in small groups. On their own, students endeavor to answer the greater question: "Who are you?" by considering the following: "What subject positions make up who you are? What influences in your life have affected and continue to affect who you are today? How do those influences contribute to your identity?" After ten minutes of freewriting, students form small groups to discuss their responses to these questions. Discussion is lengthy, but the goal is for students to think critically about their identities and be able to explain to each other the societal and familial influences in their lives. After discussion students compile a list of these subject positions, which they share in the next class period.

For the remainder of the class time, I introduce students to journal writing. Students then spend the first ten minutes of every class period writing about the following topic:

---

#### In-Class Journal Assignment

Describe one specific way in which you have come in contact with some aspect of culture today. You might write about someone you meet; a place you go; the music you listen to; a movie or television program that you watch; a book, magazine, advertisement, or billboard that you read; and food that you eat; etc.

---

According to Diana George and John Trimbur in their introduction to *Reading Culture: Contexts for Critical Reading and Writing,* "[t]o read culture means *not* taking for granted such readings of everyday life. Reading culture means bringing forward for analysis and reflection those commonplace aspects of everyday life that people normally think of as simply being there, a part of the natural order of things" (3). The journal is the students' record of the cultural "conflicts" that they encounter throughout the week, and it provides a space for students to negotiate their positions within the context of that culture. For instance, one student might write about the rap song he heard on the radio on his way to school. He might choose to deconstruct the song and give specific details about the lyrics, tone, and effect the song had on him.

The goal in this journal writing assignment is not only for students to pay attention to the vast number of different cultural influences they come in contact with everyday but also to examine closely how and to what extent those influences affect them. As Phyllis van Slyck suggests in her essay, "Repositioning Ourselves in the Contact Zone," "[p]art of our responsibility, it seems to me, is to help students see that unreflective group consensus does not constitute an ethical position and that sometimes becoming an individual means standing apart from one's community and questioning its practices and values" (156). This call for self-reflection then may serve both to examine more closely how influential culture is in our daily lives and to break down the cultural biases prevalent in students who neglect to question and articulate their subject positions.

In the next class period, students begin with their in-class journal writing assignment. Then, we discuss the lists of subject positions that the students made in the previous class, and the students explain their rationale for the inclusion of each subject position. I then explain that these subject positions make up who we are as individuals and that collectively they form our cultural identities. We also discuss how these subject positions differ from person to person depending on the culture, so that one definition of "family" might include a husband, a wife, and their two children while another might consist of two women and their adopted child. By the end of the class, the students have created a master list of subject positions (hereinafter "Students' List"), which may include, without limitation, any or all of the following: family, religion, community, education, race, gender, sexual orientation, class, heritage, customs, traditions, arts, environment, among others. The class keeps a copy of the "Students' List" for future reference.

---

**First Writing Assignment**

Pick three subject positions from the "Students' List" and write an essay in which you describe yourself based on each position. Approach each subject position individually. First, describe what you think each subject position means to you. Consider how each subject position affected your identity when you were a child and how it influences you today as an adult. You should ask yourself the following questions: "What does the subject position mean to me? What role has the subject position played in my life, and what role does it play in my life today? How does the subject position continue to influence me as an adult?" Finally, describe the ways in which the culture in which you live influences your subject positions.

---

The goals for this writing assignment are that students deconstruct and articulate their subject positions so that they understand the influences of these positions; that students be aware of how culture influences their subject positions throughout their lives, that is, from infancy to adulthood; and that students recognize that who they are is a direct result of their particular subject positions as well as the cultures in which they were raised and currently live. This essay provides the basis for comparison in the final paper.

## II. Second, by using a foreign film as the class "text," students will look through the lens of another—a Mexican woman—and examine how culture determines who a person is and will become.

In *Getting Home Alive,* Aurora Levins Morales and Rosario Morales discuss "La Identidad Cultural," that is, the cultural identity of Latinos living within the United States. Drawing on Joseph Fitzpatrick's definitions of identity "as the points of reference that we use to define ourselves in relation to other people in the world" and "an awareness of who we are and where we belong," the writers elaborate on what they consider "points of reference" for the Latino: "family, religion, community, and various artistic expressions" (109). These influences, as our class has seen and discussed, are not limited solely to Latinos but may also apply to any ethnic group, including the Anglo-American. Cultural identity, then, is a malleable construct that constantly shifts and changes depending on an individual's exposure to a variety of cultures. As a person moves within and without various communities, s/he chooses, often without recognition, whether or not to incorporate certain aspects of that culture into her/his identity.

While personal influences such as family, religion, community, and customs and traditions contribute to the identity of a person, the cultures of peoples from different ethnic groups are also influential. For van Slyck, "[d]iscussions and writing assignments can, I believe, be shaped to open new perspectives so that students can experience the 'conflicts and struggles' of those who occupy subject positions quite different from their own" (152). The idea is that a multicultural pedagogy will assist students as they begin to articulate their subject positions and negotiate differences when these positions "clash" with someone else's. Gregory S. Jay adds to this discussion in "The End of 'American' Literature: Toward a Multicultural Practice":

> In sum, a multicultural pedagogy initiates a cultural re-vision, so that everyone involved comes not only to understand another person's point of view, but to see her or his own culture from the outsider's perspective. This decentering of cultural chauvinism can only be healthy in the long run, especially if it leads each of us to stop thinking of ourselves as subjects of only one position or culture. (274)

Cultural biases are prevalent in students whose exposure to different cultures is often negligible. In her essay "Contact, Colonization, and Classrooms: Language Issues via Cisneros's *Woman Hollering Creek* and Villanueva's *Bootstraps,*" Mary R. Harmon describes her first-year students as predominately white, from small towns or rural areas, and with minimal travel outside of their local region. In Harmon's class, these students read multicultural texts that forced them to "encounter Englishes and other languages with which they are unfamiliar and which they often have been taught either to dismiss or to regard as inferior" and compelled them to "grapple with lifestyles and cultures much different from most of their own" (200). A multicultural approach to the writing classroom, then, initiates students into a cultural conflict, a contact zone where differences may cause contention and discordance. However, out of these struggles arise new insights into both the cultural identity of the "combatant" as well as the students' own cultural identities. After reading *Woman Hollering Creek* and *Bootstraps* and negotiating their own positions within the contact zones created by these texts, Harmon's students "demonstrated more thoughtful, less judgmental, more open responses to the languages, story modes, and cultures of the texts" (210). My hope is that as my students grapple in unfamiliar contact zones, they will recognize not only the importance of respecting different cultures, as Harmon's student did, but also that multiple subject positions and cultures constitute their identities and that they are more than simply Anglo-Americans.

In the third week of class, we watch Alfonso Arau's film *Like Water for Chocolate* (1992), which is based on Laura Esquivel's novel of the same name. The film is set in early, rural Mexico and centers on the everyday life of Tita and her relationships with her domineering mother, two sisters, and the two men in her life. As the youngest daughter, Tita cannot marry but must take care of her widowed mother until the latter's death. She is also given the onerous responsibility of preparing the food for daily meals and social events, including the wedding of her own true love to her oldest sister. The film's focus on the roles of women within the family, as well as the importance of food, sex, and relationships, illustrates the traditions and customs of Mexican culture. This culture is significant to the Anglo-American student because of the rising number of Latinos/as living within the United States today.

Based on statistics taken from the 2000 U.S. Census, there are over 35 million people (12.5% of the total U.S. population) living within the United States of Hispanic or Latino descent; the largest group is from Mexico (7.3%, or 20.6 million) (U.S. Census Bureau). As the number of Latinos/as in this country continues to increase, simultaneously, their cultural influences are becoming more and more pervasive. This is especially true since, according to the California Identity Project, Latinos/as are not assimilating fully into American society but consider themselves Americans in the sense that "being American implies being Latino, speaking Spanish, and conserving the family" (Hayes-Bautista 40). While they may call themselves Americans, many Latinos/as still hold on to the culture of their homeland. They, "[i]n contrast to the European immigrants [,]…continue to base their identity on the family, culture, religion, and language" (40). Thus, Latinos/as are part of a rapidly growing group in the United States whose strong cultural backgrounds deserve our immediate, undivided attention.

After watching *Like Water for Chocolate*, the class discusses the film, focusing on prevailing cultural issues such as the role of food, sex, family, relationships, the roles of men and women within society and the family, how men and women dress, traditions, and customs. My hope is that this discussion informs students about a different culture with which, despite their close proximity and possibly daily exposure to it, they might not be very familiar. I also hope to help them confront any cultural issues with which they might be struggling and negotiate their own positions in relation to this culture.

---

**Second Writing Assignment**

Choose an issue that was brought up during class discussion or that you think is controversial, and write an essay in response to it. You should answer the following questions: "How do you feel about this issue personally? How do(es) the character(s) react to that issue? What does the issue say about the culture? How does this issue affect the character(s) involved? Does the issue change your perspective of it?"

---

In this second essay, students have another opportunity to reflect on something from the film that may have caused them "conflict," especially if they were unable to respond fully to this particular issue during class discussion. This essay provides the space for confrontation and negotiation of the students' positions.

In the fourth week of class, we focus attention on the cultural identity of Tita, the main character of the film. In their small groups, students talk about and create a second list of words to describe what they perceive as the influences in Tita's life; this is called "Tita's List." I will suggest that they return to the "Students' List" and add any of the words from this list that apply to "Tita's List." Then, as a class, we discuss Tita's subject positions and create a second master list based on what the students say constitutes Tita's cultural identity. The items on "Tita's List" are very similar to those on the "Students' List," and I hope that the students will see cultural similarities and differences between themselves and Tita based on these lists and small group and class discussions.

---

**Third Writing Assignment**

Pick one of the subject positions on "Tita's List," and write an essay explaining how that subject position influences Tita. For example, if you choose to write about the *family,* describe how the *family* influences and affects Tita's identity. You should answer the following questions: "What do you think this subject position means to Tita? What role does the subject position play in Tita's life? How does the subject position affect both who Tita is and who she becomes at the end of the film? How does Tita's culture affect this subject position?" (You may want to pick one of the same subject positions that you wrote about in your first writing assignment because your final writing assignment will be to pick one subject position that appears on both the "Students' List" and "Tita's List" and compare your personal position within that subject position with Tita's position within it.)

---

My goals for this writing assignment are that students consider another person's perspective about a subject position that they may or may not have in common; that students see the similarities and differences between themselves and others; and that students consider how a person from another culture is affected by his/her culture. Continuing with the example in the writing assignment, the student might write about the influence that Mama Elena plays in Tita's identity. S/he could reflect on how Tita's mother neglected her emotionally from infancy, forced her into a life of servitude, refused to allow her to marry her childhood sweetheart, and terrorized her even after death. The student might discuss how these actions contribute to who Tita is, how she changes throughout the film, who she is at the end, and what this says about her. Finally, the student might consider how Tita's culture affects her relationship with her mother. The purpose of the assignment is to get students to think about how Tita's culture and her subject positions within that culture work together to create her identity.

# III. Finally, students will compare what they have learned about their own cultural identities with what they have learned about the influence another culture can have on that identity, as well as how one's cultural identity affects and influences the cultural identities of others.

---

**Fourth Writing Assignment**

Pick one subject position listed on both the "Students' List" and "Tita's List," and write an essay describing both your personal position and Tita's position within that particular subject position. You should answer the following questions: "What is your personal position on this subject position? What do you think Tita's position is on this subject position? How is your position both similar to and different from Tita's? How do these similarities and differences affect your perception of the subject position you chose? How might your cultural identity influence Tita's? How might Tita's cultural identity influence yours?" Your essay should conclude with your opinion about how one's culture affects his/her subject positions.

---

This final paper is a synthesis of the prior writing assignments, and students are encouraged to refer to and use pertinent sections from their three prior essays, journals, and in-class discussions to assist them in their papers. The final paper should reflect an awareness of the students' own subject positions and how these positions compare and contrast with Tita's. For example, continuing with the subject position of the family, first, the student would write about his/her own position in the family, his/her role in the family, how the family has influenced him/her, and how the family has contributed to his/her cultural identity. Then, s/he writes about Tita's position within Tita's family, the role of the family in her life, how the family has influenced her, and how the family has contributed to her cultural identity. Next, the student compares his/her position to Tita's, looking at both similarities and differences. In addition, the student should answer how, if s/he came in contact with Tita, s/he might influence her subject position and also how Tita might influence the student's. S/he should close with her/his opinion about the effects culture has on one's subject positions. My goals are that students will be more aware of their own subject positions as well as the subject positions of others from both similar and different cultures; that students will understand their differences and be cognizant of potential biases; and that students will perceive how they influence and are influenced by different cultures and how that culture affects their subject positions.

I hope that by using a multicultural approach in the writing classroom, students may become more aware of their own cultural identities and the different subject positions that make them up so that when faced with "conflicts," they will know how to respond appropriately: negotiating positions without fear and dread. Hopefully, through self-reflection and a negotiation of positions, students will better understand their own cultural identities so that in future classes and in life, they will be cognizant of the fact that their own biases affect their worldview and others'. I also hope that students will be able to perceive more clearly how their identities are influenced by different cultures in their daily lives, and, as a result, that students may learn more about their own cultural identities through an awareness of the cultural identities of others. Also, if students are able to examine another culture, they will be able to analyze future texts with confidence and relative ease in spite of the conflicts that will inevitably ensue. My final desire is that students will see their personal biases and find ways to eradicate, not perpetuate, them so that they may have more tolerant perspectives of peoples of different cultures.

## Works Cited

George, Diana, and John Trimbur. Introduction. *Reading Culture: Contexts for Critical Reading and Writing*. 4th ed. Ed Diana George and John Trimbur. New York: Longman, 2001. 1-4.

Hairston, Maxine. "Diversity, Ideology, and Teaching Writing." *CCC* 43 (1992): 179-93.

Harmon, Mary R. "Contact, Colonization, and Classrooms: Language Issues via Cisneros's *Women Hollering Creek* and Villanueva's *Bootstraps*." *Professing in the Contact Zone: Bringing Theory and Practice Together*. Ed. Janice M. Wolff. Urbana, IL: NCTE, 2002. 197-212.

Hayes-Bautista, David. "Latino Contributions." *Americanos: Latino Life in the United States.* Ed. Edward James Olmos, Lea Ybarra, and Manuel Monterrey. Boston: Little, 1999. 40.

Jay, Gregory S. "The End of 'American' Literature: Toward a Multicultural Practice." *CE* 53 (1991): 264-81.

Lu, Min-Zhan. "Conflict and Struggle: The Enemies or Preconditions of Basic Writing?" *CE* 54 (1992): 887-913.

---. "Professing Multiculturalism: The Politics of Style in the Contact Zone." *CCC* 45 (1994): 442-58.

Morales, Aurora Levins, and Rosario Morales. *Getting Home Alive*. Ithaca: Firebrand, 1986.

Pratt, Mary Louise. "Arts of the Contact Zone." *Profession 91* (1991): 33-40.

Schriner, Delores K. "One Person, Many Worlds: A Multi-Cultural Composition Curriculum." *Cultural Studies in the English Classroom.* Ed. James A. Berlin and Michael J. Vivion. Portsmouth, NH: Boynton/Cook, 1992. 95-111.

United States Census Bureau. "QT-P3. Race and Hispanic or Latino: 2000." *U.S. Census Bureau American Factfinder.* 15 Mar. 2005 <http://factfinder.census.gov/servlet/>.

Van Slyck, Phyllis. "Repositioning Ourselves in the Contact Zone." *CE* 59 (1997): 149-70.

# Evaluation, Plus: Using the Review Assignment to Move Students from Passive to Active Learners

## *Sarah Huffines*

On a beautiful spring day as the semester was nearing its last few weeks, I found myself in a composition classroom facing by-then familiar faces. We were talking about the Black Eyed Peas song, "My Humps," an insanely popular song at the time, driven by a powerful beat and a nearly monotone but syncopated and quickly-delivered vocal track. My students are always up for a laugh, so I thought a discussion of this ridiculous song could be useful but lighthearted. I grabbed a copy of the lyrics and a relevant article from Slate.com and enjoyed my walk to class. I should have known then what would be waiting for me. On this spring day, the campus was full of visitors: bright-eyed skinny teenagers, slightly disoriented and mortally embarrassed, and their accompanying parents, smartly dressed in business casual and perhaps internally calculating the ratio between the quality of the college and its tuition. When I walked into the classroom with a discussion of "My Humps" planned and ready to go, naturally, there were parents visiting my classroom that day, sitting in the back seats with good posture and a general air of expectancy.

I read through some of the lyrics – "my hump, my hump, my lovely lady lumps"—and skipped over some of the other lyrics—"I'm a get, get, get, get, you drunk, get you love drunk off my hump" (Black Eyed Peas). I'll admit it: I blushed. I tried to sound articulate and distant when I read the lyrics. I tried to enunciate the title specifically so that it never sounded as though I was talking about *my* humps. I hoped that the parents weren't on the board of trustees. But I also knew that this was a chance to test my belief in using popular culture in the classroom, a chance to articulate why "My Humps," or any song for that matter, is worth talking about.

Students, particularly freshman composition students, need help with the transition from high school to college, a transition from passive receivers of information to active engagers in arguments, from students who passively consumed knowledge in high school to students who can use their critical thinking skills to judge information and make new arguments based on what they find. In his well known study *Forms of Ethical and Intellectual Development in the College Years*, William Perry traces the growth of college students' thinking through nine different developmental stages. In the first stage, he writes, "[the] assumption of [the] dualistic structure of world [is] taken for granted, unexamined" (endnote). Though his primary focus is on the dualistic nature of these students' world views, he does spend some time addressing the way these students' perceive their own thoughts. He writes of the progression away from stage one, the unexamined stage: "The progression is from thinking to meta-thinking, from man as knower to man as critic of his own thought" (71). Ultimately, Perry traces the development from embeddedness to actualization, from an assumed knowledge to a knowledge made real. To borrow a phrase from educational theory, students need to move from the "known to the new," and they certainly know pop culture. They've watched it on television, Googled it, downloaded it onto their iPods, and then blogged about it. Theirs is a generation in touch and entertained, and teachers wanting to reach students where they are can use that knowledge. Specifically, an evaluation assignment that asks students to critique popular culture and examine the implications of their arguments helps them become the sort of thinkers that college demands.

## The Evaluation Argument: An Overview

"Evaluations are everyday arguments," write the authors of *Everything's an Argument*, a popular rhetoric and composition textbook that devotes thirty pages to "Evaluations" (Lunsford 176). They continue, "Today rituals of praise and blame are part of American life. Adults who'd choke at the very notion of debating causal or definitional claims will happily spend hours appraising the Miami Hurricanes or the Fighting Irish" (177). They are certainly not alone in that claim. "People make evaluations all the time," according to another textbook, *Good Reasons* (Faigley 153). Just as evaluation arguments are common in our society, writing about evaluations is common in so many composition textbooks. A quick look at any publisher's available composition textbooks reveals whole chapters devoted to evaluation; even an online rhetoric and composition "wikibook," created by internet users devotes significant space to evaluation. It is a foundational topic in composition classrooms—right alongside chapters about clarity, rhetorical analysis, or arguing by definition.

This importance is why, like so many other composition teachers across the country, I assign an evaluation paper to my students every semester. To qualify for just a moment: I recognize that there are some problems in assignments that have an end product in mind (in this case, an evaluation by criteria), rather than focus on process or self-expression, and I also recognize that this may appeal to the more traditional or classic rhetorical approach to composition. However, composition theories are not necessarily contradictory, and the evaluation paper, as an end product, is worthwhile for several reasons.

First, as the textbooks mention, the evaluation paper teaches students something about argumentative public discourse. Letters to the editors, arguments about zoning ordinances, or simple restaurant reviews: evaluations are everywhere, and students will encounter them. Asking students to participate in public-like writing activities (even in artificial constructs like the classroom) shows students the credibility of the assignment, helping them to recognize that they are not writing some invented, context-less, and therefore pointless assignment, but rather practicing at a *real* thing, with *real* world consequences. An evaluation paper gives students a concrete context and a larger sense of purpose.

Second, the evaluation paper is an occasion to talk about and generate criteria, a skill that is useful for developing critical thinking skills. Ken Bain, in his book *What the Best College Teachers Do,* connects public discourse with critical thinking skills when he writes that "Many outstanding teachers think of their courses as ways to help students learn to reason well and to join a conversation that flourishes among people who do" (80). The problem of evaluation does go far beyond academic life: What makes something particularly good or bad? What makes legislation good or effective? What makes a good tradition? As students learn to generate criteria, they learn to question the assumptions that go into decision making processes; they learn how to create their own tool kit for future evaluations they might make, a tool kit that will equip them with necessary cognitive abilities.

Third, with an evaluation paper students can choose a topic they are interested in and then have the opportunity to think about those topics. Asking students to follow their own interests is particularly valuable in a freshman composition course. For example, if a student has a curiosity about manatee habitats, he or she can evaluate a certain piece of legislation or environmental policy. Students can be invested in the topic for a few weeks, see if they are interested, and then if they are, go on to pursue coursework or perhaps even a major in that topic. If they realize that they are not interested, then they have not invested too much time. At the beginning of their college careers, facing a time in their lives where their success often depends on being interested in something, students can try out ideas.

Finally and perhaps most importantly, in evaluation papers students are not just asked to think about something, they are asked to make a value judgment; they are asked to take a stand. So many students have not had practice at this. In her article, "The Millennial Teacher: Metaphors for a New Generation," Kristine Johnson writes that students of the millennial generation (those who graduate high school after 2000) are highly respectful of authority and therefore more likely to defer to others' opinions. She writes, "More than any generation in living memory, millennials are happy to accept authority and dutifully jump through hoops in order to achieve" (8). She writes of one student's inability to see the need for any kind of change at his institution: "students do not always know how to ask questions respectfully that constructively challenge authority" (17). Students who do not know how to take a stand on an issue are intellectually impoverished, and an evaluation assignment teaches them that skill, helping them take a stand.

## Review as Evaluation

I do not ask my students to do just any sort of evaluation argument, though. I ask them to write evaluation arguments that involve popular culture; I want them to write reviews of music, movies, books, or television shows. Writing a review has the benefits of any other evaluation argument—participation in a form of public discourse, the generation of criteria, the construction of value judgments, and allowing the pursuit of interests—while only slightly limiting what students can write about. In nearly every major magazine, newspaper, website, or blog, students can come across reviews, so the genre is certainly not new to them. Instead, the assignment asks them to join a conversation they may already be familiar with. In their evaluations, students can argue why a particular movie might be the best "twenty-something male has trouble shaking adolescence" film of the last decade. Or why the new album from their favorite musician does not quite measure up to their expectations. With the review format, students are engaging with the popular culture that already surrounds them. In addition to the traditional review format, though, I ask them to take the reviews one step further than they would ordinarily like: I ask them to make a larger cultural argument within their paper. The assignment sheet prompts them by introducing the genre of reviews.

Writing evaluative papers on different expressions of popular culture encourages a critical eye toward those things which surround students every day, those things of which they may not always be consciously aware. However, having students write reviews does more than give them the chance to write about something familiar. It gives them the chance to think through their reasons for liking or disliking something. In argumentative papers and presentations, it is inevitable that I will get the Mac vs. PC papers, the you've-got-to-see-this-movie presentations. They constantly evaluate, constantly consume, but not much thought is put into it. In my initial discussion with students, they often do not know how to approach or support their opinions. For example, a student came into my office and said he wanted to evaluate the last good movie he saw, *The Holiday*. I asked him, "Okay, what makes this a good movie?" There was a silent and painful pause before he replied, "I don't know. It just is." It took multiple conversations to get him to think about what made that movie good, conversations that went back to criteria—to thinking about what makes *any* movie good. Without good reasons for liking or disliking certain things, students can never get beyond being passive receivers of marketing, fickle consumers, without a basis for their opinions. Writing evaluation papers asks them to question why they feel the way they do.

---

**Assignment #2: Evaluation Essay**

What makes something good or bad? At the end of every year, magazines and newspapers compile "10 best lists" or even "10 worst lists," letting readers know their picks for the best movie of the year, the best albums, or the best books. But what makes something like an album good? The ability to execute something technically perfect? Or does daring matter more than execution? Does innovation trump tradition? And what qualifies lyrics as "good"? As you can see, there's a lot to consider for even a music review.

For this assignment, write a review – an essay evaluating some piece of artwork (movie, music, television show, or book). Write the review as though it would be placed in a magazine or some other popular format.

This essay should include:
* An argument – is this piece of art good, bad, or somewhere in between?
* Some sort of orientation for the reader, as most reviews have – context, description, or plot summary (but don't give away the ending!).
* Support for your argument – in other words, an evaluation by criteria.
* A gesture towards a larger cultural argument – what does it mean that this is good or bad?

---

In addition to writing a simple review, though, asking students to think about the larger cultural argument puts them in the good company of thinkers who wrote about what art should be or what it might mean—from Aristotle to Tolstoy. Ken Bain writes that highly effective college teachers often have high expectations of their students: "Students will be buoyed by positive expectations that are genuine, challenging yet realistic, and that take their work seriously" (72). Asking them not just to evaluate but to think about the implications of their criteria and the implications of their entire evaluations means taking their ideas and their ability to make ideas seriously. It lets them know that they can have a hand in some big ideas.

When I ask the students to "gesture towards" the larger argument, though, I am acknowledging some of the limits of what they can do. Only the most philosophically-minded students would be ready to tackle the "what is art for" or "what should art do" questions knowing that they would have to fully support it. A gesture towards a larger culture argument is less committal and more about asking them to make explicit some of the assumptions behind and implications of their evaluations. Reviews do this sort of gesturing all the time, actually. For example, in my composition course we recently read a review of Norah Jones's album, *Not Too Late*. In the review, author Jody Rosen argues that Jones should stick to what she does best, that rather than "trying to push her music into 'hotter,' more expressive territory," "she should be playing to her strength, emphasizing her cool and reserve," even if that means earning her nickname of "Snorah Jones" (Rosen par 6). The implication? That artists should work within their realm of expertise, to not try so hard. In the same course, we read a review of the television show, *Lost*. The author of this article, while largely critical of the show, does praise it for being "ambitious" and for staying true to the ambiguity of story-telling (Brownfield). The implication here might be that artists taking risks and failing are more virtuous than those who do not take risks but succeed. Seeing these examples lets students know that their arguments could be touching these larger ideas.

Students often respond to this prompt with satisfying results. One student, in her review of *The DaVinci Code,* mentions that she enjoyed reading the book but felt unsatisfied afterwards. She takes this argument one step further to speculate on our culture's celebration of a book that is all thrill and low on substance. Another student reviewing her favorite British television series, *Midsomer Murders*, argues that art that plays with genre by mocking it perhaps does just as much as anything else to celebrate that genre. The students demonstrate quality thinking on this assignment when they are pushed to do it, when they are asked to first do something familiar (think about a movie or piece of music), then do something less familiar but entirely feasible (write a review), and finally be pushed to examine the implications of their thoughts and opinions—the implications on the wider world.

## So Where Does This Take Us?

As mentioned previously, students, and particularly younger students, often come into the classroom with a passive approach to learning. They are consumers of information—a useful metaphor here, for it touches on students' attitudes towards entertainment and popular culture and the way that attitude might influence their approach to learning. In his book *Consumed*, Benjamin Barber writes of our "radical consumerist society," in which spending and conscious consumption are virtues and brand identity manages to meld with personal identity. Barber paints a dire picture of a consumer culture out of control. This hyper-consumerism relates to the matter at hand, though, in what Barber outlines as the infantilizing effects of this culture, an infantilization that works against the natural intellectual development that Perry describes.

Barber points to adults playing video games, the popularity of cartoons for adults, and what he sees as the general denial of aging, but there is more to it than that. For him, infantilization plays out in the dogmatic dualism of politics, in "age without dignity . . . work without discipline, play without spontaneity, acquisition without purpose," and so on (6-7). He reduces all these nuances to "three archetypal dualisms that capture infantilization: EASY over HARD, SIMPLE over COMPLEX, and FAST over SLOW" (83). These are exactly the values that our students find themselves faced with as they are making the transition from adolescent thinkers to those who can actively and constructively participate in the college world. In an environment where media and advertising seem to hold students in the easy/simple/fast adolescent model, popular culture, and specifically the review assignment provide the meeting place to catch students with what they know and move them into new territory, from consumers into makers of arguments, students prepared for the hard/complex/slow world of college.

## Conclusion

So on the spring day when I found myself talking about "My Humps" to both my class and a few visiting parents, I had the chance to truly test my commitment to using popular culture in evaluations. We talked about the song for a few minutes, hearing the students' thoughts on it, and then I brought out a review from Slate.com writer, Hua Hsu. He writes:

> [The Black Eyed Peas'] current single, "My Humps," is one of the most popular
> hit singles in history. It is also proof that a song can be so bad as to veer toward
> evil . . . "My Humps" is a moment that reminds us that categories such as "good"
> and "bad" still matter. Relativism be damned! There are bad songs that offend
> our sensibilities but can still be enjoyed, and then there are the songs that are *just*
> *really bad*—transcendentally bad, objectively bad. (par. 1 and 4)

In this moment, and a funny moment at that, Hsu gives the readers a glimpse into other, larger, arguments—arguments about subjectivity and meaning, about art and standards—and then he moves on to the rest of the review, critiquing the song, comparing it to other bad but popular songs, and generally hoping that it would go away soon. But in that small moment, the article essay moves from a consumer position—"it is widely believed to be the most successful unsolicited single in history"—to a critic's position, a movement I hope that my students can make, and a movement that the parents seemed to appreciate as well.

## Works Cited

Bain, Ken. *What the Best College Teachers Do*. Cambridge: Harvard UP, 2004.

Barber, Benjamin R. *Consumed: How Markets Corrupt Children, Infantilize Adults and Swallow Citizens Whole*. New York: Norton, 2007.

Black Eyed Peas. "My Humps." *Monkey Business*. A&M Records, 2005.

Brownfield, Paul. "'Lost' Writers Know Just Where They Are." *Los Angeles Times* 7 Feb. 2007: E1.

Faigley, Lester, and Jack Selzer. *Good Reasons with Contemporary Arguments*. 2nd ed. New York: Pearson Longman, 2004.

Hsu, Hua. "Notes on 'Humps': A Song So Awful It Hurts the Mind." *Slate*. 6 Dec. 2005. 2 May 2007 <http://www.slate.com/id/2131640/>.

Johnson, Kristine. "The Millennial Teacher: Metaphors for a New Generation." *Pedagogy* 6.1 (2006): 7-24.

Lunsford, Andrea A., John J. Ruszkiewicz, and Keith Walters. *Everything's an Argument*. 3rd ed. New York: Bedford/St. Martin's, 2004.

Perry, William G., Jr. *Forms of Intellectual and Ethical Development*. New York: Hold, Rinehart and Winston, 1970.

Rosen, Jody. "Brunch Goddess." *Slate*. 2 Feb. 2007. 2 May 2007 <http://www.slate.com/id/2158869/>.

# Fastest Pen in the West: Using Quickmuse in the Composition Classroom

## *Aaron Herschel Shapiro*

Ever since Dana Gioia's *Can Poetry Matter?,* there has been a great deal of argument over the use-value of poetry and its status as an art form. Some theorists, like Gioia, argue that poetry has passed its prime and largely divorced itself from popular discourse. Others, such as Cary Nelson, Michael Thurston, and Joseph Harrison, argue that poetry has never *not* been a popular art and that only the New Critics' focus on aesthetics made it appear adrift. Citing examples of public and activist poetry, they assert that—Auden aside—poetry can and does make things happen (Chasar).

But if poetry has a social function, the question remains: what use is it in the composition classroom? Many composition specialists, from Paulo Friere to Wendy Bishop, make the case for using creative writing to help students develop their own voice and reflect on their lives. The free-verse lyric, formally open and primarily concerned with the self in contemplation, epitomizes this kind of expressive writing. As such, it can be a powerful tool for opening students up to their potential as writers. However, a new website, Quickmuse.com, has introduced another layer of functionality.

Quickmuse was developed by Ken Gordon and Fletcher Moore in 2006 as "a linguistic jam session" where established poets "riff away on a randomly chosen subject" (Gordon, "About," par. 1). Writers are allowed fifteen-minutes to compose, and when the clock runs out, so does their virtual ink. The real innovation here, however, is a program nicknamed "the Poematic" which records every key-stroke made during the writing process and allows visitors to play back the composition from opening word to final period. In so doing, the Poematic brings viewers "closer to the moment of composition than they have ever been before" (Gordon, "About", par. 1).

For students, and all writers, the benefit is immense. At the click of a mouse, visitors have the kind of intimate access to writing practices that Sondra Perl and Nancy Sommers needed a laboratory to produce. They can actually *see* how stray ideas and phrases alter the direction of a piece. They can watch writers adjust diction, tone, or point of view, and question the effects of those changes. They can even watch writers get stumped— moments that humanize the writing process even as they suggest ways of escaping a block.

In short, Quickmuse offers a palpable experience of writing as dynamic and recursive. By reflecting on their own processes in conjunction with Quickmuse, students gain insight into strategies of generation and revision. Moreover, they learn to see writing as *in flux*: not the expression of a fixed idea, but a site of negotiation where language and meaning shape each other. Since its inception, Quickmuse has published forty-six poems by approximately thirty contemporary poets. Kevin Young is here, and Paul Muldoon; Charles Bernstein and Marge Piercy; Mary Jo Salter, Carol Muske-Dukes and David Kirby. Each of their poems affords dozens of teachable moments that can be used to illustrate both broad concepts of writing well and specific writing strategies.

# Real Writing: Using Quickmuse to Demystify the Writing Process

When introducing Quickmuse to a class, I begin with an exercise in demystification. I ask students to take three to five minutes and jot down their ideas about writing, and the traits they feel define a writer. Most often I find they've imagined the writer sitting down and spitting out a finished piece without effort, error, or editing. Their list of traits often includes words like "creative," "talented," and "inspired."

This image implies that in order to write one must be gifted with genius or on intimate terms with the muse, leaving students feeling they can't write, that they aren't writers. Yet they do write: emails and text messages, notes to each other in class, graffiti on bathroom stalls. They compose with confidence in those genres. When I raise this issue, my students counter that these are not examples of real writing. Real writing is fiction, essays, poetry, or a paper for class. Real writers write important thoughts with elegance and precision. They get A's.

Real writers, it seems, write brilliantly always, and they do not make mistakes. I want to disabuse my students of this misconception. I want them to realize that errors are potentially "portals of discovery" (Gordon, "Improvisers," 2), that no piece of writing is perfect, and that creativity isn't a straight line. Quickmuse, with its revisions, deletions, false starts, and dead ends, provides the perfect opportunity, allowing students to pull the curtain back on a finished piece of writing and see the writer turning cranks and pulling levers, huffing and puffing over the machinery of language. To give them an example, after introducing the site, I play back former poet laureate Robert Pinsky's untitled poem composed on May 30, 2006.

Here, Pinsky responds to an excerpt from an interview with Miles Davis about Charlie Parker. As the Quickmuse stopwatch begins ticking, Pinsky jumps in with, "Lots of crap written about artists like Parker" (line 1). He then flounders, typing nothing for seven long seconds, followed by a tentative "my" that is deleted four seconds later. He stutters from "my" to "I" to "he was" to "he had" where he finds his voice and finishes with "He had the generosity of an artist" (2). Two sentences. One minute twelve seconds gone.

At this point, I pause the playback and ask my students if what they have just witnessed corresponds to their idea of writing. The answer is usually "no," but Pinsky's stuttering does correspond with my students' *experience* of writing. They, too, have stared at the blank page and felt equally blank, and they easily identify with Pinsky's uncertainty. What seems so amazing, however, is the way that uncertainty can suddenly blossom into wonderful language. The next question is, how do writers—and how can my students—find the words?

# Riding The Words:
# Using Quickmuse to Encourage Freewriting and Flow

To answer this we look to Pinsky's second line, "He had the generosity of an artist." It is clear from Pinsky's opening that he has no preset idea to express and that his artistry is not without "mistakes." It *is* generous, however. Generous enough to try different openings, choose one that felt compelling, and follow it without knowing where it would lead. In this poem, Pinsky's writing depends on his willingness to begin without direction, treating the writing process as free play.

Further, Pinsky writes most smoothly when he is responding to what his poem calls "a honk in an unexpected place"—an image, word, or turn of phrase that catches his ear and demands attention (11-12). Pinsky's second line is one of these, and enables the rest of his poem. The principle here is to listen for the honk, to be alive to the moments when we have written something surprising.

As Ken Macrorie points out in *Telling Writing*, those moments arrive unconsciously: the result of intense personal engagement (1-2, 7). To cultivate them, we must allow ourselves to write without a plan. We must be generous, allowing ourselves to write without knowing what we will say or how we will say it. I ask my students if they practice this kind of generosity in their own writing.

Usually, they do not. At least, not when writing academically. In struggling to write "correctly" within the norms of a formal essay, my students often lose touch with the sense of flow so apparent in Pinsky's poem. In fact, they may be unwittingly working from the linear process model: trying to know what they will say before they write. This focus on fixed expression kills their writing, shutting down its potential for growth and shackling it to a single idea. It is the opposite of Pinsky's generosity.

Freewriting is an ideal way for students to put generosity back into their writing. To paraphrase Peter Elbow, freewriting encourages students to approach writing more organically and honestly; though the writing may ramble, it may also stumble into clarity and even poetry (Elbow 7-9). Like the improvisational practices on Quickmuse, freewriting can unblock flow and encourage those miraculous honks. To bring that point home and help my students get into the practice, I introduce the following two assignments.

## Assignment 1: In-Class Writing

Using Pinsky's second line as a prompt, I ask students to exchange "He" for "I" and write for fifteen minutes on what "the generosity of an artist" might mean for them. When the time is up, I invite students to share their work and talk about how it felt to write without an agenda. The variety of responses makes for lively discussion and demonstrates how the words themselves evoke new ideas and associations even as they are written. Working from Pinsky's poem provides a dramatic example of Janet Emig's assertion in "Writing as Learning" that writing is "epigenetic," a recursive process of discovery wherein ideas overlap, bump into, and compel each other (127). Beginning from this perspective, students are encouraged to ride the words, accepting the uncertainty of the blank page and trusting their instincts to propel their writing.

## Assignment 2: The Freewriting Notebook

To truly establish a sense of writing as play, and to practice flow, students need to freewrite frequently. With this in mind I require students to keep a freewriting notebook, writing for at least fifteen minutes every day. These notebooks are not graded, but are included in class participation. To promote consistent entries, I offer weekly prompts for in-class writing and encourage students to choose their own prompts as well.

Quickmuse is an excellent source for prompts. Every poem on the site grew out of a prompt, and viewers can access them without reading the poem. Prompts can be anything, from a sales receipt found on a street corner to another poem. By finding prompts in their own lives, students make the connection between writing and living that makes writing a social act, a way of "using language to make sense of the world" (Lindemann 5). I invite them to write on anything at all: an image from a magazine, a television commercial, an old shoe dangling from a telephone line, the smell of socks and moldy pizza permeating the dormitory. Anything will do, so long as they write with engagement and honesty—and without stopping.

## Bridling the Words:
## Using Quickmuse to Teach Meta-Cognition and Craft

Though freewriting is fun, and essential to building confidence and developing flow, my students inevitably notice that the poems on Quickmuse (not to mention the essays in their textbooks) do not read like their notebook entries. While improvised, they are nevertheless highly crafted. The next step in using Quickmuse in the classroom, then, involves examining that craft.

Quickmuse allows viewers to crawl inside the writer's mind and discover what William Stafford calls "portable principles" (104), i.e., broad concepts and strategies that students can apply to writing in multiple genres. Those principles are not only visible in the words that appear on the screen, but also can be felt in the pauses the writer takes and the changes he or she makes, providing students with a model of how awareness of craft shapes the writing process.

As students learn to ask questions and analyze the writing on Quickmuse, they also increase their awareness of the choices they make in their own writing. This kind of self-awareness, or meta-cognition, is key to the generative and revising process, and helps students evaluate their work and push it forward (Martinez 33-4). In addition, because Quickmuse allows students to see meta-cognition as an ongoing part of the writing process, it provides them with a model for applying their growing knowledge of craft without stifling their creativity.

For students to use Quickmuse in this way they must learn to read a writer's pauses and revisions and abstract the principle at work. In-class discussions on Quickmuse poems are invaluable here, promoting the kind of analysis I hope my students will do on their own. To facilitate that analysis, I have developed guidelines for watching Quickmuse, along with a worksheet that contains a graph for quantifying revisions and deletions (based on those used by Sommers and Perl), and a series of questions designed to encourage critical thinking about the writing process.

## Speed Reading the Muse:
## Guidelines for Watching In-Process Poems

Watching Quickmuse takes a great deal of attention and requires multiple viewings. The poems move either very fast or very slow. In real time, each composition takes about fifteen minutes, and while Quickmuse includes a 4x speed function that allows the viewer to watch a poem in approximately three and a half minutes, it is easy to miss revisions at this speed. Additionally, watching a poem develop this quickly gives viewers an unnerving and inaccurate sense of the writer's facility. Sometimes the most telling moments occur when the writer is stuck and takes a minute or two to find a direction and move on. It is worthwhile to sit through the pause to get a sense of how much uncertainty and effort has gone into producing the next word or line. I recommend that students watch the poems a few times at both speeds, using the 4x speed to get a sense of what is happening and what moments they would like to focus on, and the real time function for the closer analysis required to fill out the worksheet in *Figure A*.

## Measuring Poetry:
## A Worksheet for Quantifying Process

Quantitative analysis may seem anathema to reading poetry, but the purpose here is not to come up with a literary interpretation, or even to engage directly with what is being said. Rather, the purpose of the following worksheet is simply to get students to slow down and consider the words one by one as they appear on the page. Cataloguing the choices made during a Quickmuse improvisation with the worksheet in *Figure A* is like making a tandem jump with an experienced skydiver; tandem jumpers may not get to pull the rip cord or direct the landing, but they do gain an intimate knowledge of what happens during freefall. The sample worksheet below has been partially filled out to reflect the opening two lines of the Pinsky poem discussed earlier.

**Student's Name:**
**Date Viewed:**
**Date Written:** 5/30/06

**Title:** None
**Author:** Robert Pinsky

| Time (in 30 second increments) | Words Written | Words Deleted | Revisions |
|---|---|---|---|
| 0-30 | Lots of crap written about artists like Parker. | | Line #: |
| | | | From: |
| 30-60 | My<br>I | X<br>    X | To: |
| 60-90 | He was | X | |
| | He had the generosity of an artist too, though. | | |

*Figure A*

# Riddles of the Sphinx:
# Questions for Abstracting the Principles Behind the Process

There is really no way, short of telepathy, to be 100% sure of what is happening in a writer's mind as he or she writes. However, the revisions, deletions, pauses, and maniacal scribbling fits of the process can be highly suggestive. The questions in *Figure B* are designed to encourage students to think beyond the black and white of the page and imagine the struggles and questions behind the chosen words. This list is not definitive, and I encourage teachers and students alike to add to it.

---

**Questions for Reading Quickmuse**

- What prompt was your poet given, and how did he or she engage that prompt in the poem?

- How does the poem begin? Smoothly, or with difficulty? What do you imagine gets your poet started and allows them to start filling in the page?

- When is your poet writing most quickly? What honks propel the writing?

- Looking at the writing before and after a pause, how do you imagine the poet got from one line to another?

- Does your poet ever get stuck? If so, why? How did he or she get unstuck?

- Looking at your poet's revisions and deletions, how do those changes alter the way you read the poem?

- What rhetorical conventions appear in the poem? Does your writer use storytelling, logical argument, emotional persuasion? How do these approaches affect the writing; for example. Do they change the writer's speed, diction, or tone? How do these conventions fit together within the poem?

- What qualities and techniques can you see in the writing of the poem that you would like to apply or have already applied in your own writing process?

---

*Figure B*

## Quickmusing:
## Analyzing Poems at Home and in Class

Using the guidelines, the worksheet, and the questions, teachers may pick Quickmuse poems for in-class discussions and exercises, or they may turn their students loose to watch and analyze the poems for themselves. I prefer to combine these approaches, selecting a poem now and then to illustrate specific issues (more on this in a moment), and requiring students to watch and analyze at least five poems during the course of the semester.

### Assignment 3: Reading Quickmuse: The Home Game

As mentioned, this assignment asks students to choose five poems to watch and analyze throughout the semester. These analyses do not have to be essays. They are musings on the processes observed and can take the form of journals, lists, freewritings, or another form of informal writing. They must, however, engage the poem as well as the questions on process, and they must be accompanied by a completed worksheet. Because students' understanding of the process behind any one poem will deepen the more they watch it, I tell my students that they need not try to finish the response all in one sitting. Instead, I suggest they watch the poem more than once and write a quick response each time, noting whatever occurred to them as they watched the poem unfold. I also recommend that each response be dated. This way, students end up with a complete record of their experience with the poem. The notes students take over the course of this assignment have a further application: they form the basis of a reflective essay that I give at the end of the semester (see Assignment 5).

## Talking Quickmuse Blues:
## Using Quickmuse to Illustrate Issues of Craft

Though students will discover different principles from every poem, teachers can browse the site and choose poems to highlight aspects of craft in class discussions. Because reading poems may seem an odd way to approach writing essays, a word needs to be said here about the difference between these genres—or rather, about their similarity. While poems rely less on linear logic than story, sound, and image, and while they employ a looser syntax and an openly subjective point of view, they nevertheless operate along the same principles of strong writing.

In fact, as Shirley Brice Heath argues, the modern expository essay is a close relative of poetry. It is a descendant of the epigram, a form of poetry stressing clarity and brevity, as well as the movement from an initial premise through supporting evidence to a well-argued conclusion[7] (108). Poems and essays have diverged over time, but as Anthony Petrosky says, even now they "exist . . . in a common landscape" whose prominent features include a strong voice, personal engagement, and the use of particulars to ground a narrative or argument (209).

---

[7] Curiously, the conclusion of an epigram is called "the point." The modern usage of "point" to describe the main idea or thesis of an argument (as in "what is the point of this essay?") first occurs in 1643 and seems to be linked to Ben Jonson's adaptation of the epigram in his 1597 book, "Essays" (Heath 112).

In class discussions, I use Quickmuse to explore all three of these features, as well as issues of organization and point of view.[8] The site is rich with teachable moments, and I have no doubt that teachers will discover additional applications as they browse. Due to the requirements of length, however, I have limited my sample discussions to a single example focusing on the connections between poetry and essay writing.

### The Poem as Essay: Organization and Genre Switching
### In-Class Discussion on "Untitled," Robert Pinsky, May 30, 2006

This discussion focuses on the Pinsky poem described earlier in this essay. When I first introduced the site, my students were skeptical about the idea that looking at a poem could show them how to write an essay. For them, poetry meant creative self-expression—a kind of writing entirely divorced from the research and argumentative essays they had written in their other classes. The discussion, along with its accompanying exercise and assignment, uses that skepticism as a jumping-off point and provides a guide to students' work with Quickmuse over the semester. The goal is to encourage students to see that writing conventions may apply across different genres and to recognize how those conventions give shape and direction to the writing process.

### In-Class Exercise: The Outline in Essays and Poetry

After watching the Pinsky poem, we compare it to the general outline of an expository essay (introduction, body, conclusion). Writing the outline on the board, I then ask my students to place each of the poem's stanzas within that outline. As they do, they realize that the two forms are nearly identical. Pinsky's opening five lines fit the introduction and even include an implied thesis: "He had the generosity of an artist" (2). The next few stanzas illustrate the thesis via anecdote and are synonymous with the body and supporting points of the expository essay (6-18). Finally, the last two stanzas return to the thesis and extend it, leaving the reader with a memorable image—a saxophone resting "severe and flawed" in its case—that localizes the poem's argument and brings home its point about the universality of artistic potential (18-24).

## Extending the Discussion:
## How Free is Freewriting?

Making these connections between the poem and the expository outline not only gives students practice in recognizing conventions across genres, but also offers a clue to Pinsky's quick composition. Pinsky's flow is not entirely free. Like the jazz musicians in his poem, Pinsky uses his knowledge of writing conventions to give his writing form and direction from the outset. Even as he stays within the confines of the outline, however, he remains attentive to those surprising "honks" that give his writing life and energy. He even switches conventions, moving

---

[8] Try Paul Muldoon's September 20, 2006 poem, "Potatoes" for a lesson on point of view. Halfway through the poem, Muldoon changes his perspective from third to second person. Also, Bill Zavatsky's poem from February 7, 2007, titled "Nucular," is excellent for lessons on specificity and support.

from didacticism to narrative and back whenever he needs to illustrate a point. For students, this suggests that the requirements and conventions of a particular genre are exchangeable and need not be stumbling blocks. Instead, they are methods for channeling flow and for plotting out the general development of a piece of writing.

Finally, the dual focus of Pinsky's composition—recognizing and following the *honks*, and honoring writing conventions and the reader's expectations—is typical of the poems on Quickmuse and provides a powerful model for students' own struggle to shape and direct their writing. Integrating these concerns is certainly not easy. It is a high-wire act, a tense and precarious balance between the requirements of genre and audience and the integrity of the writer. To give my students a bit of hands-on experience with this death-defying feat, I ask them to turn to their freewriting notebooks.

## Assignment 4

Once my students have written a number of entries, usually about half way through the semester, I ask them to comb through their notebooks and select one entry (or a combination of entries) to revise in a genre of their choosing. The end product may be a series of poems, a play, a narrative, or an essay, but it must contain 800 to 1000 words and conform to the norms of the genre. This requires students to know what those norms are, and I ask them to choose a model either from our textbook, from Quickmuse (if they have chosen poetry), or from their own reading. Students present their model, along with their notebook entries and intended genre, for approval. Once I have approved their projects, I ask them to bring a first draft to class the following week, and we continue to workshop this project through multiple drafts in peer editing groups[9].

Unlike the notebook assignments, the final version of this assignment will be graded. The pressure this adds to the revision process encourages students to rework their entries extensively, and gives them a sense of how freewriting can be reshaped to adhere to the more stringent requirements of a finished work.

# Wrapping Up:
# Reflecting the Muse

Writers do not "find the words" so much as the words find them (Macrorie 2). Though this sounds suspiciously like genius, inspiration is available to all writers who allow their unconscious to work for, or better, *with* them (Macrorie 1). But tapping the unconscious and recognizing inspiration (those honks, again) is only half of the writing process. The other half involves the conscious and careful decisions writers make as they respond to and revise their writing. As Macrorie suggests,

> Both the writing and responding are complex. To do them well, we must act
> unconsciously at that moment; but to extend our ability to do them well—to

---

[9] This assignment works best in a classroom based on the portfolio model where students have time to produce two or three drafts and go through a few different workshops. However, it can also work in a more structured classroom, and even without the peer groups, as long as teachers allow students time for revision.

move it toward habit—we need to be conscious of what we've done . . . When we are living at our highest capabilities, experiencing life to the fullest, we're alternating between unconscious and conscious behavior. At our most exciting and powerful moments these two forces come together and fuse. (8)

Because Quickmuse allows students to watch writers in action, it gives them a unique window into that moment of fusion not only in the work of the writers it hosts, but in their own writing as well. In their in-class discussions and at-home analyses, students work on the conscious side of this equation, acquiring an understanding of the principles that inform strong writing. By freewriting and watching the poems, they work on the unconscious element: learning to trust themselves as writers, to let their thinking flow into words, and to be open to those flashes of insight that propel their writing into unexplored territories. The Quickmuse experience, then, combined with class assignments, fosters that acute double vision required to successfully navigate the writing process.

### Assignment 5: Mirror, Mirror, On The Page . . .

At the end of the semester, after my students have had extensive experience watching and responding to the site, I ask them to write a 1,000 word reflective essay addressing the following questions:

- How have your ideas about writers and writing changed as a result of watching and responding to the compositions on Quickmuse?

- How has your own writing changed over the course of your work with Quickmuse? What "portable principles" and/or freewriting techniques have you adapted into your process?

- Given your answers to preceding questions, how would you assess the effect Quickmuse has had on you as a writer?

## Works Cited

Chasar, Mike. "A Full Nelson? Getting a Grip on Cultural Criticism of Modern American Poetry." *Word for Word* 9 (2006). 19 Feb. 2007. 29 Mar. 2007 <http://www.wordforword. info/vol9/Chasar.htm>.

Elbow, Peter. *Writing Without Teachers*. 2nd ed. New York: Oxford UP, 1998.

Emig, Janet. "Writing as Learning." *CCC* 28 (1977): 122-28.

Gioia, Dana. *Can Poetry Matter? Essays on Poetry and American Culture*. St. Paul, MN: Graywolf, 1992.

Gordan, Ken. "About." *Quickmuse.com*. Ed. Ken Gordon. 17 May 2006. 4 Apr. 2007 <http://www. quickmuse.com/about>.

---. "Improvisers and Revisers: An Experiment in Spontaneity." *Poets & Writers* 4 Apr. 2007 <http:// www.pw.org/mag/0605/gordon.htm>

Heath, Shirley Brice. "Rethinking the Sense of the Past: The Essay as Legacy of the Epigram." *Theory and Practice in the Teaching of Writing: Rethinking the Discipline*. Ed. Lee Odell. Carbondale: Southern Illinois UP, 1993. 105-31.

Macrorie, Ken. *Telling Writing*. 3rd ed. Rochelle Park, NJ: Hayden, 1980.

Martinez, Valerie. "Missing Link: Metacognition and the Necessity of Poetry in the Composition Classroom." *Writing on the Edge* 12.2 (2001): 33-52.

Lindemann, Erika, and Daniel Anderson. *A Rhetoric for Teaching Writers*. 4th ed. New York: Oxford UP, 2001.

Perl, Sondra. "The Composing Process of Unskilled College Writers." *Cross-Talk in Comp Theory: A Reader*. 2nd ed. Ed. Victor Villanueva. Urbana, IL: NCTE, 2003. 17-42.

Petrosky, Anthony. "Imagining the Past and Teaching Essay and Poetry Writing." *Encountering Student Texts: Interpretive Issues in Reading Student Writing*. Ed. Bruce Lawson, Susan Sterr Ryan, and W. Ross Winterowd. Urbana, IL: NCTE, 1989. 199-220.

Pinsky, Robert. "Untitled." *Quickmuse.com*. Ed. Ken Gordon. 30 May 2006. 28 Apr. 2007 <http://www.quickmuse.com/archive/landing.php?poem=15tTPzuBPDmVLYLMokffOhMpreRA1>.

Sommers, Nancy. "Revision Strategies of Student Writers and Experienced Adult Writers." *Cross-Talk in Comp Theory: A Reader*. 2nd ed. Ed. Victor Villanueva. Urbana, IL: NCTE, 2003. 43-54.

Stafford, William. *You Must Revise Your Life.* Ann Arbor: U of Michigan P, 2000.

# Graphic Novels in the Composition Course:
# Are They Really Novels?

## *Clifton Kaiser*

While teaching the classics is often fun for teachers, students get easily turned off by what they perceive as old, stuffy books. I have wondrous dreams of being able to teach Fitzgerald's *Tender Is the Night* and Ellison's *Invisible Man*, but they are long works to fit into an already tight schedule in a composition course. Typically, unless I persistently administer reading quizzes, many of the students either do not read the entire novel or else they do not read deeply. They do not pay close attention as they read, instead pushing ahead zombie-like just to reach the end.

To combat this, teachers have several options. One engaging option is assigning a graphic novel. I often joke with my students that "graphic novel" is just a fancy term for a comic book. Actually, this is true to a point. Graphic novels, which are also known as *manga* in the Japanese form, are comic books, but they are typically longer, and they frequently eschew superheroes, instead preferring fairly weighty matters such as the Holocaust, the first atomic bomb test, and coming of age in late 20th-century Iran.[10] As Will Eisner, the unofficial father of the graphic novel states in his groundbreaking work *Comics & Sequential Art*, "The future for the graphic novel lies in the choice of worthwhile themes and the innovation of exposition" (141). Eisner offers this further assessment of graphic novels:

> The future of this form awaits participants who truly believe that the application of sequential art, with its interweaving of words and pictures, could provide a dimension of communication that contributes—hopefully on a level never before attained—to the body of literature that concerns itself with the examination of human experience. (141-42)

This future that Eisner wrote about in 1985 has arrived.

## Increasing Popularity and Respect

The graphic novel genre and market are growing rapidly. In 2001, sales of graphic novels were estimated at $75 million, but in 2005, sales reached nearly $250 million (Twiddy). Yet while sales are increasing, the respect in academic circles is rising at a much slower pace. James Sturn taught for four years at Savannah College of Art and Design, which at the time was the only institution that offered a graduate program in "sequential art" (or comic-book art). In a 2002 commentary in *The Chronicle of Higher Education*, Sturn bemoaned the lack of respectability from which this art form suffers. Similarly, scholar Paul Buhle noted in a 2003 *Chronicle* piece

---

[10] Actually superhero-based comics have in recent years dealt with fairly serious matters. In 2006, the comic publishing company DC announced that Batwoman was lesbian. Rival publisher Marvel, in its 2006-2007 *Civil War* series, tackles the issue of the Patriot Act similar to the way the popular NBC television series *Heroes* does.

that comic artists still struggle for respect, but he also suggests that comics might achieve status as an official discipline in the same way that film studies have become a discipline. Furthermore, he suggests, comics just might be one of the ways that the older generation of academics can relate to the young students these days.

## Literature with a Visual Element

In addition to covering, as Eisner puts it, the "worthwhile themes," graphic novels employ the same literary techniques as traditional novels, and then they add a layer of visual literacy to the mix. Gretchen Schwarz argues that "to read and interpret graphic novels, students have to pay attention to the usual literary elements of character, plot, and dialogue, and they also have to consider visual elements such as color, shading, panel layout, perspective, and even the lettering style" (59). Sequential art does have a set of conventions that take some acclimation. Students who are not familiar with comic books or comic strips may need a brief instruction about these conventions. With a basic understanding, the students can then proceed to analyze the way graphic novelists manipulate these conventions for literary effect. For example, in Gene Luen Yang's *American Born Chinese*, a mythical being tries to escape reality, which Yang illustrates by having the character break out of the physical line of the graphic cell or panel.

To be clear, it cannot be said that all graphic novels are more complex than traditional novels. A graphic novel is a very different entity from a novel by Henry James or Edith Wharton. Yet graphic novels do provide another avenue towards literacy and critical analysis. Given its inclination towards worthwhile themes, "the graphic novel offers teachers the opportunity to implement critical media literacy in the classroom—literacy that affirms diversity, gives voice to all, and helps students examine ideas and practices that promulgate inequity" (Schwarz 62).

## Significant Examples of Graphic Novels

No discussion of graphic novels can go without mentioning what is arguably the most important graphic novel to date: Art Spiegelman's two-volume set called *Maus*, which won a Pulitzer Prize in 1992. Spiegelman is the son of Holocaust survivors, and *Maus* relates his father's survival story. On one level it is a Holocaust survival story that is gripping and worthy of being told. Still, it is more than that. It also has an element of metafiction as Spiegelman writes and illustrates himself interviewing his aging father about the Holocaust. So *Maus* thereby becomes Spiegelman's own story of coming to terms with the Holocaust, his father's mortality, and his familial bond. Finally, Spiegelman masterfully employs metaphor by drawing each ethnicity as a certain type of animal. The Nazi Germans are cats and the Jewish people are mice. *Maus* is quite popular, and I suspect that graphic novels since *Maus* may suffer from the anxiety of influence. Nonetheless, *Maus* works very well in the classroom as history, autobiography, and metafiction.

Students also respond very well to Marjane Satrapi's *Persepolis*, which is a two-volume autobiographical account of the Iranian author/illustrator's upbringing during the Iranian Cultural Revolution of the late 1970s and early 1980s. Satrapi's artistic style in *Persepolis* is less intricate than *Maus*, but *Persepolis* still tackles very serious issues. Students find common ground with the witty protagonist, but they also get a glimpse of real people living in Iran (whereas the news these days mainly focuses on Iran's nuclear defiance instead of the lives of everyday Iranians).

As mentioned, the graphic novel has achieved a fair amount of popularity, and so it is difficult to enumerate all of the wonderful offerings. Briefly though, let me list a few other meritorious examples. One of the most recent graphic novels of note is *American Born Chinese* by Gene Luen Yang. Its three separate stories about discrimination and cross-cultural encounters strikingly merge in the final chapter—so much so that to say more would spoil the secret. Yang's graphic novel is the winner of the American Library Association's Michael L. Printz Award for Excellence in Young Adult Literature, and it was also a 2006 finalist for a National Book Award. *Ghost World* by Daniel Clowes is a dark tale of two Generation X girls, and *Blankets* by Craig Thompson is a touching coming-of-age memoir. There are even graphic novel versions of Franz Kafka's *The Metamorphosis* by Peter Kuper and *The 9-11 Report* by Sid Jacobson and Ernie Colon.

## Practical Suggestions for Using Graphic Novels

So how does a teacher begin to use graphic novels in the classroom? In his famous piece of literary criticism "An Apology for Poetry," Sir Philip Sidney proclaims that the goal of poetry is to teach and delight. For most students, comics are a source of delight but not so much a source of learning. I assert that if you can get students to see past the delight of the comic medium, you will be able to teach them the lessons in the same way as you would with any other novel. To this end, let me offer a few practical suggestions. Implementing graphic novels is not difficult, but I recommend taking a slow approach for students who have never read one either in or out of the classroom. In general, I recommend first discussing the comic genre in all its forms with the students. After a discussion about comics in general, the students should be ready to read a graphic novel, but it is helpful to review and draw attention to literary elements and terminology as they do so. Let me explain this process in more detail and offer some specific assignments relating to graphic novels.

### Analyzing Comic Strips

The first step in using graphic novels is getting students acclimated to the genre. Before giving the students the first reading assignment in a graphic novel, ask them to bring in an example or two of their favorite comic strip (such as *Dilbert* and *Garfield*). It is okay if they bring in a comic strip that they liked as a child or ones that are below their grade level. Look at several of the examples they bring in, and ask them what they like about these comic strips. Try to turn the discussion to whether the comic strips are intended solely to entertain; ask them if there is any practical value or lesson to be learned from them. Whenever possible, point out literary devices being used. For example, *Dilbert* is a prime example of satire. Quite often comic strips use puns in the dialogue. Plus, most comic strips rely on irony as their source of humor. Consider the classic example from Charles Schulz's *Peanuts* where Lucy promises that *this time* she will not pull the football away from Charlie Brown just before he kicks it. Even an occasional reader of *Peanuts* can recognize the dramatic irony: Lucy again will pull the football away, and Charlie Brown again will go flying through the air. Verbal irony also abounds in comic strips: characters frequently say one thing but mean something else entirely, or else the listening character misreads the speaker's comment. If there are comic strips that most students have read, it is possible to have them write a short character analysis on the main character wherein they describe the character's key traits and motivations. I sometimes bring in that day's newspaper funnies page and have small groups of students search for literary devices. The key is to get students to see that the comic medium uses literary devices, and this exercise has the benefit of having them practice and review literary devices.

Another fun—and brief—exercise that students enjoy regarding comic strips is to have them fill in the words for an existing comic strip. I pick a single, three-cell comic strip from a recent newspaper, use white correction fluid to blot out the words, and then photocopy the comic strip. I give each student a copy and ask the students to fill in the words. They do not have to try to figure out what words the artist originally used; rather, I encourage them to be creative and make up their own version. Typically I display a few of them on the overhead projector. I do not force them to be clever. This exercise is not meant to pressure them. Instead, it is a fun way to get them even more acclimated to the format, and it can take as little as ten minutes to complete.

## Analyzing Political Cartoons

Unless it has already come out of the comic-strip discussion naturally, at this point I usually bring up the case of political cartoons. Again, I either have students bring in a political cartoon, or I bring some in myself. Each weekly issue of *Time* and *Newsweek* has a few examples of them, and these are also accessible on the magazine websites if you have internet access and a projector in your classroom[11]. Transitioning from comic strips to political cartoons works well because students know that political cartoons, while sometimes amusing, definitely serve a deeper purpose. In this discussion, as in the previous one about comic strips, I try to get students to recognize literary devices like satire and irony in the political cartoons. In this way, students can see that cartoons can both delight and instruct.

## Analyzing Comic Books

After a discussion of comic strips and political cartoons, you may find it useful to discuss comic books (such as those that have superheroes in them). Ask if any students used to read or still do read any comic books. I typically have at least a few students who do. Ask those students what comic books they like and what they like about them. You might also ask them to bring in one or two of their favorites, though be sure to specify that the comics must not contain any inappropriate material for the grade-level (I usually preview them as well before letting the students show them to the class). Also ask those students whether any of the comics they read handle serious topics such as the controversy over the Patriot Act or genocide. For the students who do not read comic books, try to include them in the discussion by asking if they have seen any of the recent superhero films like *Fantastic Four*, *X-Men*, and *Spider-man*, and then ask them if there are any serious issues raised in those films. Technology permitting, you might show a clip or two from one of the films where a serious issue is discussed. Usually with some guidance, I can get students to see that both comic books and superhero films address serious topics.

---

[11] Political cartoons are available on the *Time* website at http://www.time.com/time/cartoonsoftheweek/ and they are available on the *Newsweek* website at http://www.msnbc.com/comics/.

## Analyzing Historical Context

Depending on the graphic novel you choose, you may want to provide a historical context. For instance, when I teach Marjane Satrapi's *Persepolis*, I usually break the class down into small groups and assign each group a specific topic to do a short (5 minute) presentation on in class. For *Persepolis*, this usually includes reports on the Islamic Revolution of 1978-1979, Reza Shah, Reza Pahlavi, Islam, ancient Iranian history (which can be broken up into any number of date ranges to fit the number of student groups), and recent Iranian history (1980-present).

# Beginning the Graphic Novel

By this point, students should be ready to tackle a graphic novel, although the approach should be both slow and deliberately focused on literary elements. Before you assign any reading as homework, try reading the first few pages together as a class. This is useful for a couple of reasons, not the least of which is that some students will need to practice reading. Although it may seem simple, you may need to stress that graphic novels are typically composed of cells or panels (the 'boxes') just like comic strips, and a reader should proceed just like a regular novel— from left to right and from top to bottom on the page. It is useful as well to point out—if applicable to the graphic novel you choose—the difference in font and design between speech, thought, and narration as well as between shouting and a regular tone. As a short exercise, I ask small groups of students to examine the opening pages and come up with a list of all the emotions they see on the faces of the characters. I give them a graphic organizer like the one pictured below and ask them to describe the way the artist conveys that emotion.

| Emotion | Character | Description of the Facial Expression | Location (page # and cell #) |
|---|---|---|---|
|  |  |  |  |
|  |  |  |  |
|  |  |  |  |

## Reading the Graphic Novel On Their Own

After reading and examining the first few pages as a class, the students should be ready to proceed individually with the reading. For the first couple of reading assignments, I ask students to pay close attention to the standard literary elements: plot, setting, imagery, point-of-view, symbolism, and tone. This provides another opportunity for small-group exercises. Students come to class having read the assignment, and I break them up into small groups, assign each group one literary element, and have that group examine the assigned reading for their element. They then report their findings back to the class. Analyzing the tone usually leads to interesting discussions because the tone is conveyed heavily through visual means. For the first few instances of this exercise, you may need to guide the group assigned to tone. Point out that they need to consider the color choices, shading, sharpness, font, and even size of the cells. For example, a standard convention in comic books and graphic novels is to emphasize a critical moment in the narrative by devoting an entire page to it instead of just a series of cells on the page. With guidance, the student will soon be able to point out visual details with acuity.

## Analyzing Critical Cells and Passages

As the students make their way into the graphic novel, you should continue to devote time and attention to both the narrative and the visual elements. One exercise that I use is to tell students to identify an important cell from the homework-reading assignment. By "important," I specify that it has to have a critical function in the context of the chapter or larger work. It might, for instance, show the character coming to a realization or demonstrate some sort of change in the character. Sometimes the importance will be in what the character says, and sometimes it will be due to the visual depiction in the cell. This is very similar to an assignment I use for traditional novels where I ask my students to read a section of the novel and identify an important passage from the reading. In both cases I require the students to write a short explanation about why they chose that part. There is an in-class variation of this exercise as well. For the in-class variation, I break the class into small groups, assign each group a page range from the graphic novel, and have each group identify a key cell in that page range. The group must elect a spokesperson to report back on which cell they chose and why.

## Analyzing Genre

Genre can be a useful approach as the students near the end of the graphic novel. Both *Persepolis* by Marjane Satrapi and *American Born Chinese* by Gene Yang are coming-of-age stories. This makes for a great opportunity to pair a graphic novel with a coming-of-age traditional novel like Judith Ortiz Cofer's *Silent Dancing: A Partial Remembrance of a Puerto Rican Childhood*, Mark Twain's *The Adventures of Huckleberry Finn*, Jamaica Kincaid's *Annie John*, or Zora Neale Hurston's *Their Eyes Were Watching God*. Art Spiegelman's *Maus* can be framed in the context of Holocaust-survival literature, and it can be paired with *The Diary of Anne Frank* or Elie Wiesel's *Night*. By placing the graphic novel in the context of a genre, and by pairing it with traditional novels of the same genre, students can see the graphic novel as an entity worthy of literary analysis.

## Writing a Literary Analysis

When students follow the careful, deliberate process described above, they end up being very prepared to write a literary analysis essay just as they would for a more traditional novel. The constant attention to literary elements makes the students realize that graphic novels have the same development as traditional novels, so they are able to write about theme, character development, and symbolism in the same way. Consider some comments taken from an essay written by a student of mine named Samantha. She wrote these about Jin, the coming-of-age protagonist in Gene Luen Yang's *American Born Chinese*:

> When he changes his hair to fit in better, it does not make people forget he is a Chinese-American; it makes people think he is a Chinese-American with a weird hair style . . .
>
> However, because deep down Jin truly feels like he is not good enough for [Amelia], he accepts his own phony reality and never asks her out again.

There is no way to tell that these comments are necessarily about a graphic novel instead of a traditional novel; the literary analysis is the same. Samantha is examining Jin's motivations for changing his looks—he is trying to look more 'American' instead of 'Chinese-American,' but the effect is superficial. Another one of my students, Beth, wrote an essay that analyzed the Biblical allusions in Yang's graphic novel. Yet another examined Yang's use of Chinese mythology. Thus, it is clear that with the proper introduction, students can see and write about the literary elements of graphic novels.

One of the most creative versions of a literary analysis was done by a student named Caitlin. She wrote a literary analysis in the format of a graphic novel. She has a proclivity for illustrating, so I encouraged her in this effort. She wrote about how Marjane Satrapi's *Persepolis* is a coming-of-age novel. In her graphic novel, she partially copied—by hand—some critical cells from *Persepolis,* but then she added herself to the scene in the form of a researcher, complete with a lab coat and a clipboard! All of the scenes she duplicates have the corresponding page number from *Persepolis*, and she even used an outside source which she cites in a footnote fashion. Below are some cells from Caitlin's essay/graphic novel entitled "Persepolis as a Coming-of-Age Novel." On the left is a sample that places Caitlin in the foreground of a copied image from Satrapi's work, and on the right is a cell entirely of Caitlin's own making:

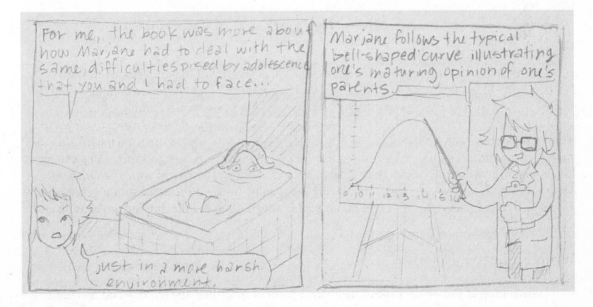

## Implementing Technology

An added bonus to using graphic novels is that it can often provide the opportunity for students to use technology in their writing. I still require students to quote from the graphic novel they write about, but I also encourage them to use images from the graphic novel as well. Provided the students have access to a scanner and a word-processing program, students can insert cells into their essays to use as examples. Sometimes even the scanner part is unnecessary; the website of its publisher, First Second Books, has samples from *American Born Chinese*[12], and students can save these images to their computers. Of course, in both cases the images are used only for educational purposes in the student essays. This is a great time to teach the students about copyrighted images. If you, as a teacher, are unfamiliar with how to scan images or insert them into documents, you might ask your school's technology staff to demonstrate, or you might ask one of your technology-savvy students to teach it to the class.

## Implementing Alternative Exercises

Aside from the standard literary analysis essay, there are numerous other exercises that you can use in conjunction with graphic novels. My favorites include having the students create their own page for a graphic novel and having the students write a prose version of a section of a graphic novel. These two exercises are explained in more detail below.

Having students create their own page of a graphic novel works well despite the fact that numerous students will proclaim their inability to draw. For this exercise, I offer two variations. The first variation is to have the students create a page that could appear in the graphic novel we are reading. In other words, with some guidance, they find a place in the graphic novel where some of the plot is compressed, and then they create a page that fills in that gap. It is akin to reclaiming a scene from the proverbial cutting room floor. I usually break the class into small groups of about three students each, and I give the students the following steps to follow:

1. Pick a point in the graphic novel where you will create and 'insert' your page.
2. Before beginning any illustration, decide what will happen in this scene. List 3 possibilities.
3. Write the dialogue or narration for the scene. Remember to keep it to a bare minimum since space is very limited.
4. Pick one of the possibilities and break it down into an appropriate number of cells (from 1 to 6). A single cell that takes an entire page signifies a critical event or action in the story. Using six cells is most useful when you want to show more physical activity or a significant change or progression.
5. Sketch each cell using basic illustrations like stick figures and common shapes. In your group, decide what would be the best "camera angle" for each cell. Refer to the graphic novel we are reading for reference.
6. Convert the sketched cells to the final version. Each student must be responsible for at least one cell. In the case of a single-cell page, then each student must be responsible for a portion of the cell. You can create your cells separately and then tape them together onto a single page to create the finished version.

---

[12] Samples from Gene Yang's *American Born Chinese* graphic novel and more information about Yang himself can be found at the publisher's website: http://www.firstsecondbooks.net/geneYang.html

For the first variation of the create-your-own-page exercise, I usually use class time for steps 1-5 so that I can guide them and answer questions. Step 6 works well for homework because the planning is all done by this step.

The second variation of this project is to have the students create a page or a couple of pages of an autobiographical graphic novel. This works well in conjunction with an autobiographical essay, which is a fairly standard assignment in English classes. After they have finished their autobiographical essay, have the students illustrate the essay in graphic novel form. Ambitious students may want to do this task individually, but it works well with small groups where each group chooses only one of the members' essays to illustrate. If time permits, you can have the students create the entire graphic-novel version of their essays; otherwise, you might have them create just a scene or two from their essays.

The second exercise involves the students creating the prose version of a scene from the assigned graphic novel. In this exercise, the students pick a scene from the graphic novel, and then they "convert" it to a scene written in the format of the traditional prose novel. To avoid having the students feel overwhelmed by the task, I encourage them to approach the task in the following steps:

1. Write a summary of what happens in the scene. [This helps students to practice their skills at summarizing.]

2. For each separate cell, brainstorm a vivid description. Be sure to carefully consider the colors and shading as well as the sharpness of the lines used in the cell. Remember to use any of the five senses (sight, smell, hearing, taste, and touch) that are appropriate, and create at least one unique comparison (simile or metaphor) per cell. [This helps students practice descriptions and comparisons.]

3. For each separate cell, describe in a sentence or two the tone. It may be the same for several or all of your cells, depending on which cells you are "converting." Again, consider the colors and shading as well as the sharpness of the lines used in the cell. [This helps students practice gauging the tone.]

4. Put it all together (your summary, description, and tone) into prose. Use the same perspective (first-person or third-person) as the graphic novel. [For this final step, I usually try to have on-hand an example of a first-person prose novel and a third-person prose novel so the students can reference them.]

## Handling Trouble Spots

Quite frankly, there are not very many troublesome aspects to using graphic novels in the classroom—provided that students proceed slowly and stay focused on literary elements. In fact, one of the chief problems I've encountered is preventing the students from reading ahead. Many students are driven to finish the graphic novel in just one or two sittings. This often causes them to favor plot development over more sophisticated literary elements. Fortunately, because it takes less time to read a graphic novel, students are more inclined to re-read it for a closer analysis, and re-reading is a task I have always found challenging when assigning traditional novels. Nevertheless, there is one particular note of caution that should be stated. This note of caution is echoed in Schwarz's article and in nearly every recent article about graphic novels. Educators and librarians have to be careful in selecting and placing each individual graphic novel. Some graphic novels contain fairly adult content matter, so previewing a graphic novel is an absolute necessity before teaching it.

Having used both traditional novels and graphic novels in my composition classes for many years, I can say that students have much preferred the graphic novels. Again, I am not arguing that graphic novels can or should replace traditional novels, but they certainly can become part of an effective curriculum, and they often work well when paired with a traditional novel. Graphic novels can, in Sidney's words, both teach and delight.

## Works Cited

Buhle, Paul. "The New Scholarship of Comics." *The Chronicle of Higher Education* 16 May 2003: B7-9. <http:// chronicle.com/free/v49/i36/36b00701.htm>.

Clowes, Daniel. *Ghost World*. Seattle: Thompson & Groth, 1997.

Eisner, Will. *Comics & Sequential Art*. Tamarac, FL: Poorhouse, 2001.

Jacobson, Sid, and Ernie Colon. *The 9-11 Report: A Graphic Adaptation*. New York: Hill and Wang, 2006.

Kuper, Peter. *Franz Kafka's* The Metamorphosis. New York: Crown, 2003.

Millar, Mark. *Civil War*. Illus. Steve McNiven. New York: Marvel, 2007.

Mitchell, Caitlin. "*Persepolis* as a Coming-of-Age Novel." Unpublished essay, 2006.

Purdue, Samantha. "Robots in Disguise." Unpublished essay, 2007.

Satrapi, Marjane. *Persepolis: The Story of a Childhood*. New York: Pantheon, 2003.

Schwarz, Gretchen. "Expanding Literacies through Graphic Novels." *English Journal* 95.6 (July 2006): 58-64.

Spiegelman, Art. *Maus: A Survivor's Tale I: My Father Bleeds History*. New York: Pantheon, 1986.

Sturm, James. "Comics in the Classroom." *The Chronicle of Higher Education* 5 Apr. 2002: B14-15. <http://chronicle .com/>.

Thompson, Craig. *Blankets*. Marietta, GA: Top Shelf, 2004.

Twiddy, David. "As More Graphic Novels Appear in Libraries, So Do Challenges." *Associated Press State and Local Wire* 15 Nov. 2006. LexisNexis Academic. Middle Tennessee State University. 3 Mar. 2007 <http://web.lexis-nexis.com.ezproxy.mtsu.edu>.

Yang, Gene Luen. *American Born Chinese*. New York: First Second, 2006.

# The Graphic Novel: Writing as Close Focus

## *Kevin Haworth*

With one foot in popular culture, and the other in traditional art and literature, graphic novels present interesting opportunities for the writing classroom. On one hand, both historical and contemporary examples of comic books and comic strips can be read as cultural artifacts for their representations of gender roles, minorities, social mores, and many other things. In this way, these texts can be problematized, examined, and written about within a cultural studies framework, prompting students to, as Diana George and Diana Shoos suggest, "become critical readers of a culture and its popular productions" (202).

On the other hand, the narratives told by the best graphic novels, augmented by the creative interplay of text and image, allow students to see their own lives reflected in these books. As a teacher of literature as well as composition, I am sympathetic to Gary Tate's urge to give students the opportunity to "think and talk and write about human lives outside the academy" (321). Too often, a division is made between pop culture (i.e., 'low-rent culture') and literature ('high-rent culture'). I would argue that graphic novels occupy a useful, though by no means unique, space in this debate, embodying low-rent and high-rent culture at once. This allows them to be used by writing teachers with a cultural studies approach, a more traditional literary approach, or a combination of both.

In either case, we are fortunate enough to be living in a boom era for the graphic novel. The term itself is relatively recent, and not quite synonymous with the more modest "comic book." Simply put, a graphic novel is a long comic book, though often one with a higher level of quality, production, and ambition. I use the terms rather interchangeably with my students, along with others such as sequential art, because each term can encourage students to think in slightly different ways about what they are reading. But whatever the label, the depth and variety available in the medium has increased steadily since Art Spiegelman's two-volume *Maus: A Survivor's Tale* in 1986 and 1991 brought new awareness of the genre. In addition to Spiegelman's Holocaust narrative, recent graphic novels have explored such significant topics as Iran's Islamic Revolution from a young woman's perspective (Marjane Satrapi's *Persepolis* volumes), capital punishment (Kim Deitch's "Ready to Die"), queer issues (Alison Bechdel's *Fun Home*) and many others. Of as much interest to my students (if not more) are narratives of the teenage/college age years such as Daniel Clowes' *Ghost World* and Charles Burns' *Black Hole*. By the time Ben Katchor won a MacArthur Fellowship in 2000, following the publication of *Julius Knipl, Real Estate Photographer*, the emergence of the genre was well established.

Rocco Versaci has written quite persuasively about the way that the accessibility and subtle complexity of graphic novels can be used to encourage reluctant readers. This is true for reluctant writers as well. Again, a number of different approaches can be used. The emphasis that many graphic novels place on personal narrative —the struggle to tell one's own story —can serve as a starting point for students' own expressivist writing. At the same time, the sophisticated aesthetic and narrative techniques employed by the better graphic novels can provide the basis for source-based, academic writing that prepares students to examine both images and text. As one of my students wrote, imperfectly but not wholly inaccurately: "comics are a balancing act of the visible and the imagination." That balance can be a very productive one for writing teachers to explore.

I will present here some steps to establishing a common critical vocabulary about graphic novels—necessary for students to think and write well about these works—as well as some writing prompts for both expressivist and source-based writing from my experiences using graphic novels in my own classroom over the last two years.

## Slowing Down

One of the points of caution in teaching graphic novels is that like other forms of visual rhetoric (photographs, advertisements, film, et al.) students typically believe that they can read them very quickly and still get "the whole story." Our students are surrounded by images—from television to t-shirts—and consider themselves fluent in the visual reading process, if they consider it at all.

This concern is common to all teachers who use visual texts. As Joel Foreman and David R. Shumway note regarding their teaching of images from the *New York Times Magazine*, "The speed and ease with which we consume a visual text tends to conceal the fact that the mind is extremely active in the second it takes to scan the page of the magazine" (245). It takes time and effort to reveal this activity to students, who may resist deep examination of visual texts they have seen their entire lives. There is an added concern with comic books as some (though certainly not all) readers have experienced them as an essentially juvenile, simple medium. Combine these multiple elements of lowered expectations, and there exists the potential for some very superficial reading as well as superficial writing.

Thus, as with much popular culture, writing about graphic novels might well begin with the breaking down of assumptions. I pursue this in two parts. One is to establish a simple critical vocabulary (which can be expanded upon later in more depth). I often hand out Matt Madden and Jessica Abel's "Basic Comics Terminology," produced for the National Association of Comics Educators, on the first day of discussion. This simple mockup of a comics page by two well-known illustrators uses callouts to introduce students to terms such as panel, bleed, gutter, splash page, and thought and speech balloon. Almost all students are basically familiar with the visual layout of a comic strip or comic book, even if they have never thought much about it. As a result, I find that they are able to employ this new terminology very quickly, both in discussion and in their writing.

The second part is to consider the basic unit of comics layout—the panel—for all its potential visual and textual information. The panel is the basic unit of meaning in this art form, and it is to the graphic novel what the sentence is to written text: the first building block of complex thought. As such, a close reading of a single panel can be used to encourage students to both read and write more carefully and specifically.

The key here is to assist students through initial in-depth readings of single panels, to build their skills and to counteract their urge to read quickly and move on. I often introduce students to this concept using a web (online) comic titled *Nine Planets Without Intelligent Life*, by Adam Reed, which is a witty and erudite episodic journey undertaken by, well, robots.

A small but important element of *Nine Planets* is that it scrolls sideways on a computer screen, generally revealing one panel at a time. If technology allows, one approach can be to project it on a screen at the front of the class. This allows a teacher to limit the area of focus and keep the students involved in a single panel at a time.[13]

The panel shown here is the third one of the very first episode of *Nine Planets*, from a sequence titled "Ubermensch." It is preceded by a quotation from Fredrich Nietzche, along with some simple exposition, and is part of a sequence in which the figures in the panel, two factory robots, realize that they are building improved versions of themselves—essentially constructing their own obsolescence.

The wordless nature of this panel forces students to construct meaning based solely on visual cues, a process that can be assisted by the instructor. Drawing on Donald McQuade and Christine McQuade's work, I ask students questions such as: What is the figure and what is the background? What is relationship between the two? What are the distinct areas of visual focus within this single panel? What patterns of shape and shadow, and color can be seen? What is wholly within the frame, and what only partially? Why?

This pedagogy of close focus, for lack of a better term, can be linked quite quickly to interesting writing challenges. Since I do this exercise toward the beginning of the class term, I often pair it with a (seemingly) basic writing exercise. Using the brainstorming information on the board, students are asked to sum up the panel in one sentence. This becomes surprisingly hard to do. Since together they have generated far more information than they can include in one sentence, this exercise leads to a series of discussions that are at the core of many writing decisions: What to include? What to leave out? What is really important, and why? And how do you order that information thoroughly, but succinctly? This writing exercise builds on the close inspection of a single comic panel by focusing attention on a single sentence—in this case, their own. This establishes a level of attention for small detail, with many clear benefits for both the reading and the writing that follows.

From a single panel, students can be encouraged to move to the next step—understanding the narrative possibilities of a single page. I have followed the *Nine Planets* exercise by providing students with a page copied from a graphic novel in which all the text has been blanked out, leaving only the artwork to suggest the relationship between characters. (I typically use a page

---

[13] If a classroom is not equipped with the capacity to project a web site on a media screen, teachers can photocopy a single interesting panel from any work and hand it out to students to perform this exercise.

from Clowes' *Ghost World*, featuring two teenage female characters in a cold suburban environment.) Working individually or in groups, students are asked to reinvent the dialogue that flows between the two characters. The students inevitably produce very different—even opposing —versions of what is happening on the page. This exercise conveys to them the complexity of the relationship between text and image; as Scott McCloud discusses in his influential study, *Understanding Comics*, itself presented in a graphic novel format, the relationship can be additive, parallel, or interdependent, or one of several other choices. Just as importantly (if not more so), the exercise points to the intricacy of how people relate to each other, using verbal cues (i.e., dialogue) and visual cues (conveyed by the artwork) that can be supportive of each other, opposed to each other, or a complex combination of both.

A more student-focused variation on this last exercise involves each student bringing a series of their own related photographs to class. The students then lay the photos out on a page, graphic novel-style; using some or all of the textual possibilities at hand, including speech balloons, thought balloons, or narrative boxes (the 'voice-over' of the comic book), the students "write the story" suggested by the photographs. On one level, this is basic storytelling exercise. At the same time, each of the narrative choices can lead to discussion, such as: What should be said aloud? What should be only be thought? Whose voice should be heard? Who is kept silent? If a voice over is used, who is telling the story, and— very importantly—why are they telling it?[14]

## Writing the Self

This last exercise speaks to one of the central strengths of graphic novels in the writing classroom— their ability to prompt students to write thoughtfully about their own lives. As Charles Hatfield points out, autobiography is one of the most common, albeit complicated, elements of many graphic novels. The author/narrators of books such as *Maus* and *Persepolis* position themselves within their stories and openly struggle with how and why to narrate their lives. For writing students who struggle to tell their own stories, seeing accomplished authors such as Spiegelman and Satrapi grapple with many of the same issues is inspiring and empowering. And "see" it they do, for the graphic novel medium allows for both autobiography and self-portrait, a powerful combination that Scott McCloud suggests is at the core of why many readers identify strongly with comics.

In addition, the curious position held by comics in both literature and popular culture makes them accessible to students in thinking about their own lives. Comics yet suffer from a "considerable lack of legitimacy," as Thierry Groensteen argues. But it is this lack of legitimacy that can inspire students who are unsure of the legitimacy of their own experiences and the value of writing about them (29). With their roots in outsider art, typified by R. Crumb, by Art Spieglman's early work, and by others, graphic novels offer marginalized students a voice that may not be found either in more traditional writing texts, or in mainstream pop culture that idolizes the exceptional. (As one eighteen-year-old male student told me, "I can relate to Crumb because he's weird like me.") Despite growing mainstream acceptance, many contemporary graphic novels still illustrate life on the social, sexual, and economic margins. These examples

---

[14] There are software programs, such as plasq's Comic Life 1.3, that allow students to perform this exercise via computer.

reflect experiences many students have had—often ones they may be reluctant to discuss in the classroom—and thus can provide these students with a launching point for writing about the self.

For a final essay, I try to draw together these strains and encourage the students to use the many graphic novel excerpts and full texts we have read as a lens through which to focus their own narratives. The prompt:

---

**The Comic Book and YOU**

Explore the following question: which comic book author would you have illustrate your life, and why? Consider questions like: what aspects of your life would you choose to have illustrated? Why? How would it be structured? How, exactly, would a particular author's style and techniques serve to represent you and your experience? Think of yourself as the author and your chosen artist as your illustrator.

---

Like the author/illustrators they have read, students must respond by making significant decisions about how to frame their own narratives. In choosing a graphic novelist to illustrate their lives (something they find quite fun), they must articulate decisions about tone, style and other aesthetic elements. A student who chooses the seemingly plain drawing style of Scott McCloud imagines himself or herself quite differently than one who sees the highly stylized work of someone like Charles Burns as appropriate for their story. The same is true for the many narrative decisions they must make: Do I focus on one day? One hour? One year? Where do I begin? Where do I end? Who do I include? Who do I leave out? What 'scenes' from my life best illustrate my story? And why?

When I have given this assignment, one or two adventurous students have responded by constructing an essay wholly or partially in graphic novel form. These are intriguing, if not always successful. More often, though, students respond with a three to four page prose essay that I find more revealing than the standard writing classroom fare. Some of this stems from the relatively safe space of the final essay, in which one does not necessarily have to face teacher or fellow students again. But I choose to believe that reading graphic novels prompts a level of introspection some students may be unable to access otherwise. The first time I gave this assignment, two students (out of twenty) wrote powerfully about coming out about their sexual orientation, choosing quite different artists (Chris Ware and Adrian Tomine) as their personal illustrators. The second and most recent time, an eighteen-year-old woman narrated a three-day period that had culminated in her having an abortion, just a few weeks before the class had begun. In doing so, she referred several times to Debbie Drechsler's "The Dead of Winter," which we read in class and which covers much the same topic. It is worth noting that this same student earlier wrote a four-page critique of Drechsler's work without ever noting its relevance to her own life.

It is at moments like these that our students reflect the multiple and confusing spaces that graphic novels inhabit: literate and popular, visual and textual, childish and yet very adult. In chapter four of *Understanding Comics*, titled "Show and Tell," Scott McCloud depicts that early grade school moment when to show was to tell, and vice versa. It is a moment of storytelling liberation that he has chosen never to leave.

## Works Cited

Bechdel, Alison. *Fun Home: A Family Tragicomic*. New York: Houghton, 2006.

Burns, Charles. *Black Hole*. New York: Pantheon, 2005.

Clowes, Daniel. *Ghost World*. Seattle: Fantagraphics, 2001.

Deitch, Kim. "Ready to Die." *McSweeney's Quarterly Concern* 13 (2004): 136-41.

Drechsler, Debbie. "The Dead of Winter." *McSweeney's Quarterly Concern* 13 (2004): 208-13.

Foreman, Joel, and David R. Shumway. "Cultural Studies: Reading Visual Texts." *Cultural Studies in the English Classroom*. Ed. James A. Berlin and Michael J. Vivion. Portsmouth, NH: Heinemann, 1992. 244-61.

George, Diana, and Diana R. Shoos. "Issues of Subjectivity and Resistance: Cultural Studies in the Composition Classroom." *Cultural Studies in the English Classroom*. Ed. James A. Berlin and Michael J. Vivion. Portsmouth, NH: Heinemann, 1992. 200-10.

Hatfield, Charles. *Alternative Comics: An Emerging Literature*. Jackson: UP of Mississippi, 2005.

Katchor, Ben. *Julius Knipl, Real Estate Photographer: Stories*. New York: Little, Brown, 1996.

Madden, Matt., and Jessica Abel. *National Association of Comics Arts Educators*. 25 Apr. 2007 <http://www.teachingcomics.org>.

Groensteen, Thierry. "Why Are Comics Still in Search of Cultural Legitimization?" *Comics & Culture: Analytical and Theoretical Approaches to Comics*. Ed. Anne Magnussen and Hans-Christian Christiansen. Copenhagen: Museum Tusculanum/U of Copenhagen, 2000. 29-42.

McCloud, Scott. *Understanding Comics: The Invisible Art*. New York: HarperPerennial, 1993.

McQuade, Donald, and Christine McQuade. *Seeing and Writing 2*. Boston: Bedford/St. Martin's, 2003.

Reed, Adam. *Nine Planets without Intelligent Life*. 31 Mar. 2007 <http://www.bohemiandrive.com/comics/npwil.html>.

Satrapi, Marjane. *Persepolis: The Story of a Childhood*. New York: Pantheon, 2003.

Spiegelman, Art. *Maus: A Survivor's Tale I: My Father Bleeds History*. New York: Pantheon, 1986.

---. *Maus: A Survivor's Tale II: And Here My Troubles Began*. New York: Pantheon, 1991.

Tate, Gary. "A Place for Literature in Freshman Composition." *CE* 55 (1993): 317-21.

Versaci, Rocco. "How Comic Books Can Change the Way Our Students See Literature: One Teacher's Perspective." *English Journal* 91.2 (2001): 61-67.

# Inspired Artists and Office Drones: Taking Literacy Narratives to the Movies

## *Bronwyn T. Williams*

For most of us there have been the occasional moments in our lives when events seemed to be unfolding just like a scene in the movies. Perhaps it is a romantic moment watching the sun set, or winning the game in the last seconds, or doing an acrobatically comic pratfall. Yet for all the moments that might seem like they are scripted from the movies, the moments when we sit down to write don't, at first glance, seem to connect to common images from the screen in the same way. Writing in movies is often portrayed as the inspired act of the tortured artist. When Sylvia Plath (Gwyneth Paltrow) or Virginia Woolf (Nicole Kidman) sit down to write in films such as *Sylvia* (2003) or *The Hours* (2002) we see them in splendid isolation, writing with pen and ink, as lyrical music rises, and we hear the actresses reading in voice over the authors' words in unbroken, graceful phrases. By contrast, I am sitting at a computer, the room is a mess, the phone is ringing, and it seems like each line I type I have to go back over time and again, rewriting it until I don't hate it quite so much. There is nothing unbroken in my writing, little that feels inspired, and no voice in my head that sounds like Gwyneth Paltrow's.

While it is true that film portrayals of authors are often romanticized visions of inspired genius that seem detached from the writing experiences of most mortals, there are other portrayals of literacy practices, of reading, writing and the values they represent, that are more complicated and interesting. These more complex representations of literacy can be used in the writing classroom to open up for students different ways of thinking about how they read and write in the world. In this essay I will describe how and why I use popular movies when I teach literacy narrative assignments in first-year writing classes. I use movies as a means of helping students connect their individual experiences with reading and writing to larger cultural questions of how literacy is defined and who gets to use it as a means of granting or withholding power. I want students to create a dialogue between their individual literacy histories and the cultural and historical forces that have shaped and will shape their literacy practices. The more students understand about how these forces have influenced their experiences with reading and writing the more able they will be to make critically informed choices in the future knowing that reading and writing are always negotiations between private thoughts and desires and public ideologies.

## "Individual" Experiences with Literacy

I am a fervent advocate of literacy narratives and have for years assigned them in almost all the courses I teach at every level, usually at the beginning of the semester. I may vary the focus of the assignment, depending on the course, but I always find value in having students reflect on their experiences with reading and writing. In this essay I am going to focus on my literacy narrative assignments in first-year writing courses. Literacy narratives are one way to make students conscious of the role literacy has played in their lives before they walk into a first-year writing classroom. The assignments remind students that they are experienced writers and readers who have been engaging in these activities for years. Literacy narrative assignments also help reinforce the focus of the course as one about the activities of writing and reading in the world, rather than simply about correcting grammar or reading literature.

As a teacher I find students' literacy narratives reveal for me not only their experiences, but also how and why they feel as they do toward writing and reading. The stories students tell about can be thrilling, such as narratives of supportive parents or creative teachers who nurture and encourage adventurous writing and reading. Very often, however, the narratives are wrenching, such as the student who drew pictures on a story she had written only to see her second-grade teacher toss the story into the trash can with the admonishment, "Big kids don't draw pictures on their writing" or the student who loved writing until a grammar-obsessed teacher drove out the passion through daily grammar drills and worksheets. These more troubling tales offer me insights into potential sites of student resistance to my pedagogical goals and approaches for the class. Students are usually too savvy to come right out and tell me that they don't want to do this kind of reading or that kind of writing. But they will often, in their discussions of past writing experiences, tell of both how and, more to the point, *why* they dislike a particular kind of literacy practice. Understanding the source of such resistance allows me to consider how to construct my assignments in creative ways that might engage such students.

Still, as valuable as I have found the literacy narrative assignment, as much as I have enjoyed reading them, I had remained discontented with one aspect of the assignments I used and the essays students wrote. When students wrote about their individual experiences they portrayed them as purely *individual* in nature. In other words, if a student wrote about a teacher who was difficult, or inspiring, to work with, the essay portrayed the teacher's actions and student's responses as if they were solely a result of the unique personalities of the two individuals involved. Individual actions were the consequences of individual choices. The difference between a positive or negative experience with literacy was a matter of the luck that placed a student in the company of a person who was either supportive or not just because the person decided to be. Rarely did students attribute the motivations or actions of others to cultural definitions of literacy and the institutional demands shaped by such definitions.

It is neither a surprise nor a criticism to note that students interpreted their literacy experiences as a series of individual choices and events. We live in a culture that explains events through the ideal of the individual. We preach the doctrine of individual responsibility and celebrate achievements as growing from individual efforts. The focus on individual actions as the lens through which to interpret events and actions explains our resistance as a culture to ideas such as systemic racism or gender roles. First-year college students, who are just emerging from an adolescence in which their developmental and cultural influences reinforced ideologies of individualism often are particularly resistant to thinking about culture as having any influence in their values, perceptions, or actions. Popular culture reflects this emphasis on the individual in many ways, such as the lone action hero in films or, as I noted above, the lone author.

In terms of literacy the students' essays reflect the still dominant cultural conception of literacy as a set of a-contextual, stand-alone skills (Street). The students still see their reading and writing as a series of autonomous literacy events which are sometimes positive, sometimes not, with little predictability to, or explanation of, the outcome aside from personality differences. Such perceptions stand in vivid contrast to the social theories of literacy that have become more persuasive in the fields of literacy and rhetoric scholarship. David Barton and Mary Hamilton argue that we should regard literacy as a social practice in which the observable "events" of reading and writing are inextricable from the values, attitudes, social structures that shape our responses to such events. For Barton and Hamilton:

> Practices are shaped by social rules which regulate the use and distribution of texts, prescribing who may produce and have access to them. They straddle the distinction between individual and social worlds, and literacy practices are more usefully understood as existing in the relations between people, within groups and communities, rather than as a set of properties residing in individuals. (7)

I realized that what I was not seeing in students' literacy narrative essays, and in all fairness not asking for in my assignments, was an exploration of how their experiences with reading and writing had been influenced by cultural institutions and social relationships. I realized that I wanted them to explore how their experiences with literacy in school had been shaped, not just by the personalities of their teachers, but by the institution of education. I wanted them to understand that social relations of power had a role in determining who could read and write and for what purposes. I wanted to help them see that whether reading or writing felt fulfilling was not only a matter of personal taste or artistic genius, but often rested on cultural and historical definitions of literacy and its purposes. Most of all I wanted them to understand that every time they read and write, how that practice would take place and be assessed and valued would be situated in specific cultural contexts.

Although others have realized the potential of literacy narratives for helping students analyze similar questions of culture and writing (Eldred and Mortensen, Soliday, Kamler), I was also concerned that I not make students feel as if culture is entirely deterministic. The unfortunate approach of some pedagogy that purports to engage students in questions of culture and social relations is to treat students as unfortunate dupes, powerless puppets of dominant ideologies. Even worse, the students are made to feel silly for having enjoyed popular culture in the first place. Students understandably often resent and resist such approaches. My goal is more traditionally Freirean. I believe in valuing people's abilities to understand their own experiences and work with them to connect those experiences to the questions they raise, rather than shape them to any single agenda. Instead of feeling hopeless or powerless, I hoped that by helping students connect their experiences to the cultural expectations of literacy they would be better able to make critical choices about their writing. Whether they wanted to conform to or resist cultural expectations, I wanted them to be able to understand those expectations more clearly, rather than bump into them by accident, blame them only on individual personality differences, and feel frustrated.

## Literacy Practices on Film

Developing the ability to step back from individual experiences and see the cultural framework that helped shape such experiences is not an easy task for any of us, however. This is why I find myself going to the movies. On the one hand, movies reflect and reproduce our culture for us. As Andrew Light points out, movies, like other popular culture texts, create complex portrayals of how we see ourselves and others that don't "merely represent individuals and groups but also help to actually create understandings of who we think we are, how we regard others, and how members of groups identify and understand their group membership and their obligations to that group" (9). In mainstream movies, even slapstick comedies and gory horror films, we in the audience see a recognizable world with characters who act in generally familiar and comprehensible ways. If popular movies did not reproduce our culture in ways we could comprehend, they would not be appealing to mass audiences. Though we know movies are fictional and not direct representations of the lives most of us inhabit, we accept the world, characters, and actions we see in movies as consistent with the ideological truths and values that shape our lives. Much recent film criticism that has explored how movies reinforce ideas about gender, class, race and other identity characteristics is grounded in the premise that movies reproduce our dominant cultural values for us.

What I have found useful in the classroom, particularly in terms of literacy narratives, are the ways in which literacy practices are portrayed in movies. Although we don't always take explicit notice of it, it is much harder to find a movie without literacy represented in it than it is to find one where people are reading or writing. Movies are filled with moments of people reading and writing. Some of these scenes are central to the movies and involve characters identified as writers while others are brief, almost incidental to the main plot, and involve characters from action heroes to comic foils. The motivations for reading and writing and the results of those actions can vary from film to film. Even so, the pervasive representations of literacy reproduce dominant ideas about literacy that have an effect on our cultural conceptions of reading and writing from issues of identity to institutional practices (Williams and Zenger). The literacy practices displayed on the screen and consumed by the public are part of the ideological construction of what is considered literacy, what social goals it serves in what institutions, how it is perpetuated, and what cultural power is determined by who is considered literate. Of course ideology is not uniform and not adopted unquestioningly by every person in society. Still, if we focus on the literacy practices of characters in movies we open a window to the social practices of literacy in which we all engage.

The advantage movies, like other texts, have in the classroom when it comes to talking about culture and literacy is that they are representations of culture and of the lives of others from which we can gain some critical distance. We can't freeze the moments in our own lives and step outside them to ponder what is happening as we can with film. The advantage movies have as a popular culture text, however, is that students have extensive experiences in reading and interpreting mainstream movies. This experience gives them the ability to talk about movies with both a sophistication and an authority that they might not bring to poems or literary texts. Movies offer scenes of reading and writing that students can examine and against which they can compare their ideas about their own literacy practices in a fairly low-stakes conversation.

## Who Gets to Read and Write In the Movies?

I begin the literacy narrative assignment in the first week of class with invention prompts and mini-assignments of several kinds. All of these invention activities are focused on getting the students to write about their reading and writing experiences in as much detail as possible.

First we brainstorm lists in class of the kinds of reading and writing people have done, locations where such activities happened, artifacts that have been involved from books they've read to neighborhood newspapers they wrote, and other people who may have been involved. We discuss literacy events both in and out of school at various ages, prompting the students to think beyond literary and school-sanctioned texts to include work, play, and other experiences as well.

From the lists I ask the students to choose items that resonate for them and begin freewriting, both to accumulate details about the events, people, and places they remember and to begin to explain how they felt about the experiences. We do the freewriting over more than one class session, and I often assign additional freewriting between class sessions.

I then assign students to write scenes and descriptions from the most compelling material that has emerged in their invention activities. These are out-of-class writing assignments that we also work on in class in terms of shaping the scenes and providing adequate detail as well as adding a sense of how the students felt about the experiences. The invention and craft-oriented exercises I use during these class sessions I have drawn over the years from a number of sources (Murray, Rule and Wheeler, Wheeler). I do not, at this point, ask the students to put the scenes, descriptions, and reflections together into an essay draft. I do not want them to make choices of what will go into the draft yet and possibly preclude other ideas. Instead I want them to accumulate detailed material about their reading and writing experiences.

It is at this point in the literacy narrative assignment that I introduce movies into the mix. I specifically use film clips to engage students with questions of how communities define literacy, how settings and motivations influence reading and writing experiences, and how institutions determine which literacy practices are valued. I like to start with films that connect to some of their childhood memories to give them a sense of how attitudes about literacy are shaped from early in their lives.

In something as simple as the opening song in the Disney animated film *Beauty and the Beast* (1991), the character of Belle walks through town, nose in the book, oblivious to life around her. While others are baking bread and buying vegetables, Belle walks, reads, and dreams that "There must be more than this provincial life." Meanwhile, the townspeople around her watch her pass and sing:

> Look there she goes that girl is so peculiar
> I wonder if she's feeling well
> With a dreamy, far-off look
> And her nose stuck in a book
> What a puzzle to the rest of us is Belle (Ashman and Menken 1991)

I hand out the lyrics to the students and we watch the clip more than once (I always have students watch scenes more than once, taking detailed notes the second time, just as I would want them to do with a print text). I ask what the townspeople think of Belle. When I discuss movies with students in this context, I focus the questions on the relationships between characters or the events in the scenes rather than what the students think of the film. I want to take advantage of the critical distance film offers rather than turn the conversation toward student preferences of the film. I also ask them to list what qualities the community attributes to literacy and how those are the same or different than how Belle seems to regard reading.

What I want to touch on during the discussion, and am willing to chime in with if need be, is the distance that reading creates between Belle and the other people in the town. There is a distinction between the way she sees the world and the way the world sees her, and reading has a role in both of these. For Belle, her desire to escape the "provincial life" is mirrored in her desire to read fantasy books about "far off places, daring swordfights, magic spells, a prince in disguise." Literacy for her is empowering and lifts her gaze beyond the limits of those around her, just as we writing teachers always say it will. For the townspeople, however, Belle is regarded, as deeply engaged readers are, as absent-minded, out of touch. She is a puzzle and evokes a certain sense of wariness. The townspeople sing:

> Now it's no wonder that her name means "Beauty"
> Her looks have got no parallel
> But behind that fair facade
> I'm afraid she's rather odd
> Very diff'rent from the rest of us
> She's nothing like the rest of us
> Yes, diff'rent from the rest of us is Belle (Ashman and Menken 1991)

Not only is her commitment to reading somewhat suspect, in a way intellectuals are often portrayed in popular culture, but this is magnified by her gender identity. It strikes the town as unusual that a beautiful woman is also such a devoted reader. The tension between the value the community places on literacy and Belle's view of literacy is clear. The community sees literacy as puzzling, trivial, and suspicious while Belle sees it as fulfilling and empowering. We then talk in class about the arguments to be made for both of these positions. I want the students to think about how literacy practices can be perceived differently in different contexts, how individuals may feel at odds with community values. I want them to understand why each side might have reached the conclusions it has.

To finish this class session I have the students look at the material they have written about their experiences to see if there were times when the values they placed in a literacy practice (or did not place it in) were different from others' values. What was the community definition of literacy in that circumstance? Why did each side hold the position it did? Did this lead to misunderstanding or frustration? Why? I don't ask for finished essays, just exploratory writing analyzing the experience from this perspective.

## Identities and Institutions

For the next class I bring in clips that I hope will complicate their ideas about the identity of "writers." Popular culture in reflecting the culture at large often portrays writers as inspired, if occasionally tortured, geniuses. Yet, as I mentioned in my introduction, the reality of writing is quite different, even for professional writers. More to the point, however, is that anyone who writes is a "writer." What determines the culture's perception of that act is the situation in which it takes place. How is the writing valued? How is the writer valued? What motivates the writer? Is the experience of writing pleasurable? Is it empowering or oppressive?

While there are many films that feature scenes of people writing, two that I like to put in stark contrast to each other are *Shakespeare in Love* (1998) and *Office Space* (1999). Of course *Shakespeare in Love* has a variety of scenes about writing, but one particular sequence displays the myth of the inspired genius in all its glory. In the film Shakespeare (Joseph Fiennes) has fallen in love with Viola de Lesseps (Gwyneth Paltrow) even as she is disguising herself as a boy to play the part of Romeo. In a scene set a few days after they have consummated their love, we see them stealing kisses back stage as she rehearses. With great effort he withdraws from her embrace as she begs him not to go. He answers, "I must, I must" and races to his room, which looks like the romantic ideal of the isolated writer's garret, barely able to sit down before he has begun writing. He begins to write with quill and ink the *Romeo and Juliet* balcony scene, which begins in voiceover (always a cue in movies that the writer is producing inspired art) then cuts to Viola reading the scene with Will as they lie in bed together, and then cuts to her speaking the final lines of the scene at rehearsal as the rest of the cast looks on amazed at the poetry Shakespeare has produced. When I discuss this scene with students they are quick to recognize the hallmarks of the inspired genius that are present, from the inspiration of a muse to the lonely writer's room, to the ability to produce art in a single, unrevised burst of genius. Of course they all know that Shakespeare is a genius, perhaps the greatest cultural symbol of the romantic vision of the inspired author. Students are able to identify how writing in this scene is portrayed as personal, liberating, emotional, and as pleasurable as love and sex, and to come up with other examples from film and television of similar scenes.

Once we have discussed *Shakespeare in Love*, I then show them the first scene from *Office Space*. *Office Space* is a satire of contemporary white-collar office life and takes place in a high-tech company in a nameless, placeless suburban office park. Like the comic strip *Dilbert* or the television series *The Office*, the focus of the film is on the gray, grinding drudgery of the employees in their gray cubicles. In the first scene in the office, early in the movie, Peter (Ron Livingston) is criticized by his supervisor (Gary Cole) for having made a mistake with his paperwork:

> Lumbergh: We have sort of a problem here. Yeah, you apparently didn't put one of the new cover sheets on your TPS reports.
> Peter: Yeah, I'm sorry about that. I forgot.
> Lumbergh: Um, Yeah. You see we're putting the cover sheet on all TPS reports now before they go out. Did you *see* the memo about this?

Peter no sooner finishes this conversation than two other supervisors criticize him for the same mistake. As this scene sets up, literacy throughout the film is never empowering. Instead it is represented as a set of meaningless tasks imposed upon employees by an inept and uncaring management. From the puzzling obsession with cover sheets to the slightly menacing inspirational banners on the office walls (Is This Good For The Company?), to personnel files used to terrorize employees, the literacy practices in *Office Space* are portrayed as relentlessly tedious and exhausting.

In discussions about *Office Space*, students sometime struggle at first with identifying the motivations and perceptions of literacy. They recognize that reading and writing are happening, and are not supposed to be pleasant, but are unsure how to identify the reasons for the differences with *Shakespeare in Love*. What I often do to help highlight the cultural expectations and values that shape each scene is ask students, in groups, to write a scene that somehow combines elements of the two movies. For example, they can put Shakespeare in the office cubicle and write about how his supervisors respond to his writing of the *Romeo and Juliet* balcony scene. Or they can turn Peter from *Office Space* into a playwright and see how his actions change. These scenes are fun to create, but also allow us to identify more clearly which cultural factors have changed for each character and the effect those changes have had on their literacy practices. I then ask the students to look again at the writing they have created about their experiences and write about what situational and cultural factors made the experiences empowering, oppressive, pleasurable, or enervating.

I finish the use of movies with the literacy narrative assignment by exploring the role of institutions in shaping how literacy is valued and controlled. I want students to understand that is not simply enough to know how to read and write, but that certain kinds of literacy are valued by certain institutions and others are not and understanding the difference can be the key to power in society. To generate this discussion I use a scene from the film *Changing Lanes* (2002). The plot of the film is fairly ridiculous, but for the scene I show all the students need to understand is that the character of Gavin Banek (Ben Affleck) is a wealthy corporate lawyer and Doyle Gipson (Samuel L. Jackson) is a clerical worker seeking custody of his children. The scene I show contrasts their literacy experiences at a courthouse. First, Banek strides through the lobby of the courthouse unhindered by authority and enters a spacious and quiet courtroom with subdued lighting. The few people in the room are well dressed in suits and speaking standardized, middle-class English. Banek produces some legal documents and then is flustered when he finds that he no longer has the file he needs. He explains to the court how he lost it in a voice and manner that make it clear he expects the judge to accept his explanation. The judge is disappointed, but respectful toward Banek and gives him until the end of the day to retrieve the file.

By contrast, we then see Gipson enter the courthouse through a loud and chaotic lobby and a gantlet of X-ray machines and metal detectors. The waiting area outside the family court he is visiting is filled with people in sweatshirts, jeans, flannel shirts, and other work or casual clothes. The room is loud and people are arguing, a number speaking languages other than English. The only people who are shown reading or writing are officials such as lawyers or clerks. Gipson is late, just as Banek was, but when he enters the cramped courtroom the judge is unsympathetic and awards custody to Gipson's ex-wife. The room is cramped, with bright fluorescent lighting, plain walls, and institutional furniture. People talk over one another, and the feel of the setting is chaotic and stressful. Gipson tries to present his case to the judge, pulling out a legal pad and starting to read a handwritten narrative about the need for young boys to be near their father. "The streets of this world are lonely for boys without their father," he reads. "I have grown and I have recognized my mistakes." The judge, however, looks through other official papers as Gipson reads his statement and looks up only long enough to dismiss him and call the next case. Gipson leaves the courtroom in a frustrated, barely suppressed rage, and dumps all his papers in a trashcan.

I ask students why the two men are treated so differently at the courthouse. Students quickly point out how the differences in race and class between the two characters also result in differences in cultural power. When we watch the scenes again, I ask them to pay particular attention to how their literacy practices either enhance or undermine their power. This leads the conversation toward how the men are influenced by the knowledge of the literacy practices accepted by the institution of the legal system. Banek understands the literacy demands of the courtroom he has entered and knows that the work he wants to accomplish cannot happen without the specific missing document. He understands what kinds of documents count as evidence and can produce cultural power in this institution as he points out to the judge that the documents he does have on hand have been properly signed, notarized, and witnessed. Gipson, on the other hand, does not understand the literacy demands of the courtroom he has entered. His somewhat rambling personal narrative is dismissed by the judge, as well as the audience, as inappropriate for a legal institution. The emotional, personal appeal Gipson is making does not count as evidence in the courtroom. The literacy practices that matter are the judge's; the documents that matter are the ones the judge is shuffling through as he ignores Gipson's plea.

Through the discussion of this film we can begin to address questions of how institutions and their ideological interests influence what literacy practices are considered to have cultural power. We list different institutions and discuss the kinds of reading and writing that are or are not valued in each. We talk about the constraints that people working in those institutions are under in terms of the literacy practices they accept. I ask them if the family court judge in *Changing*

*Lanes* is being cruel, or if he has no choice given the institution in which he works but to reject Gipson's narrative as evidence. When it works well the students begin to see how institutions shape behaviors as much as personalities do. That the curriculum of a high school teacher is often well outside her or his control is but one outcome I want students to consider. I then ask them to look at the experiences about which they have written and write about how institutional interests have shaped any of those experiences. Obviously schools figure heavily in their writing, but churches, businesses, sports leagues, and other institutions show up as well.

## Connecting the Individual with the Social

By this point the students have a great deal of material about their literacy experiences, from descriptions of scenes and emotions to reflections and analysis. Now I move students toward creating a draft of a full essay. We spend some time in class engaging in organizing, cutting, and pasting activities that help the students find the ideas and details that are most central to what they want to say and then building around those with other pieces they have. The truth is, by the time we have watched and discussed the films and students have written about those discussions, they are usually bursting with ideas they want to write about. The greater challenge is helping them focus in on the ideas that will create a coherent essay. When I begin to read their drafts, I am struck both by the clarity and vitality of their scenes and descriptions as well as the thoughtful reflection and analysis on those events. Most of the students have at least begun to complicate their interpretation of their reading and writing experiences as being more than just individual moments. Their writing shows how they are connecting their individual experiences to social conceptions of literacy and how those are influenced and reproduced by popular culture, issues of identity, and social institutions.

The assignment sequence I describe above results in more than thoughtful and complex literacy narratives, however. After the writing, movies, discussion, and more writing that begins the semester, students are also ready to think about how literacy operates in the university and beyond. They are ready to think and talk in more depth about how social situations influence how and why they write and read. Far from finding this discussion of culture and literacy discouraging, they talk about how much more they understand about why some literacy events in the past have been frustrating or disappointing and others successful. They have more control over how they approach writing opportunities when they understand the social relationships and power dynamics that mark all literacy practices. An additional benefit of the assignment is that, as the semester moves along, the scenes from the movies provide the class with common textual references about literacy. Whether we are discussing issues of audience, voice, focus, style and grammar, or other concepts, the students keep bringing up these movies, and others that have come up in conversation, to illustrate and refine their ideas.

Movies are often said to represent our dreams or nightmares, reproducing common cultural myths for our individual interpretations. For that reason movies are useful tools for thinking about our ideas about the relationships between individuals and society. Of course life is not like the movies, and there is truth in that cliché for which I am often grateful. Yet when brought to an assignment like a literacy narrative, movies do offer us representations, however incomplete, of how our culture sees itself. When we can ponder these film representations of literacy practices with our students, we can open a productive conversation about how we all negotiate the delicate social dialogue of writing.

# Works Cited

Ashman, Howard, and Alan Menken. "Belle." *Beauty and the Beast.* Dir. Gary Trousdale and Kirk Wise. Disney, 1991.

Barton, David, and Mary Hamilton. *Local Literacies: Reading and Writing in One Community.* London: Routledge, 1998.

*Beauty and the Beast.* Dir. Gary Trousdale and Kirk Wise. Disney, 1991.

*Changing Lanes.* Dir. Roger Michell. Paramount, 2002.

Eldred, Janet C., and Peter Mortensen. "Reading Literacy Narratives." *CE* 54 (1992): 512-39.

*Harry Potter and the Chamber of Secrets.* Dir. Chris Columbus. Warner Bros., 2002.

*The Hours.* Dir. Steven Daldry. Miramax, 2002.

Kamler, Barbara. "Literacy Narratives of Crisis and Blame." *Literacy and Numeracy Studies.* 9 (1999): 65-73.

Light, Andrew. *Reel Arguments: Film, Philosophy, and Social Criticism.* Boulder, CO: Westview, 2003.

Murray, Donald M. *The Craft of Revision.* 5th ed. Boston: Thompson/Wadsworth, 2004.

*Office Space.* Dir. Mike Judge. Fox, 1999.

Rule, Rebecca, and Susan Wheeler. *True Stories: Guides for Writing from Your Life.* Portsmouth, NH: Boynton/Cook, 2000.

*Shakespeare in Love.* Dir. John Madden. Miramax/Universal, 1998.

*Sylvia.* Dir. Christine Jeffs. Capitol/Focus, 2003.

Soliday, Mary. "Translating Self and Difference Through Literacy Narratives. *CE* 56 (1994): 511-26.

Street, Brian V. Introduction. *Literacy and Development: Ethnographic Perspectives.* Ed. B. V. Street. London: Routledge, 2001. 1-18.

Wheeler, Susan. "Exercises for Discovery, Experiment, Skills, and Pay." *Nuts & Bolts: A Practical Guide to Teaching College Composition.* Ed. T. Newkirk. Portsmouth, NH: Boynton/Cook, 1993. 67-100.

Williams, Bronwyn T. *Tuned In: Television and the Teaching of Writing.* Portsmouth, NH: Boynton/Cook, 2002.

Williams, Bronwyn T., and Amy A. Zenger. *Popular Culture and Representations of Literacy.* London: Routledge, 2007.

# Pop Culture and Pedagogy: Using Urban Legends in the Composition Classroom

*Allison A. Hutira*

The idea of using popular culture in the classroom can be a source of contention among academics, with its effectiveness and usefulness questioned. However, using urban legends provides a way to get the students' attention and provide them with instruction concerning the basic concepts of writing and researching, enabling students to use their familiarity with urban legends to understand and relate to the writing process without sacrificing the pedagogical or theoretical aspects of composition. Instead of merely discussing subjects such as structure, organization, or argumentation, these concepts can be applied to the genre of urban legends in a pedagogical manner to facilitate students' understanding and to keep them (and the teacher) interested.

I first began using urban legends in my writing courses as a new teacher, and fifteen years later I still incorporate them into my courses every semester to provide a starting point for discussions in the classroom and to explain and discuss not only the legends but also concepts about literature and writing. Urban legends fit well into a basic composition course as well as a research-based course and can be introduced early in the semester or at any point during the course. I tend to use them early in the semester because I have found that doing so promotes a sense of community, creating a "safe zone" where students are more prone to share and discuss their ideas and opinions: there really are no "right" or "wrong" answers when discussing their experience with urban legends since there are so many individual legends and even versions of the same legend. This enables students to become used to sharing their ideas while listening and responding to others' ideas without being overly judgmental, since no one version of an urban legend is the "right" one.

Urban legends can be used informally, as an enjoyable assignment that ties in with Halloween, but they can also be used in a more formal manner to illustrate such concepts as style, word choice, presentation of ideas, critical thinking, writing a thesis, and developing a persuasive argument as well as researching, analyzing, and using secondary sources. Assignments about urban legends can be tailored to the needs of a specific class or lesson, and new and experienced teachers will find them a useful and productive resource for any English course, whether its focus is composition, research, or literature.

When I was a new teacher, I had wanted to do something fun with my class for Halloween, and in addition to a discussion of the holiday itself, from its history to its evolution in pop culture, I used urban legends to have a discussion about how individuals gather and process information through their personal experience and how this results in differing perspectives and opinions. My idea was that most of them would have at least some familiarity with the genre and that this would help them appreciate how they naturally gather and process information and how changes and developments in society have affected urban legends, producing more stories and more versions of the same story. This was successful, as most students, even those who did not usually offer much to the discussions were more than willing to share what they knew and to listen to others and learn new urban legends. Realizing that this was a pedagogical gold mine, I lengthened and developed the scope of that first assignment to address specific aspects of composition.

To begin the assignment on urban legends, I present the students with a preliminary assignment.

---

**Use any of the following questions to guide you as you write your journal:**
1.  What is an urban legend, exactly? How would you define it?
2.  Where do urban legends come from?
3.  What is the function of urban legends in society? Why do you think that they exist in the first place? Are they to entertain, to scare, to try to explain the unexplainable, or are there other possible reasons?
4.  Which ones have you heard before? Where did you hear them? From whom? In what context?
5.  Are there any urban legends connected to your hometown?
6.  Do you know of any urban legends connected with this campus?
7.  Are urban legends believable? If not, why do they continue to exist?
8.  Which urban legend is your favorite? Why? Be specific.
9.  How do logic and reason function with urban legends—or are they devoid of logic and reason? Explain.
10. What is significant about urban legends, in your opinion? What makes them interesting, important, and worth discussing?
11. Are urban legends a thing of the past, or are they still being created today? Explain and provide examples.
12. What films, TV shows, or TV series have either dealt with or used urban legends?
13. What news stories from recent years come to mind when thinking about urban legends? (Think Wendy's chili.)
14. What have you found of interest in your research? Go beyond the websites I provided, and feel free to ask family and friends about what urban legends they're familiar with or have heard from others.
15. List any other questions that you have or that would make good discussion questions for class.

---

This assignment calls for outside research that can be easily done on the Internet, but the assignment can also be tailored to involve no outside reading or research. From this students realize that they already have a vast store of information to use to do some concentrated critical thinking. I have my students do some basic web research to show them the enormous amount of information available, to get them used to researching, and to provide practice sifting through, analyzing, and using source material. I also have them see what the university library or local libraries have to offer concerning urban legends to prevent them from relying solely on the Internet for their source material. All of this relates to the papers they have to write during the semester, when they have to choose a topic, develop a thesis and argument, and use secondary source material to support their ideas. Some students have even developed papers on the topic of urban legends since they were so interested in the class assignments concerning them.

After completing this assignment, we usually spend one or two classes discussing their answers, and the response is always overwhelmingly positive. A "comfort zone" is created because the same urban legend can have different versions, and I let them know that no matter what their input, there is no pressure to be "right" or fear of being "wrong," since everyone knows something about urban legends but no one is expected to be an expert. This frees up the tension that is sometimes felt, and the students are able to bring personal experience to the discussion in a comfortable atmosphere. I also bring my own personal experience, having heard my first urban legend in grade school when a classmate earnestly told a group of us that his older sister, who was in high school, had a friend who had taken a hamburger from a certain fast food chain to school, analyzed it in the biology lab, and the meat was proven to be . . . kangaroo! As a ten-year-old, I found the story to be fantastic and creepy, and this is probably why it sticks in my memory. Many students have similar memories to share as well as a similar understanding of the definition of an urban legend, the purpose of such legends, and how they function in society, which always generates a productive discussion. Students get excited, share information, and respond to each other, adding their ideas and opinions as well as information, which is the atmosphere I want to promote in the classroom. This atmosphere is useful later in the semester when we begin discussing the essays and when they begin working on their own papers.

I like to begin the discussion of the preliminary questions as a general response so students do some critical thinking and use the knowledge concerning urban legends that they already have from their personal experience. This enables them to begin developing, organizing, and presenting their own ideas and opinions through expressive writing and verbally in the classroom. This part of the discussion blends well with other concepts, such as argumentative writing. A comparison of their various definitions of an urban legend helps students understand the need for being specific, for defining terms and concepts, and enables them to appreciate the similarities and differences of their perspective as compared with their classmates' perspectives and knowledge, shown here in excerpts from my recent research class' responses to the assignment:

An urban legend is a story that appears mysteriously and spreads spontaneously in various forms and is usually false; it contains elements of humor or horror and is popularly believed to be true. Urban legends are a kind of folklore consisting of stories often thought to be factual by those circulating them. Urban legends are sometimes repeated in news stories and, in recent years, distributed by e-mail. People frequently say such tales happened to a "friend of a friend"—so often, in fact, that FOAF has become a commonly used phrase to describe this type of story. Urban legends are not necessarily untrue, but they are often false, distorted, exaggerated, or sensationalized. –Edward W. Horodyski II

An urban legend is modern folklore believed to be true by the people who preach about them. I would define an urban legend as an incredible story that may be true or false, but gets exaggerated by the people who tell the story. As the story grows older, the more unbelievable the story becomes. Most urban legends are not stories with happy endings, but rather a story with gruesome details that would make someone run out to warn their family and friends. Urban legends are a way for people to try and explain the unexplainable. Every culture has their own urban legends that people create. The stories carry their own traditions as they are passed down to later generations. –Charles Housteau

> In my view, urban legends are created through inductive reasoning . . . an urban legend is an exaggerated story that is often based on some fact. Urban legends do not necessarily have to be true, but they are also not pulled out of thin air. Usually, urban legends are stories that were created and have traveled and changed over time to become even more exaggerated and explain a reason as to why something happened. Anyone can create an urban legend, but almost always one being told starts off with my friend's friend knew someone who . . . –Rebekah Sturgiss

> An urban legend is a story, picture, or video that is just realistic enough that it may be true, and just crazy enough that it may be false. They are stories that are purported to be realistic accounts of actual events; however, the overwhelming majority of urban legends are false. Many are tied to a specific place or region and are just local legends. Others are more widespread. Many urban legends either play off of our fears by relating a tale of some horrific incident occurring to someone, or they are meant to present some kind of moral lesson or champion some moral value. Others are purely for entertainment. –Jeff Cowles

> An urban legend is a short story that is told by word of mouth, often containing the elements of humor or horror, as it becomes distorted each time it is told. In most cases there is no real way to confirm if it is true or not. I believe they are stories to entertain people or they are scams to make money. –Kyle Banna

A discussion of their definitions of an urban legend is generally lively and gets them used to debating ideas rather than resorting to snap judgments. Students are willing to listen to each other and learn instead of immediately disagreeing with an idea or opinion that they do not hold, using phrases like "OK, but the way *I* heard it was . . ." or "I never heard *that* version before . . . that's interesting" instead of "No, you're wrong" or a similar negative response. This method of debating ideas is particularly useful when the class begins discussing various essays and topics and promotes debate and discussion. This also leads into the next part of the discussion, which deals with analyzing the facts and information for logic, reason, and logical fallacies. This can be done with virtually any urban legend, from a "classic" like "The Hook," where two teens parked on lovers' lane either leave the area just in time, finding a bloody hook on the car door handle when he drops her off at home (or, in some versions, where the boyfriend goes to investigate and ends up a victim, hanging above the car with either his fingers or feet scratching against the roof of the car) to more recent urban legends, such as the hoax surrounding a photograph that was supposedly taken as one of the planes was approaching the World Trade Center, showing a smiling tourist on top of the WTC while a plane ominously approaches in the background (for the infamous photo, additional information, and other versions of the photo, including one where the "tourist guy" is aboard the *Titanic*, see <http://urbanlegends.about.com/library/blphoto-wtc.htm>).

Using urban legends with which the students are already familiar enables the class to analyze the content for logic and reasoning, using their critical reading and thinking skills as well as sharpening these skills for future assignments. A detailed discussion of such urban legends as the "tourist guy" on top of the WTC enables them to understand the process of analysis as they move from their initial shock and emotional reactions to the photograph, which seems horrific at first, to a logical analysis of the feasibility of the existence of such a photograph. The discussion can then be geared towards the effect of technology on urban legends, since there are many hoaxes surrounding various photos and e-mails circulating today. As some students commented:

> The Internet is a fast and easy way to spread these legends. Sending someone an e-mail with a "send this along to ten of your friends and you'll receive something good in the next few days" is common nowadays. We all want to believe these e-mails, so we send them to our ten friends hoping that something good will happen in a few days when we really know that nothing is going to happen in a few days . . . Urban legends will continue to be told, and people will continue to believe them. –James LaCivita

> Urban legends can originate from any number of sources. The most common is probably people who just want to create trouble and/or entertain themselves. The tools of modern technology make this infinitely easy for them. Thanks to complex photo software it is relatively simple to alter a photo and make it look like whatever you want it to look like. An excellent example of this is also my favorite urban legend that I found online. It is supposedly an actual photograph of a shark attacking a helicopter somewhere off the coast of South Africa. In actuality, the photo of the helicopter was taken in San Francisco (the Golden Gate Bridge is in the background), and the shark was photo-shopped in. At the bottom of the story, they show the same photo with a soda vending machine photo-shopped in over the shark in order to illustrate how simple it is to produce a doctored photo. –Jeff Cowles

Examples of hoaxes involving photographs, websites (such as manmeat.com, a website hoax that offered recipes and cooking tips for human flesh), emails, and other forms of technology are easily accessed and used in a class, and the students enjoy finding them and even experimenting with them, as with the last student excerpt. Other students also recounted their experiences with various legends, including the urban legends "Helpful Hands (Ghost Children at a Train Crossing)" and "Bloody Mary," among others:

> I have one urban legend that is just up the road from my house. You are supposed to be able to take your car down this old dirt road at 12 midnight on a Saturday night and shut your car off, roll down your windows halfway, turn on your parking lights and put your car in neutral. Now this is a dirt road and where you have to stop is right in the middle of a gully at the very bottom of both hills. Supposedly a family that lived down by that gully was killed one night in their house that was set on fire by some young kids. Once you stop your car and shut it off and do all the nonsense things you have to do, you wait 15 minutes and according to what "my friends" told me the family will come out and push your car up the hill backwards. I only went once to this place and nothing happened when I went, so of course I don't believe it. –Edward W. Horodyski II

> When I was a child, almost every sleepover consisted of someone trying to muster up enough courage to say "Bloody Mary" or "Candy Man" repeatedly in the bathroom mirror . . . –Brittany Sujka

One urban legend that comes from around where I live is called Zombieland. Zombieland is a small area off of Route 224 in Pennsylvania. The little cemetery that is located there contains a statue of Mary, the Mother of God. Much of the legend dwells around this statue. It is said that the statue is seen in two positions, with her arms folded as if praying and with her arms spread as if raising her prayers to heaven. The myth goes that when one sees her arms spread out, Mary is accepting souls into heaven that night in Zombieland, but if her arms are folded then all is safe. Another part of the legend has to do with the one-lane bridge. Rumor has it that while on the middle of the bridge, if a car is turned off and the windows are open, one can hear the sound of babies crying. Stories have also been told of the sound of smacking against the car that takes place while on the bridge. The one night I ventured off to Zombieland, the statue of Mary had her arms folded and the driver refused to stop on the bridge. However, the one strange thing that did occur was that right after we crossed the bridge, a thick fog settled on the land. It was eerie, but we didn't make too much of it. –Ryan Novotny

I have heard many urban legends in my time. Living in Boardman, I have heard about Zombieland, although I'm not really sure what is supposed to be there. I have also heard of the "green man," which apparently is a real man in Ohio who was electrocuted and his skin turned green due to a reaction with electric shock. One urban legend which has entertained me at many a slumber party with my fellow teenage girls is that of Bloody Mary . . . Although there are many theories of how to get Bloody Mary to appear, a mirror is always included in the ritual. This is, of course, so that the image can appear in something . . . –Tamara Halaweh

If you stand in front of your bathroom mirror in the dark and chant "Bloody Mary" six times starting at the stroke of midnight, two red eyes will appear in the mirror. The eyes are supposedly the spirit of a girl who was killed by a cruel joke gone awry. This is a common urban legend that most people have heard of, but few have ever tried it themselves. Others like me are too afraid to see if it is true. I am sure that if I go into my bathroom on a dark night and say "Bloody Mary" six times, nothing is going to happen, but because of this urban legend, I am too scared to try it. –Alexis Sciola

Since almost every city, town, or campus has its own urban legends, students are eager to research and discuss these. A simple web search often produces many sources, whether about the students' hometowns or local areas, and they enjoy learning more about the urban legends associated with their hometowns, especially if they were unfamiliar with them previously. Students also get good practice in researching on the Internet, in the university library, and their local libraries. I also encourage them to ask family and friends about urban legends, if they have not already, to use personal interviewing techniques, since interviewing is often an overlooked technique by students.

Other aspects of writing that urban legends are useful in explaining include style, word choice, presentation, and purpose. Urban legends can have different purposes and have varying degrees of significance, as the following students explain:

What I believe to be the most significant about urban legends is the fact that many of them have no specific origin. They always seem to be gathered from a friend's uncle who heard from his mom that her uncle's cousin found out from their sister . . . and so on. Therefore, they are always altered a little every time they are retold. It is kind of like the game children play called "Telephone." The resulting story is usually very far off from the original legend. That is what makes them so interesting. The stories gather more, or something is changed about them, and they become more out of the ordinary. This makes people want to discuss them . . . I found one interesting story on a site called Urban Legends & Superstitions (http://urbanlegendsonline.com/index.html). It was the story behind the Sloppy Joe. Legend had it that a butcher, Joe, and his wife, whom he loved very much, owned a diner. One night the butcher came home to find his wife and best friend together. He was so mad that he ended up killing them both. He then used his meat grinders to grind up their bodies. Joe invited the parents of his best friend and wife for dinner to tell them that his wife had left him and ran away with the best friend to get married. For dinner, Joe served his ground-up wife and best friend in a sauce mixture. Although the parents were surprised and confused, they still ate and loved the dinner. His mother-in-law made the comment, "This is delicious, but it is kind of sloppy, Joe." Hence, this is how the Sloppy Joe received its name. This is also why the most common Sloppy Joe mix is called "Man-wich." It was made from the man and the "witch" in the story. I thought it was a witty explanation of how the famous story came about. –Alexis Penrose

Urban legends are devoid of logic and reason all the way; that is what makes them an urban legend—they have no sense to them but you just want to believe them. Urban legends are significant because they make life unpredictable. They make you think twice and keep your brain moving. Urban legends are worth discussing because people have different thoughts about things, and sometimes it's good to get people's ideas on things. –Ashlee Schier

I think that urban legends have many different sources. Some of them surfaced after tragic events, such as wars and/or natural disasters, while some surfaced more as old wives' tales to keep their children out of trouble; this is why urban legends serve many purposes. Some legends surfaced throughout the years as a warning of bad things that can happen as a result of bad behavior . . . Other legends surfaced for pure entertainment . . . My favorite urban legend is probably the legend that says if you eat Pop Rocks and drink a Pepsi, your organs will explode. This story is my favorite because it seems absolutely ridiculous and makes me laugh every time I hear it. –Krista Cunningham

After discussing urban legends and using them to relate various writing concepts, instructors can use them to segue into many other topics or assignments, depending upon whatever aspects of urban legends or writing an instructor wishes to pursue. Other useful assignments include researching local legends or campus legends, since there are very few university campuses which do not house a ghost, scary tale, or legend of some sort. The assignments can be expanded to other genres, such as myth, legend, folklore, monstrous creatures (such as Bigfoot, Champ, the Loch Ness Monster, and the Jersey Devil), and the media. Celebrity urban legends are prevalent, especially with deceased celebrities such as Elvis, Jim Morrison, Tupac Shakur, and Marilyn Monroe. The plethora of information readily available on the internet makes for a productive research assignment.

Films also offer a myriad of possibilities, with a vast array of horror films such as *Candyman*, which is similar to the "Bloody Mary" legend, and *Urban Legend*, which uses various urban legends to advance its storyline. There is also the "curse" associated with *Poltergeist* and the unfortunate demise of a few of the actors in the film. Films such as *The Wizard of Oz* have multiple urban legends associated with them, and the urban legend of a man who supposedly hanged himself on the *Oz* set is even supposed to be the grandfather of the boy ghost that is supposedly seen in *Three Men and a Baby*. The possibilities for assignments, research, and discussion in relation to film are limitless, as are the possibilities for discussing television.

Various television shows address urban legends, either by including elements in their storylines or by pursuing the "truth" behind them. Shows such as *The Unexplained*, *In Search Of*, and *Mythbusters*, to name only a few, explore the reality and truth associated with legends, as this student explains:

---

Every week on Mythbusters, [Adam Savage and Jamie Hyneman] use their knowledge and skills to test the validity of various rumors and urban legends in pop culture. Their myths have covered everything from the several uses of Coca-Cola to the best ways to remove dried cement from a cement mixer . . . This program helps make science more interesting for those who are not usually inclined to that subject. It applies theories and scientific procedures to show the practical purposes of something a person may not have cared to learn about while in school. People are drawn to urban legends because they are a form of gossip, as offbeat as they are . . . the variety . . . and . . . the preposterousness of the legends should be enough to keep Mythbusters on the air for years to come. –Abbie Twyford

---

Other shows purely for entertainment also use urban legends in their storylines; these include *Are You Afraid of the Dark*, *Freddy's Nightmares*, *The Twilight Zone*, *Night Gallery*, *Tales From the Crypt*, and *Monsters*, just to name a few.

The last assignment I have used in relation to urban legends is a creative one in which the students are put in groups and challenged to create a new urban legend, hopefully unlike any of those they have heard before. The class shares their legends and discusses their degree of believability, success, and entertainment value, and most students enjoy trying their hand at creating a new legend.

Urban legends can be valuable in the composition classroom since they can be tailored to any class, teach almost any writing concept, and the results of using the same (or similar) assignments are different with each and every class. These assignments are always enjoyed by a majority of the students, and they are enjoyable for the teachers also since they produce successful discussions as well as written assignments. In addition, the material never gets old or dated since urban legends are always being created or adapting to the new technology that is being created, so using urban legends in the composition classroom is something that new and experienced teachers can use, modify to fit the needs of their individual classes, and enjoy along with their class.

## Works Cited

Bronner, Simon J. *Following Tradition: Folklore in the Discourse of American Culture*. Logan, UT: Utah State UP, 1998.

Brunvand, Jan Harold. *The Truth Never Stands in the Way of a Good Story!* Urbana, IL: U of Illinois P, 2000.

Dégh, Linda. *Legend and Belief: Dialects of a Folklore Genre*. Bloomington: Indiana UP, 2001.

Dickson, Paul, and Joseph C. Goulden. *There Are Alligators in Our Sewers & Other American Credos*. New York: Delacorte P, 1983.

Dorson, Richard M. *Folklore and Fakelore: Essays toward a Discipline of Folk Studies*. Cambridge: Harvard UP, 1976.

Ellis, Bill. *Aliens, Ghosts, and Cults: Legends We Live*. Jackson: U of Mississippi P, 2001.

Whatley, Marianne, and Elissa R. Henken. *Did You Hear About the Girl Who . . . ? Contemporary Legends, Folklore, and Human Sexuality*. New York: New York UP, 2000.

# A Sound Education: Popular Music in the College Composition Classroom

## *Robert McParland*

The enthusiasm on Jay's face was unmistakable. B.I.G. was his man, and hip-hop was his daily companion. One could see the confidence there: the brightness in his eyes, the way he lit up with a smile when he could talk about the song "Juicy" in his composition class. Equally obvious was his need for reassurance about his writing. When he wrote, Jay struggled to get the words out. When I looked for assignments from him, his brief papers arrived late. Sometimes they didn't arrive at all.

Two weeks of popular music in an English composition class are what began to turn Jay around. In his essay, he wrote that B.I.G. "turned a negative into a positive." Then he began going to the writing center. He remained engaged in class discussions and turned in his assignments on time.

Jay's classmate Cassandra was quiet and uneasy about class discussions. Indeed, she didn't talk in class at all. However, she took quickly to permission to write about her favorite band's lyrics. Whereas Jay's enthusiasm enabled him to squeeze out three pages of writing, Cassandra's passionate interest in a band resulted in seven pages. The voice one seldom heard in class was strikingly alive on the page. She wrote in her essay, "I analyze these lyrics all the time and write about them at home."

Popular songs are socially produced forms of discourse that can stir students toward writing. Not only do they engage students, but when placed side by side they generate an intertextual field that encourages exploration and allows students to feel more at ease in expressing what they value. Songs offer the multiple voices that Mikhail Bahktin has called heteroglossia. They prompt many varieties of individual response as they invite college students to explore cultural diversity and interpersonal issues. Songs enact relationships and provide students with a social field from which they can negotiate, contest, and produce meaning. The analysis of popular music can help students to inquire into the desires and hopes of people. Meanings are produced as they interact with these texts and write about the dreams, hopes, memories, and concerns expressed by the singers.

College freshmen "seldom believe that their own considered judgments are worth anything," Harvard's former writing director Richard Marius once wrote (475). To get them beyond this uncertainty, he suggested, we have to show them models of how to build an interpretive argument from texts. Following Marius's observation, starting with themes from popular songs can give students a familiar place to begin building such interpretations. Introducing popular music in the college composition classroom gives students an opportunity to work with "texts" with which they are already familiar. Indeed, as Paulo Freire and Henry Giroux observe in "Pedagogy, Popular Media, and Public Life," it is in the spaces of popular culture that a great deal of education is occurring today (vii-xii). When students bring their favorite songs, they contribute something that is alive and meaningful to them. This increasingly student-centered method encourages an empowerment of student writers. As Lester Faigley has pointed out, "Asking students to write narratives about the culture in which they participate is one way of allowing them to explore agency and to locate themselves within their culture" (218). Or, as Anne Haas

Dyson has asserted, contexts are "interactional accomplishments" in which people gain a sense of competence and agency (352-64). Teachers have to support students' "intention to communicate the stuff of their lives" (352-64). Using popular music in the classroom enables them to do this.

Songs are compact forms, expressing within a few minutes a range of emotions and ideas. They are intended to tug immediately at hearts and to get a response. For students, familiarity with songs brings a sense of authority to their writing about them, a willingness to discuss words and ideas that matter to them.

One aspect of building a bridge for first-year college students to college and to the world is to encourage their voices and to enable them to take personal responsibility for their own growth as people. When they believe they have something to say about a text, they have a confident starting place. The familiar song gives them this. The less familiar song or text then begins to challenge them to stretch toward new horizons. In each case, students engage in a form of media literacy in which they become more conscious of the music surrounding them.

Songs are a way to instigate an academic challenge and a way to let popular culture into the classroom. Because our classrooms are discourse communities implicated in a larger culture, it is useful to find ways to let that culture in. There is an inescapably social character to our classrooms and to the acts of writing and reading. A pedagogy that recognizes this social character of language and learning directs our classroom conversations into the wider communities around us. As Joseph Harris argues, "We need to imagine a different social space where people have a reason to come into contact with each other [. . ]. because they have claims that extend beyond the borders of their own safe houses" (34). Popular music is vehicle to get students from their safe houses into the wider world.

Songs bring experiences and voices other than the teacher's into the classroom. Songs are pieces of our world: mirroring fragments which reflect the language, emotions, and cultural positions of those with whom we share the world. These songs are useful not only because they are a novelty but because they are brief expressions of emotions, stances toward someone or some experience.

A classroom community is built when we interact with these emotions and ideas. When students bring their thoughts on songs into the classroom, they establish what Mary Louise Pratt (1990) has referred to as contact zones. In the contact zone there is an interplay of social worlds, themes, and ideas. An intertextuality occurs that brings the familiar to bear upon the students' encounters with new texts and new ideas. Popular songs that focus on a theme provide this intertextuality and open the classroom to the variety of student voices and interests. Listening to songs starts them on a journey of inquiry.

## Preparing to Listen

To prompt this journey, a writing instructor does not have to spend hours listening to Shakhira or Faith Hill, or become a collector of heavy metal recordings by System of a Down and Motörhead. Rather, a teacher can preview the songs that students bring into class. One can then look at the song as a text for themes that can be matched with essays from any textbook that the class uses. Song themes can help students to investigate historical, cultural, or interpersonal issues.

There are several ways to prepare your students for listening to a song. As you listen to the song yourself, ways of introducing it to your students will come to mind. Once they have listened to a song, you may find it useful to have your class work in discussion groups and then move into individual writing. Peer work on songs enables the class to share their understandings of the songs and to report back to the whole class. This shared dialogue helps the members of a class to work together through their different awareness of a song. It becomes a way that they can take charge of their own inquiry and their own learning process.

Students are best welcomed to explore the entirety of a song's message. There is a tendency among teachers to speak only about the song lyrics, in part because music is difficult to write about. Music and language are different kinds of discourse. When we represent music with words, it often becomes clear that our propositional statements do not completely grasp our musical experience. Music is dynamic, fluent, and ephemeral, whereas lyrics are often sequential, linear, and narrative. In writing, music may be treated as an object, as in the meticulous study of a score, rather than viewed as an elusive process.

It is no surprise that teachers trained in literary explication and analysis, or in historical inquiry, give song lyrics disproportionate emphasis. However, even without any formal musical training, one can broadly follow the rhythm, melody, and harmony of songs. The teacher can encourage students to listen for the overall impression that vocal timbre, instrumental solos, and production effects make. It is always helpful to remain mindful that music itself constructs and bears meaning. The atmosphere of the music contributes considerably to any song's impact and message.

It is natural of an English teacher, who is absorbed with language, to privilege the song lyric. However, it is important to have your students write their impressions of the musical language at work in the song also. Allow the song's music to make contact with these listeners.

The priority that music has in a pop song makes carefully listening to it important. Music is always a full partner in its relationship with words. It is never simply background for the explication of text. Too often music in our society becomes the aural equivalent of filling the vacuum of our elevators, dental offices, or shopping malls. Music, rather, has to be actively listened to, not simply heard like the tune we endured the last time we were put on hold on a telephone call.

So we listen: to the music and to each other. Students are asked to describe the tone of the song and the emotions that the song prompts in them. The song, played at least once, has a chance to create its impression. Then, so the students can take a closer look at the words that have been sung, they are given a copy of the song's lyrics. These are often available on CD tray cards or inserts, or on websites dedicated to pop song lyrics. (In each case, while fair use applies to classroom settings, copyright should be respected. Encourage students to bring purchased recordings rather than illegally downloaded mp3s or copied material.)

## When We Listen, What Do We Hear?

"What class is that?" a student whom I did not know asked me one day. He said that he had been listening to our class from a bench outside our classroom window. It was a great way to spend lunchtime, he said. He liked the songs.

With our window open to the world, that student sitting on the bench outside our classroom heard songs that day that were focused upon a set of themes. Perhaps he could not make out every word that was sung but he liked the sound. That is not unlike most of our students. Whereas Cassandra knew every word of her favorite band's songs, for most of us "it is the voice- not the lyrics- to which we immediately respond," as Simon Frith has argued (145). Or, as Deena Weinstein has stated, "The words of a song function for listeners. . . more as isolated words and phrases than as integral poetic texts" (125). Roger Desmond has noted that research shows that about one-third of adolescent listeners comprehend the lyrical content of pop songs. What audiences remember primarily are repeated key phrases and the chorus (278). It becomes the instructor's responsibility to reintroduce students to the song by encouraging them to listen closely.

In the community of listeners, everyone listens differently. In fact, some resistance remains to the notion that popular songs would get a listening at all in a college classroom. Despite academia's increasing concern with media literacy, or Hollywood's gestures toward *The School of Rock* with Jack Black, the integration of pop music into the curriculum has not entered the mainstream in the United States. Indeed, defenders of high culture, such as Theodore Adorno or Edward Shils, would not recommend the use of popular music in education. Allan Bloom, who complained about the effects of pop music in *The Closing of the American Mind* in 1986, would consign rock music to Dante's eighth or ninth circle of hell. The Parent Music Resource Center (PMRC) choked on heavy metal and rap lyrics in the 1980s and urged that warning labels be placed on albums.

Anyone making use of popular music in the classroom confronts this legacy. Indeed, the images and attitudes that some of popular music projects can be problematic for a teacher. Today heavy metal divides among metal-pop love and lust, speed/thrash alienation, and the misery of death metal. Hip-hop raps, scratches and pulses between positive messages, assertions of pride, foul-mouthed diatribes, and gangsta violence. A teacher is pressed to find meaningful content amid "reality" TV, packaged American Idols, podcasts, mp3 downloads, commercial radio, and the exhibitionism of self-proclaimed "entertainers." The good news is that good and useful material does exist. It is a matter of finding it and determining what one believes is appropriate in one's classroom.

## Writing On A Theme

In our classroom, we began by writing about places far away that were emotionally close to us. We shared essays by Nikki Giovanni, Anna Quindlen, and Jonathan Kozol and heard songs from John Legend, Bruce Springsteen, and Mary J. Blige about experiences of home and homelessness. A variety of different approaches to the theme of home created a forum that included what Richard Miller has called "a constant series of local negotiations and interventions and compromises," (389-408) a fluent contact zone that involves a shifting set of interactions.

The wide array of examples posted by teachers on the internet demonstrates that a teacher's methods can be varied. To unfold an historical theme, Max W. Fischer (2006), a seventh grade social studies teacher, collapses history: Sly and the Family Stone meet with ancient Greece. Cameron White (2005), a college instructor, points to the usefulness of the historical list that Billy Joel offers in his song "We Didn't Start the Fire" and to the social commentary of artists as diverse as Bob Dylan, Green Day, Johnny Cash, Nirvana, and Eminem. In lesson plans contributed by teachers and students to the Rock and Roll Hall of Fame, we see numerous intersections of blues music and American history. For Andrew Kenen and Diane Seskes of Kensten High School in Ohio, song lyrics raise issues about America's changing dreams and goals. James W. Lane of Orange High School approaches music as a document in which a song by Johnny Clegg unfolds a lesson on South African apartheid. Rebecca Harrington of Delhi, New York, suggests that Led Zeppelin's "Stairway to Heaven" can draw student interest to Renaissance minstrelsy.

A theme is relatively easy to build, if you can find a few songs. The theme of "home" invited a rich intertextuality of songs and essays. It was familiar ground upon which to start out on an essay. The recollections of home that country, pop, and rhythm and blues songs addressed provided ways to stimulate the writing of college freshmen who were experiencing their first time away from home.

The concept of home became more complicated as students began to hear each other's voices and learn about each other's homes. In their movement from home to college, they had brought their personal stories. They also brought racial difference, gender difference, and a variety of geographical locations to bear upon their essays as they began to move into reflection on the world. Essays of description and narration soon became essays of definition and comparison and contrast, as song lyrics and essay texts were set side by side. My students were asked to describe their homes and to develop a definition of what a home is. Songs were used to complicate this.

The word "home" conjures up a variety of associations and is a good starting place to begin working with songs. There are abundant numbers of songs about home that one can choose from. One can easily draw upon a variety of song lyrics and essays that reflect upon the subject of home. For example, from Wilbur Cash (*The Mind of the South*) to Johnny Cash, the literature of the American south has repeatedly featured a concern with "home" as a topic of essay, story, poetry, and song. Likewise, recent pop/R&B albums, Like John Legend's are also a source that features reflections on family life. Or one may travel to the past with Dionne Warwick singing about divorce in Bacharach and David's "One Less Bell To Answer": "and a house is not a home when there is no one there."

Home may be associated with memory and nostalgia as in The Beatles' "In My Life" in which John Lennon sings: "There are places I'll remember all my life, though some have changed." This memory and nostalgia appears in Nickelback's song "Photograph," a relatively recent hit that was familiar to my students. The speaker reminisces about his neighborhood and growing up. They were less familiar with Ringo Starr and George Harrison's 1973 song "Photograph." However, most found it easy to relate to a singer who was singing about missing someone who was "not coming back anymore" ("Photograph"). Both of these songs called up associations for the students.

What is home? When Nikki Giovanni recalls the African diaspora, she writes that home can be anywhere. Willie Nelson is "on the road again" and Billy Joel sings, "Home can be the Pennsylvania Turnpike, Indiana early morning dew" ("You're My Home").

Song lyrics act as prompts for discussion and writing on social issues as well as personal ones. We read Anna Quindlen's essay on a homeless woman who carried a picture of her "home" in her pocket. We read Jonathan Kozol's insistence that most of the homeless are not mentally ill but are severely economically displaced. We listen to Hal Ketchum's song, "My Daddy's Oldsmobile," about a family living in their car. Then we hear Dan Fogelberg's song "Windows and Walls" in which he points to an elderly woman who picks up a copy of *McCall's* and spends her lonely days staring at the windows and walls of her home.

In "My Hometown," Bruce Springsteen presents a narrator who is witnessing the changes in his hometown. We are offered images of a boy with a dime in his hand running to get a newspaper for his father. The news, however, is not all good as he grows into adulthood and he and his wife talk about "getting out." In John Mellencamp's "Small Town," the singer celebrates small town life. However, in Paul Simon and Art Garfunkel's "My Little Town," the vocalists, who wistfully recall childhood, also lament the conformity of a place where there is "nothing but the dead and dying back in my little town."

This assignment gives students the opportunity to formulate arguments. Just as claims are made by the speakers in these songs, so too can students make assertions about them and about their own homes. Evidence and demonstration can follow. Student learning of the methodologies for paragraph development can be promoted through reference to popular music. Extended definitions can be developed when songs address complex social or personal issues, or abstract concepts like home, love, or justice. Songs can be measured against one another. Their differences in lyrical approach or musical style can be used to generate comparison and contrast paragraphs.

## Teaching Structure, Voice, and Methods of Paragraph Development

If a unit of study calls for classification and division, it may be a useful exercise to have students list styles of music and categorize artists. One may then have them turn this into paragraph form. The classification of musical genres reflects our tendency to seek connections between styles that have similar characteristics. Of course, much music defies easy categorization. While pop music artists do seek a signature sound, there are usually musical differences within and between their albums. The music they make is something more than the genre marketing labels that record labels and radio stations use to identify it. Our categories may vary, as when I referred to Aretha Franklin as an R&B artist. "That's not R&B," one student insisted. "That's soul."

Pop music opens up our awareness of difference and our recognition of similar universal themes and experiences among us. Our statements of interpretation present views that are negotiated in collaboration. We cross boundaries in musical style and cultural space, sometimes looking at otherness, or unfamiliarity. This boundary crossing is the work we undertake in the contact zone. Every one of us speaks from within a subject position. By doing so, we enter the community of interpreters. Pop songs, like essays in a textbook, can initiate this dialogue.

Songs provide compact examples of how people address personal and social issues, advocate positions, or attempt to persuade lovers and friends. They are effective illustrations of subject positions. Songs about similar situations that are set side by side may contest each other. Numerous arguments can be developed about topics addressed in these songs.

Class discussion of a song's theme may help to make the content and language of the song accessible. The class may consider the tone established in the lyric, the music, and the vocalist's delivery. (Who is speaking to whom? What attitude is present and what emotions are being expressed?) Or, they might look at the images presented in the lyric. Students may talk about the situations described, or speculate about the possibilities inherent in the song. As a follow-up assignment, students might also take a direction occasionally used by songwriters: They might construct their own response to the speaker of the song by becoming the interlocutor and speaking back to him or to her in an essay.

Classes can also examine the structure of a song. By doing so, a teacher can convey to students the importance of structure in their own writing. Does the song move in a verse-chorus pattern? Or are there two A-sections followed by a B and a final A? Where is the song's bridge and how does it restate the song's theme in a different musical pattern and lyrical idea?

Voice and tone are elements of essay writing that may sometimes be difficult to teach. Listening to songs helps students to listen to their own prose. Eudora Welty, in *One Writer's Beginnings*, comments that when she wrote she always first "heard" her prose. Songs give students an opportunity to begin to train their ears to listen to their own writing. In songs, students can listen for melodic and rhythmic patterns in an effort to understand how a song works. A bolder student can try speaking a song lyric by reading it aloud. Through volume, rhythm and their approach to tones, musicians provide emphasis and musical phrasing. A vocalist, likewise, caresses or attacks vowels and consonants for emphasis. Listen for intonation and for the open vowels that the singer and the melody ride upon. When a change of intonation and stress occur together, listen for how the extension of the note may be used for emphasis.

Songs also can draw attention to feeling, which is often a missing dimension in our classrooms. Feeling charges writing with energy. Assignments become matters of concern rather than exercises dutifully expedited.

Work on popular songs encourages student interaction, encounters with multi-cultural variety, and the production of interpretations. Music, while non-semantic, can engage meaning and do cultural work. Likewise, song lyrics, by necessity, provide brief statements of subject positions that can be argued. Practiced dialogically, there is a mutual exchange involved in the unpacking of sounds, attitudes and expressions that a class finds together in songs.

When the pop song enters the curriculum, student interaction about songs can encourage a truly collaborative, student-centered classroom. The diversity of musical styles that students bring engages their classmates with the social diversity of our culture. Each song is treated respectfully, as an illustration of how a topic may be approached musically and lyrically. The teacher's role becomes one of stretching a student's thought beyond his or her preferences toward a broader spectrum of possibilities. This use of popular culture enhances student engagement and inquiry. It is sound education in the fullest sense.

## Works Cited

Bacharach, Burt, and Hal David. "One Less Bell to Answer." Blue Seas Music and Jac Music, 1967.

Baumlin, Tita French. "MTV in the Composition Classroom." *Information and Technology* (1998): 1-12.

Bloom, Allan. *The Closing of the American Mind*. New York: Simon and Schuster, 1987.

Cash, Wilbur. *The Mind of the South*. New York: Random House, Alfred Knopf, 1929.

Desmond, Roger Jon. "Adolescents and Music Lyrics: Implications of a Cognitive Perspective." *Communication Quarterly* 35 (1987): 276-84.

Dyson, Anne Haas. "On Reframing Children's Words: The Perils, Pleasures and Promises of Writing Children." *Research in the Teaching of English* 34 (2000): 352-67.

Evelyn, Jamilah. "The Miseducation of Hip-Hop." *Black Issues in Higher Education* 17.21 (2000): 24-29.

Faigley, Lester. *Fragments of Rationality and the Subject of Composition*. U of Pittsburgh P, 1993.

Fischer, Max W. "The Schoolhouse Rocks: Using Music to Engage Learning." *Education World*. 24 Jan. 2003. 5 Dec. 2007 <http://www.educationworld.com/a_curr/voice/voice070.shtml>.

Fogelberg, Dan. "Windows and Walls." Full Moon/CBS Songs, 1986.

Freire, Paulo, and Henry Giroux. "Pedagogy, Popular Media and Public Life." Foreword. *Popular Media: Schooling and Everyday Life*. Ed. Henry A. Giroux and Roger I. Simon. Granby, MA: Bergen and Garvey, 1989. vii-xii.

Frith, Simon. "Toward an Aesthetics of Popular Music." *Music and Society: The Politics of Composition, Performance, and Reception*. Ed. Richard Leppert and Susan McClary. Cambridge: Cambridge UP, 1987. 133-49

Harris, Joseph. *A Teaching Subject: Composition Since 1966*. Upper Saddle River, NJ: Prentice Hall, 1997.

---. "Negotiating the Contact Zone." *Journal of Basic Writing* 41 (1995): 27-41.

Joel, Billy. "You're My Home." *Piano Man*. CBS Songs/Columbia, 1975.

---. "We Didn't Start the Fire." CBS Songs/Columbia, 1989.

Kenen, Andrew, and Diane Seskey. STI Lesson 12. <http://www.rockhall.com/teacher/sti-lesson-12>.

Ketchum, Hal. "My Daddy's Oldsmobile." *Sure Love*. Curb Music, 1992.

Kozol, Jonathan. "Distancing the Homeless." 1988. *75 Readings: An Anthology*. New York: McGraw-Hill, 2001.

Lennon, John, and Paul McCartney. "In My Life." SONY/ATV, 1965.

Mahiri, Jabari. "Pop Culture Pedagogy and the End(s) of School." *Journal of Adolescent and Adult Literature* 44 (2000-2001): 382-85.

Marius, Richard. "Redrawing the Boundaries," *The Transformation of English and American Literary Studies.* Ed. Stephen Greenblatt and Giles Gunn. MLA, 1992. 466-85.

---. *Reflections on the Freshman English Course, Teaching Literature: What Is Needed Now*. Ed. James Engell and David Perkins. Cambridge: Harvard UP, 1988. 169-90.

McParland, Robert. "Music to Their Ears." *Instructor* 109.7 (2000): 27-30.

Mellencamp, John. "Small Town." Riva Publishing, 1985.

Miller, Richard E. "Fault Lines in the Contact Zone," *CE* 56 (1994): 389-408.

Nambiar, Subramaniyan A. "Pop Songs and Language Teaching." *Methods That Work: Ideas for Literacy and Language Teachers*. Ed. John W. Oller. Boston: Heinle and Heinle, 1993. 335-38.

Ostlund, Deborah R. "Values of Youth: Messages from the Most Popular Songs of Four Decades." *Journal of Humanistic Education and Development* 36.2 (1997): 83-91.

Pratt, Mary Louise. "The Arts of the Contact Zone." *Profession* 9 (1991): 33-40.

Quindlen, Anna. *Living Out Loud*. New York: Random House, 1987.

Simon, Paul. "My Little Town." CBS Songs/Columbia, 1975.

Springsteen, Bruce. "My Hometown." CBS Songs, 1985.

Starr, Ringo, and George Harrison. "Photograph." Capitol, 1973.

Weinstein, Deena. *Heavy Metal: The Music and Its Culture*. New York: Da Capo, 2000.

Welty, Eudora. *One Writer's Beginnings*. Cambridge: Harvard UP, 2004.

# Subvert this Image:
# Negotiating Multiple Literacies & Deconstructing
# Consumerism through Photoshop

*Jessica Ketcham Weber*

*Literacy is not static but interactive.* (Barton 432)

*Literacy education is not for the timid.* (Gee 39)

It is not surprising that in the great awash of online, digital, media-friendly, and technology-rich classrooms, questions about the place of visual communication arise. Who should teach it and where do we integrate it into our already jam-packed curriculum? Does the *it* we're talking about mean visual literacy, media literacy, or multi-modal literacies, and why do I get the feeling that digital, technological, and new media don't mean the same thing? Is it just me who gets dizzy as I find myself writing in a digital age, living in a new media world, working in a technological environment among a visual culture in a global era? Though I can appreciate the need for discipline-specific vocabulary, it might be that the specialized terms in departments of Education, Art History, English, Rhetoric and Writing, Communication Studies, Media Studies, and Mass Communication actually result in negative reinforcement and provide yet another reason for teachers to resist incorporating multiliteracies into their pedagogical and research agendas.

Amid various academic definitions of visual, media, and multi-modal literacies are those created by organizations such as The Center for Media Literacy and the American Library Association's National Forum on Information Literacy, Just Think, and Citizens for Media Literacy. Although each of these groups identifies specific interests within their conception of media literacy—raising awareness about youth/alternative media, making it easier for citizens to figure out what politicians are really saying, aiding parents concerned with violence on TV and more—there exists a common thread with academia: the necessity of incorporating intertextuality and multi-modality. It is increasingly essential to teach the ability to receive and decode intertextual messages and to create and send multi-modal ones, and the composition classroom is uniquely situated as a place to deconstruct and recreate media messages designed by the infotainment industrial complex. A pedagogy which counters the rampant consumerism and passive consumption brought about by global capitalism seems appropriately connected to the many principles of media literacy and curricular possibilities of visual rhetoric.

In keeping with the requisite interdisciplinarity of a multi-modal, critical pedagogy, this essay draws from theories of visual rhetoric, media literacy, and composition theory. I also find myself situated alongside Chomsky's views on the role of public relations, advertising, and the media in contemporary politics. My composition classroom shows signs of an integration of Boal's Theatre of the Oppressed and Friere's Pedagogy of the Oppressed. My teaching life, research life, and personal life are admittedly concerned with the same things: the role of citizens, corporate media, and alternative media in social justice and equality. Wary of the interests behind the production of meaning and manipulation of images and words, there is no better time for students and teachers to question the relationship between knowledge and perceived knowledge.

There has never been a more crucial time to revitalize the push for active, critical, innovative pedagogies.

In this essay I plan to: 1) engage composition theory, visual, media and multi-modal literacies in a dialogue with each other, 2) discuss the importance of demystifying the "artist," "activist," and "author" and the implications for the classroom, and 3) share how a particular assignment, which interrogates consumerism, advertising, and visual rhetoric, connects multi-modal literacies, interrogates everyday civic issues, and central assumptions about pop culture, politics, and identities. The premise on which this is based, the premise that I ask you to consider, is that we need to develop more interdisciplinary, multi-modal assignments and practices that attend to both deconstructing images as well as constructing new ones.

## Politics in/of the Writing Classroom

Writing is always a form of resistance. Writing doesn't answer, it offers. It unsettles. Writing requires students to navigate the spaces of their existing ideologies and the ideologies that shape them. In *Opening Spaces: Critical Pedagogy and Resistance Theory in Composition*, Joe Marshall Hardin observes that, "[g]enerally, no other class in the university asks its participants to expose and examine their own values in quite the same way that writing classes do" (59). It is this critical examination of personal values which illuminates the political nature of the writing classroom. I am often asked how I effectively and honestly bring politics into my classroom, and my response is simple: education is not politically neutral. Hardin and bell hooks, among others, have constantly asserted a similar viewpoint—that literacy reaches far beyond the reading and writing of words to the reading and writing of gender—of race—of culture. Part of critical literacy is to investigate the identities and authority of the ruling class, to be able to read the message in the medium. And yet, the ability to identify embedded messages in culture is not enough either: "separating the teaching of rhetoric and convention from considerations of ideology and value is artificial and perhaps even unethical" (Hardin 7). Compositionists such as Hardin aim to teach students how to appropriate rhetorical modes to both function in and resist culture. To founder of Theatre of the Oppressed, Augusto Boal, "no one can be satisfied with the world as it is; it must be transformed" (*Games* 47). Through attention to multiliteracies, multi-modal composition, and kinetic learning, we may re-present the world and offer suggestions to change it.

Paulo Friere asserts, "it is my basic conviction that a teacher must be fully cognizant of the political nature of his/her practice and assume responsibility for this rather than denying it" (211). Thus, I start each semester off with a conversation about the fact that writing, investigating culture, and examining our identities are all entrenched in our histories. I acknowledge that I have particular political views that may not be the same as theirs, but I make it clear that it is not my intention to sway their ideologies, simply to provide a space for questioning and analyzing them. No responsible teacher would let course content suffer for his or her own political agenda (Hardin). It is, however, irresponsible not to acknowledge that with discussions of culture come discussions of social issues, and because "education is by nature social, historical, and political, there is no way we can talk about some universal, unchanging role for the teacher [or student]" (Freire 211).

I do not suggest that the classroom be centered in hyper-radicalism, or that the members of the class go searching for subject matters that are designated "political." Instead, through the emergent critical awareness and discussion of personal values in relation to genre theory, students will begin to transform meanings for themselves. The very act of questioning dismantles authority. In his manifesto for Critical Social Theory, Zeus Leonardo writes, "quality education encourages students to become aware of, if not actively work against, social injustice" (13). How then, do we get to the topic of social injustice or political agendas in general? Through the tiny specifics, through ourselves. It is the moment hooks writes about "when one begins to think critically about the self and identity in relation to one's political circumstance" (47). While it is clear that politics are already in the classroom, there remain contradictory situations that we must be aware of. The seductive feeling of "emancipating" or "enlightening" students has no place in progressive feminist education, yet often times the rhetoric of critical pedagogy (i.e. "liberatory education" or "teaching to transgress") lends itself to this trap. Additionally, sometimes assignments, such as the typical "personal writing" in freshman composition, is unconsciously used as a stepping stone to "real academic writing." I acknowledge these two common (essentialist) pitfalls because I think that critical feminist pedagogies of action can transcend them.

Why is there no such thing as a politically neutral classroom? Because we are not politically neutral—we are wrapped and decorated with our histories and our cultures: "every performance, if it is intelligible as such, embeds features of previous performances: gender conventions, racial histories, aesthetic traditions – political and cultural pressures that are consciously and unconsciously acknowledged" (Diamond 66). Writing follows this same model. Recognizing multiliteracies in the writing classroom is natural because it is so embedded in everyday life. Highlighting the intertextual nature of the writing classroom introduces context in a rhetorical manner—a breeding ground for discussions of the media and the message.

## Media and Visual and Digital, Oh My!

Whether I'm teaching digital media and composition, media and society, or images of women, Marshall McLuhan's 1964 aphorism "the medium is the message" embeds itself into the first week of class. Regardless of the class, I always include the following diagram on the syllabus:

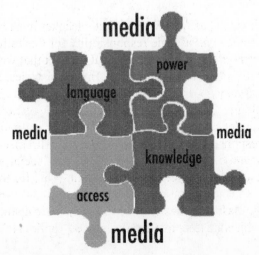

I ask the class to look at the diagram and tell me what they notice. Without fail, the first person says something like, "The colors are off for 'knowledge' and 'power.'" This is usually followed by critiques of the placement of 'language' (the blue background dips into the black outline) as well as the inconsistent positioning of all four words. Only after these comments are made does someone notice that 'the media' is not in bold. Within 5 minutes, students have demonstrated competency with balance and emphasis—two basic visual elements.[15] We then analyze as a class why color was noticed before font style and why placement was noticed after color: this is an example of what is conceived as visual literacy.

Media literacy, which is often incorrectly used interchangeably with visual literacy (or at least lumped with it as the same thing), is a different concept altogether: its focus is on decoding and analyzing communication. In other words: visual literacy + semiotics = something like media literacy. I ask two more questions about the diagram: what does the puzzle represent rhetorically and what does it mean that 'the media' is not written in bold letters? Common answers sound like "you have to know all of the pieces to understand the media puzzle" or "you have to have all the pieces of a puzzle to make it complete." Students' speculations on why the media is not in bold are always the most fiery—it's the most obvious question of interpretation: am I trying to undercut the importance, the status, of the privilege or did I just forget to make it bold? If someone doesn't bring it up first, I usually ask if they know, or if it is obvious, what my point of view[16] towards the media is. While the discussion might not seem particularly enthralling, simply articulating (oral mode) and showing (visual mode) the intertextual nature of a diagram on a syllabus (written mode) gets the point of multiple literacies across.

Media literacy extends well beyond the decoding of messages though, to a necessary intertextual understanding of how meaning is produced, constructed, and manipulated. It is not just "the [news] media" which media literacy refers to—it's also the multiple modes or mediums through which communication is rendered. Websites, billboards, television, films, and t-shirts are all texts to be read in terms of medium. I often use the example of a bumper sticker—which might take different meaning on a car versus a stop sign. Obviously rhetoric plays a large part in distinguishing media literacy from basic visual or written literacy, as does its inherent socio/political relevance. Each semester I show *Outfoxed*, a documentary detailing Fox News' consistent corporate manufactured news, as well as footage from CNN News for a comparative discussion[17] of where we get our information. Without a doubt, students love this week of class; many of them proclaim that they never thought news was different from channel to channel.

A couple of colleagues in my department express that they think I might be better suited teaching in a Mass Communication department, but the fact is that mass communication—mass messages—are not just for a Mass Communications department. Indeed, another strand of media literacy—media activists—specifically believe that all citizens should be able to have an alternate

---

[15] Though these vary slightly, there are a number of visual arts terms which are used in visual literacy such as: balance, classification, comparison/contrast, description, emphasis, metaphor, movement, narration, point of view, pattern, proportion, and unity

[16] I make it clear that the kinds of questions we are asking are applicable to all kinds of texts.

[17] While I acknowledge that a documentary on Fox does not have the same intent as randomly sampled news footage on CNN, the purpose is not to say "this one is right and this one is bad," but to discover how different they (and other news sources) are.

to getting their news from a media conglomerate—a corporation. This is not a surprising revelation for those who have watched the prevalent use of blogs and its exponential growth. Pirated radio stations manifest themselves easier through podcasting, and zines are making a comeback as the blogroll's paper counterpart. If the majority of the people are participating in alternate or independent forms of news broadcasting, of meaning-making, can they continue to be communicating from the margins for long?

A common thread that connects pedagogy, media, and politics is theory—that is, the helpful nature of theory to aid students' analysis of rhetoric and culture. However, in freshman composition classrooms (and I suspect, in other entry-level college courses) there is a hesitancy to bring theoretical readings into the classroom for no other reason articulated than "it's too hard for them [the students] to understand." A relevant Homi Bhabha writes:

> The language of critique is effective not because it keeps forever separate the terms of the master and the slave...but to the extent to which it overcomes the given grounds of opposition and opens up a space of translation: a place of hybridity, figuratively speaking, where the construction of a political object that is new, neither the one nor the other, properly alienates our political expectations and changes, as it must, the very forms of our recognition of the moment of politics. (*Location* 25)

The theory/practice binary has traversed all academic fields in a troubling way, but as Leonardo notes, "CST [critical social theory] rejects the radical distinction between theory and practice as two separate poles of a dualism" (11). This seems to attest to the lack of critical social theory in freshman composition pedagogy. When hooks says that, for her, theory was a location for healing (59), it resonates. Clearly any tools that we, as educators and students, can use to further deconstruct ourselves and our ways of knowing have a place in a writing classroom: "working the theories of knowledge and systems of truth that are working them, specific intellectuals in effect redefine knowledge and truth as worldly things and, in so doing, begin to alter the systems of statements and procedures that have produced these concepts" (Goleman 5). In some cases, the master's tools are exactly what are needed to dismantle the master's house.

## Artist, Activist, Author & Other Scary Words

One striking thing about pedagogy that focuses on multiliteracies is that it has the potential to aid in the demystification of "the artist" "the activist" and "the author." Through multi-modal composition, "artists' cultural perspectives enable them to critique cultural inscription" (Garoian 2) which in turn provides a sense of agency. Compositionists such as Hardin have suggested "pedagogy in the writing class might be made even more productive by emphasizing the student's productive role as 'author'" (12). People see authors, artists, and activists as intangible beings— reified subjects doing things that they could never do. By shattering this idea and encouraging student authorship, we can resist the way that academic culture constructs authority (of the lecture, of the text, of the original). One example of encouraging student authorship is to treat student writings as they are—texts to be read and analyzed like any other text assigned from a book or course packet. Rather than only reading students' papers in a peer review session, I prefer to treat them as conversations to the field of our subject matter. Only in an open classroom, an open space where students can establish themselves as authors of texts can progressive pedagogy be effective (Hardin). Correspondingly, when students can assert themselves as artists, the personal investment, and hence, the serious cultural critique embedded in the student's action, can allow for a restructured, invented ideology. Critical thinking is self-producing rather than regurgitative knowledge.

Composing for change in the composition classroom can both allow students to achieve agency as well as cultivate a communication style which does not merely attempt to translate what is in the world, but can allow for creation or emergence of ideas. By merging the personal and the political, writers can find those connections or intimate interests which drove them to think/write/speak/act in the first place—before diagramming sentences. As a composition teacher, I am always careful to make it clear that we won't be writing in either formal or informal language, either personally or critically, but always both (with an eye for audience). And just as I believe that there can always be an "in" somewhere for a student to find a connection to the readings or potential writing topics, Trinh Minh-ha writes, "No situation proves too small or too insignificant for a writer, since there is truly no narrow experience, only narrow representation" (29). It is this narrow representation, specifically the representation of selves and others, that we can bring together—through multiple media.

I am also careful not to sound flippant when I talk to my students about composing for change. It is scary, certainly, to begin writing in a way that questions representation rather than attempting to represent. It is also terrifying because they realize that it leaks into all parts of their lives. Many students say that they can't look at anything the same anymore; other students confess that they didn't know that they could be interested in politics, and most say that they don't want to be activists. Exploring the stigma attached is especially easier as I've found the conceptions of activism in everyday life broaden. In a consumerist society, people are making conscious daily life decisions about where to shop, what products to buy, and what to eat. The definition of activism is expanding. Activism is described as everything from simply "educating family and friends" (Sarah Chee) to "when someone acts on something that moves them" (Ayako Hagihara) or "when someone makes the choice between moving forward and perpetuating status quo" (Kim San). The extension of the meaning of "activism" has begun to diminish the stigma of "the activist." Trinh says that not taking a position is a position in itself. When we don't bring politics into the critical thinking classroom, we are taking a conservative position. If we only allow students to compose through the written word, we are taking an unrealistic position.

## An Assignment to Promote Multi-Modal Literacies

The teacher should take the risks that she asks her students to take by writing, performing, and composing in the classroom space. To keep current, I adhere to a policy of writing my own proposal for all of the assignments that I ask my students to compose. As a community, we also develop each of the major paper assignments or projects to best suit the needs and interests of everyone in the classroom—to ensure that what we are analyzing or critiquing matters. In these last pages, I will share the collaborative assignment we developed for a media, society, and consumption composition class.

After spending most of the semester interrogating issues of gender and America's "suicidal consumer binge,"[18] students were ready to take a stab at creating their own argumentative image.

---

[18] From the title of Kalle Lasn's *Culture Jam: How to Reverse America's Suicidal Consumer Binge—And Why We Must*. We also discussed the implications of essays from Naomi Klein's *No Logo* in terms of gender, globalization, and capitalism.

As I explained the third assignment, my students were relieved to find out that LSU has a free software training lab with Photoshop and I agreed to hold class there for a day. Though an hour and a half doesn't teach one everything about the program, it was enough to give students motivation to learn the rest on their own, or go back for tutoring.

Before going to the Photoshop class, students were to rummage through magazines, flip through TV channels, or concentrate on an issue that they wanted to depict visually, and bring in a written proposal for the next class period. I waited to be barraged with questions about the "correctness" of their ideas, but the emails never came. Students showed up to class the next day confident and excited to see what others' ideas were.

---

**Assignment Three: Identity Correction**

Goal: to create an argumentative image

Using Photoshop, or a similar piece of software, alter an advertisement or create your own to make an existing product/message more accurate. Think of this as a persuasive visual assignment with the goal of identity correction.

Accompanying movie: *The Yes Men*

Accompanying activity: Go to [free on-campus software training lab] for a Photoshop class

---

An equal number of students altered existing images as created ones from scratch. While the majority of the topics dealt with the dangerous implications of disinformation, some addressed "annoyingly wrong advertisements." A surprising number of students admitted to creating what may have seemed like tasteless critiques, but every single one had crafted a strong argument to back up their case. For example, one student used a picture of a strangled JonBenet Ramsey and placed it inside of a picture of Barbie doll box. Underneath the image read: "Mattel: Providing Killer Dreams For Little Girls For Over 50 Years." Another gendered image featured a skeletal model (altered by the student) on the cover of *Vogue* Magazine. Selected captions read, "STOP EATING! Experts say food may not be as vital as we thought" and "WANT to look like THIS RUNWAY MODEL? only 2 things needed: finger and toilette!" The level of intertexutality, social/cultural relevance, and competency with visual elements were all discussed in class as part of the student presentation; assessment was based on this as well.

to see a gallery of student images, visit
http://etoilebleu.com/etoilebleu/visualassignments.html

to explore the Adbusters spoof ad gallery
or to learn more about Adbusters, visit
http://adbusters.org/spoofads/index.php

In her reflection, one student wrote, "My favorite assignment throughout the entire class was the third project using Photoshop. It allowed me to create something that was all my own to express my feelings in a way that I couldn't through traditional writing assignments."

Referring to the assignment, another student said, "it helped my writing by showing me that an important basis for criticism is the recognition of a problem . . . that every aspect of language and communication revolves around context . . . and that creating a visual explanation helps you better articulate yourself in written or spoken words."

The last part of this quote is probably the most commonly heard response to my emphasis on assignments which require multi-modal literacies. Twice, students with disabilities have commented on how this kind of focus made them more comfortable and confident—an implication for future studies.

Certainly, the lack of a united terminology for media and visual literacies has prevented a cohesive coalition from forming at the university level—undoubtedly NCTE's new guideline for multi-modal literacies will give a solid backbone to the K-12 teachers who have realized the pedagogical implications of such a redefinition of twenty-first-century literacy. We saw what a lack of unification did to the Democratic Party at the US elections at the turn of the century—we've seen what a lack of unification did for identity politics and third-wave feminism. Biddy Martin writes, "our literary training and focus on language may hold out the greatest promise for new interdisciplinary discussions since it is at the level of language, of metaphor, and of rhetoric that new connections across fields can begin to be imagined" (371). Multiple terms and varying definitions aside, educators must unify in our commitment to pay attention to the way that information is manufactured and to the fact that corporate institutions are setting the agenda. Media literacy, both the visual literacy strand and the media activism strand, hold a vital place in a concerned citizen's curriculum—in a progressive pedagogy of action.

## Works Cited

Barton, Ellen L. "Literacy in (Inter)Action." *CE* 59 (1997): 408-37.

Bhabha, Homi. *The Location of Culture*. New York: Routledge, 1994.

Boal, Augusto. *Games for Actors and Nonactors*. Trans. Adrian Jackson. London: Routledge, 1992.

Chomsky, Noam. *Media Control: The Spectacular Achievements of Propaganda*. New York: Seven Stories, 2002.

Diamond, Elin. "Performance and Cultural Politics." *The Routledge Reader in Politics and Performance*. Ed. Lizbeth Goodman and Jane de Gay. London: Routledge, 2000. 66-69.

Freire, Paulo. "Letter to North American Teachers." *Freire for the Classroom: A Sourcebook for Liberatory Teaching*. Ed. Ira Shor. Portsmouth, NH: Boynton/Cook, 1987. 211-14.

Garoian, Charles. *Performing Pedagogy: Towards an Art of Politics*. Albany: State U of New York, 1999.

Gee, James Paul. *Social Linguistics and Literacies: Ideology in Discourses*. New York: Routledge, 1996.

Goleman, Judith. *Working Theory: Critical Composition Studies for Students and Teachers*. Westport, CT: Bergin, 1995.

Hardin, Joe Marshall. *Opening Spaces*. Albany: State U of New York, 2001.

hooks, bell. *Teaching to Transgress: Education as the Practice of Freedom*. New York: Routledge, 1994.

Leonardo, Zeus. "Critical Social Theory and Transformative Knowledge: The Functions of Criticism in Quality Education." *Educational Researcher* 33.6 (2004): 11-18.

Kellner, Douglas, and Jeff Share. "Toward Critical Media Literacy: Core Concepts, Debates, Organizations, and Policy." *Discourse: Studies in the Cultural Politics of Education* 26 (2005): 369-86.

Martin, Biddy. "Success and Its Failures." *Feminist Consequences: Theory for the New Century*. Ed. Elisabeth Bronfen and Misha Kavka. New York: Columbia UP, 2001. 353-80. Multi-Modal Literacies Issue Management Team. "Multi-Modal Literacies." 2005. *NCTE Guidelines*. NCTE 2005 <http://www.ncte.org/about/over/positions/category/media/123213.htm>.

Trinh, Minh-ha. *Woman, Native, Other: Writing Postcoloniality and Feminism*. Bloomington: U of Indiana P, 1989.

# Video Didn't Kill the Radio Star...

## *Laurel Taylor*

*Every college English teacher ought to tune in to a local popular record radio station once in a while, even if he must shudder throughout the whole experience.*
           *Fred Kroeger 1968*

  Students often enter the writing classroom with fear and uncertainty; the foreign feeling of a writing classroom can automatically stifle some writers. But if instructors can help students see a bridge between what they already inherently know about writing and what will be expected of them as writing students, these writers are less likely to resist new forms of writing. Any connections teachers can make between what students already know and what they will be learning in the writing classroom minimizes the stress of entering the new environment. Despite the new forms of entertainment, music is still a predominate way people vicariously express emotions. The popularity of things like iTunes, iPods, music channels, and music venues shows that despite video, the radio star is anything but dead. Since students interact with music on an almost daily basis, music functions as a logical way to connect students' daily lives and lives as writers. Not only is the genre helpful for students, it is also holds a wealth of writing instruction. The written form of a song allows songwriters to include the same literary elements utilized in "scholarly" texts and the same writing process taught in the writing classroom. The songwriting genre's place in popular culture allows songwriters to include common literary elements in their writing without the highbrow stigma attached to genres more closely associated with academia. When instructors bring in a song currently on the radio in order to look at figures of speech or metaphors, they present common academic topics within a familiar and non-threatening context. Of course, instructors need to build some bridges to help students discuss their favorite songs in academic terms. Students might have to be introduced to the terminology (synecdoche, hyperbole, peer review, etc) used in academic writing, and they may also have to see some modeling in order to become cognizant of the way they evaluate songs. Students might also need help seeing how their seemingly casual observations can be translated into writing ideas or revision strategies. All of these are minor problems, though, when looking for effective ways to discuss writing techniques.

  The need to use familiar genres while discussing writing became apparent when my students were hesitant to give each other feedback on their papers. When I asked my first year composition students to give each other feedback on their memoir essays, one student quickly responded, "I don't really know enough about memoirs to really tell people what to do with their essays." But when I played Tracy Chapman's "The Promise," the same student was the first to tell me the song was meant to be listened to when dealing with a broken heart. The analysis taking place in my classroom demonstrates the way students know the genre-specific expectations of a song, whereas they think they don't know the expectations of a memoir. The difference was obvious—he felt unsure about a literary genre but felt confident about a musical genre he had been evaluating for years. Other students quickly followed with observations about the songwriter's tone, word choice, and attitude. They then discussed how the singer's voice influenced the "feel" of the song. From there I was able to help them build connections between their observations, the textbook authors' suggestions for good writing, and their own writing. I asked them how singers create the feel of a song. Students may be hesitant to voice an opinion about a short story or a poem due to their perceived lack of expertise, but their lifetimes as informal music critics give them more authority in these discussions and can lead to much more concrete models for writing as well as renewed enthusiasm for the class.

Regardless of the song or the artist, and regardless of how good or how bad the song is, all songs and the stories surrounding them contain lessons for students. Students can learn both effective and ineffective writing techniques through a genre they have some authority on. As instructors search for a balance between relating to students and teaching valuable writing lessons, they may find the answers in their own CD players.

## Building Connections

Theorists such as Lucy Calkins and Peter Elbow have emphasized the need for students to have real world models as they develop their own writing. The concept of published authors functioning as models for students has often been applied to writers of children's books and other genres. If song lyrics are going to function as examples of good writing, students must see connections between the song and the academic essay. Students can take a favorite song and use it as an example of effective writing, looking for the mood, tone, voice, and literary devices that make that song appealing to its target audience.

As students learn to shift their attention as they listen to their favorite mix CDs, the class discussions serve as guided practice. But for these discussions about songs to truly change the way students evaluate writing and compose their own pieces, the discussions must always relate back to the students' own writing. Music is such an effective model because there are many obvious connections between the two writing forms. For example, both types of writers need to use specific details, make conscious choices about diction, and create an intentional tone in their writing. In the following classroom activities, I will show many different ways to present these similarities.

The added benefit of using published authors as guides for writing students is that even the negative feedback about the song serves as a lesson by presenting a cautionary tale. Whether the class loves a song or hates it, there are lessons to be learned. Learning what not to do can be just as helpful as learning what to do.

In the end, the question for students is, "How do we use these ideas in our own writing?" Bringing the conversation back to students' writing helps to make the songwriters clearer models for students. For example, if the students note the way the author follows the "show don't tell" approach to writing, instructors can discuss the importance of creatively presenting specific evidence. If the students note the "sappy" feel of a song, the class looks at clichés in writing. When given thinking time and a safe environment for analyzing, students can make connections without the instructor having to tell them, which leads to the type of student-centered classroom supported by Calkins and Elbow.

## Classroom Activities

Many of my class discussions about writing revolve around using song lyrics and music as teaching tools. Instructors can present songs as examples of particular writing techniques they want their students to develop or to improve. There are multiple ways to approach these studies, and they can be introduced at any point in the learning process. Instructors can emphasize a single point when students are having trouble grasping a concept by studying a song, but they can also teach the entire lesson using songs as examples. In an even more indirect approach, songs can help students discover the stylistic elements writers need to be familiar with.

Instructors can open up a general discussion of the elements of good and/or bad writing through song lyrics. People such as Fred Kroeger, who previously encouraged teachers to at least listen to the radio in order to relate to students, have used songs to exhibit problematic writing (i.e., logical fallacies). Word choice, author's assumptions, pacing, storytelling, and literary elements (synecdoche, metaphor, symbolism, etc) can all be discussed by looking at song lyrics and the music associated with them.

The oral nature of songwriting presents a unique set of challenges for writers: the text must be concise enough to keep the listener's interest, clear enough to be understood the first time it is heard, creative enough to be intriguing yet uncomplicated enough to be understood without looking at the words. Listeners tend to expect a song to fall within a certain time frame as well as conform to ideas of pace, rhythm, and order. While all writers must learn these skills, songwriters are more obviously dependent on a set of requirements. Songwriting's oral nature can be somewhat limiting, but these limitations ultimately force songwriters to develop a wide vocabulary and an open-mind towards metaphors—both admirable qualities in a writer. One Nashville-based songwriter, Laurianne Cates acknowledges the limits of songwriting and the subsequent writing challenges when she says,

> The challenge of songwriting is to take 3 minutes to tell an amazing story. Three minutes to put together what a novelist puts together in 300 pages. The goal is to create a scene that allows the reader to go to the place with you. You have to bring people there. You can't tell them in prose. The first line of the song functions like the first page of a book: it determines whether the audience checks in or checks out.

The potent writing required of songwriters makes the genre effective in the writing class. Many students have mastered the art of saying the same thing in three different ways in order to fill the word requirement—what they haven't mastered is the ability to make every word count. Short stories and essays are both genres that can accept some writing not directly related to the topic (a side story or an anecdote) without losing the audience, but songwriting does not have that kind of liberty. For students learning to center their ideas, songs are the clearest models for focused writing.

These time constraints not only promote focused writing, but they also promote precise word choice, originality, and appropriate rhythm. As Tara Leigh Cobble, a New York City songwriter suggests,

> Songwriting is also a challenge because the writer must be concerned with rhyme, melody, changes in meter, word emphasis, etc. The songwriter also can't use too flowery of language and must not reproduce what others have already done. The songwriter must say something different or in a new way and must use a creative yet direct way of expressing something.

These songwriters' observations about the multiple skills required show the huge potential for transferring songwriting skills into academic writing skills through comparisons. Students don't necessarily need to learn rhyme and meter, but they do need to learn to make their papers have a natural flow or rhythm, with a reader-friendly order, and sentence variety. Cobble's observations about songwriting relate directly to academic writing: word choice, originality, and effective language use are all important in both genres. Each of these issues could be discussed with the help of any number of composition textbooks, but these textbooks are all missing an important link—the writing examples already present in the students' daily lives. While textbooks may have well-written essays as models, these essays are foreign to most students as compared to the familiar songs that could be studied. The following are a few of the lessons my students have learned through song lyrics.

## Word Choice

Even as I try to push students to explore new aspects of familiar topics, I find they have a hard time understanding the importance of finding just the right words to explain their ideas. Song lyrics provide a great teaching tool for discussions of word choice. Because of the restrictions of songwriting, songwriters must be extremely careful in their selection of words. Because of the musical component of a song, songwriters must think about multiple aspects of the words they use: the sound of the words and the syllable-level "feel" of the words. For example, many of my high school students spend much of their writing time writing about their thoughts on love, friendship, and parent relationships. While all of these topics are valid, I often challenge them to be specific. Don't just tell me that love involves challenges; tell me what kind of challenges. Don't just say that love makes you feel things; tell me what you feel. In an attempt to help my students understand the type of unique writing I am looking for, I play the beginning of Sara Bareilles's song "Love Song." Bareilles responds to people's advice on love by saying "Head under water/And they tell me to breathe easy for a while/the breathing gets harder/even I know that" (Bareilles). After hearing one author's frustration over bad advice, one of my students set off to come up with a more specific example of the feeling she has while in love.

Students may not have to worry about the rhyming element of their words, but they do have to learn to be aware of how the words they use influence the "feel" of their writing. This feel is created by both the sound of the words and the meaning and context of the words. In songwriting, if the lyrics become too abstract, the meaning gets lost, whereas if the words are too simple or overused the listener loses interest. Cobble has a continuum she visualizes when thinking about word choice:

I---------------------------------------------I---------------------------------------------I

Too used                      more creative                   Too creative

Cobble's continuum works for essay writing as well. Students must be creative enough to keep their audiences' attention without being so abstract that they confuse their audiences. Other musicians are also aware of the delicate balance in word choice. Jody Bilyeu, songwriter for the Springfield-based band Big Smith, knows this balance: "The wording needs to be interesting, but not forced." Academic word choice must also find the balance between grabbing the reader's attention and not seeming out of place.

They also must be aware of variety and specificity in their work, much like these songwriters. Songs like Smog's "Cold Blooded Old Times" contain clever word choice by taking a familiar phrase, "Cold Blooded" and matching it with another common phrase "Old Times." The juxtaposition of the cruelness associated with "cold blood" and the nostalgia associated with "old times" provides enough originality to intrigue the reader, but the clichéd elements of the phrase convey bigger thoughts than the literal meanings of the words. The phrase makes a brilliant point about the pain associated with thinking back on old times when the memories are "The type of memory that turns your bones to glass." The song's verses give two specific examples of memories like these: those of a father leaving his family and those when a boyfriend meets his girlfriend's old lover. By using the verses to develop stories of cases in which old times would be cold blooded, the songwriter causes the phrase of the chorus to have an extra impact. Phrases like, "How can I stand/ and laugh with the man/ who redefined your body" and "Father left at eight/ nearly splintering the gate" create situations in which the nostalgia associated with the past is no longer good.

Even bad songs can work by demonstrating the negative impact of using overused ideas or clichéd phrases. Inevitably, every time I bring in a song, at least one student will say they don't like the song. For example, several students were critical of the overly-present piano in Sara Bareilles's "Love Song." From that we discussed the importance of subtlety.

These are just a few examples of the way songwriters find unique and original ways to discuss common emotions and experiences. Almost any song will have some kind of unique word choice that could serve as a model.

## Tone

Beyond the actual words themselves, students can also learn about using words to create an image or a feeling. Songwriters select different types of words depending on the type of song they are writing. For example, if a songwriter is writing about sex, the words he/she selects will depend upon the seriousness of the song and the genre he/she is writing for. The biggest way that word choice, on this level, influences student writers is seen in the distinctions between their personal and academic lives. Students are aware of the difference between the language they use around their friends and the language they use in the FYC class. This semester, as my students prepared to write their diagnostic essays on the second day of class, one of my students asked me if I would "flip out" if they used contractions. This student obviously has some concept about the differences between casual conversation in which contractions are constantly spoken and "formal writing" in which contractions, at least in his mind, may not be acceptable. Students and songwriters have some common ground in that they both have to be aware of not only the meaning of the words they are using and how those words fit together, but also the tone of the words chosen. For example, in casual conversation about a celebrity dying, someone may use expressions like "kicked the bucket" or some other less sensitive phrase, but when writing a paper about the death of a friend or family member or writing a song about a similar incident, these expressions would be seen as out of place. Two songs that deal with death in drastically different tones are "Goodbye Earl" by Dennis Linde and "Whiskey Lullaby" by Bill Anderson and Jon Randall. "Goodbye Earl" is a comical song about an abused woman killing her husband. Since the song isn't serious, the writers can say "Earl had to die." The somber topic of a man driven to alcoholism over a woman in "Whiskey Lullaby" requires a gentler approach to death. The song says, "He put the bottle to his head and pulled the trigger." While both songs deal with death, the differences in tone and subject require the writers to communicate in different types of language.

When discussing tone with my students, I have brought in songs like Ben Harper's "Oppression" and two covers of the old Beatles song "Blackbird." When discussing "Oppression," my students were able to see the way the repetition of the word Oppression and pacing of the drum beats can help communicate the tone of the song. By playing two covers of the same song ("Blackbird" by Paul McCartney) my students were able to see the variety of tones that can be set with the same song. We then discussed the options writers have when dealing with similar topics.

## Organization

Songs not only present important lessons about tone and word choice, they teach good lessons about organization. Students must learn to put their thoughts together in a logical way so they can draw readers in and then convince them to follow along. Songwriters must do the same thing in their writing—maybe even more so given the oral nature of the genre. This orality requires songwriters to make very conscious and deliberate decisions regarding the order in which they present and develop their ideas throughout a song in order to clearly communicate a complete thought in a short amount of time. Bilyeu says songs must follow a certain order to make sense:

> Verses and choruses in alternation, and sometimes a bridge or a breakdown somewhere in the middle. Intro and outro at the edges. There's a certain necessity to the form that you need to have a really good reason to break up.

Bilyeu's song "No Sir," which he co-wrote with his brother Mark, demonstrates this organization. The song opens with an instrumental section before beginning a story about a racist police officer. The song also provides an "outro" by slowing the tempo of the song and fading the voices of the singers. The song provides the musical equivalent of an introduction and a conclusion, which usher the listener "into" and "out" of the song.

The order of a song contains the same elements as an academic essay; the elements are just presented differently. Cates gives a more specific connection between songwriting and essay writing by discussing not only the order but also how a thesis emerges in a song. Songs have central themes developed over the course of the song, just as papers develop a single point or idea (thesis) throughout the text. Songwriters also address the same idea from various angles within a single text. Cates sees the chorus as equal to a thesis—the idea presented multiple times in the work. The secondary ideas (verses) are those leading to the chorus and providing insight on the topic, just as topic sentences and paragraph development lead to new views of the thesis. The first verse leads to the main point. The second verse goes deeper than the first and moves the idea or the story along. This allows the chorus to seem fresh. The bridge then offers a deviation from the rest of the song. If the thesis is moving along in a linear way, the bridge jets off a bit for a new view and then connects and gives one more aspect to the chorus (Cates).

Cates refers to the song "Jesus Take the Wheel" by Carrie Underwood as an example. The first verse tells the story of a woman driving home for Christmas. Her baby is in the backseat and the roads are icy. As she hits an icy part of the road and loses control of the car, she cries,

> Jesus take the wheel
> Take it from my hands
> Cause I can't do this on my own

> I'm letting go
> So give me one more chance
> Save me from this road I'm on
> Jesus take the wheel.

The chorus provides the thesis—the woman is giving up control to a higher power. In the second verse, the car stops spinning and the woman has a spiritual moment in which she goes from asking Jesus to take control of her physical situation to asking Jesus to take control of her emotional or spiritual life. Once again the chorus is sung and this time it has an additional meaning. The "road" is now a metaphor for life and the "wheel" represents the controlling tool of her life. The thesis remains the same throughout the song, but the second chorus expands the idea from the physical to the metaphorical meaning. In the same way, students must have a single focus, but must approach it from multiple angles. If a student is writing a paper about the value of teaching foreign languages in elementary schools, the student may need to combine personal experiences, research, and logical arguments in order to make a point. He/she is using a variety of angles, but the focus remains the same.

## Lessons beyond Words

Almost any songwriter can tell you about the power of music. The lyrics may provide the idea, but the music provides the emotion of the song. Stephen Carter address the power of music in his discussion of using the Beatles's music in his classroom, when he notes that "She's Leaving Home" loses something when it is reduced to just the lyrics (231). Cates confirms Carter's stance by noting, "Lyrics as poetry don't have the same impact. The singing makes the listener attach to it. It adds to the performance" (Cates). Both of these writers are aware of the way voice and tone are communicated in a song: through the music.

I underestimated the importance of the music when I first used song lyrics in the classroom. Since I was asking student writers to bring in examples of good and bad writing, I thought we only needed to look at the words on the page. Looking back, I see my ignorance. There must be something beyond the words in order for the words to impact the reader; this is true in both the academic and musical writing genres. As previously discussed, there must be a tone, an objective, a voice. When instructors bring both music and song lyrics into the classroom, they can open up a discussion of much more than just a modern form of poetry—tone, voice, and pacing can all be taught through the power of music.

## The Assignment

After spending time in class discussing songs, I often assign a paper revolving around songwriters and music. In the writing classes I teach, I often create assignments requiring students to convert their life experiences into various formats. In this particular assignment, students must write a memoir through their musical tastes. They have three options: (1) make a soundtrack of your life and write a paper taking the audience through the soundtrack, (2) write about one artist whose songs have had a particular influence on your life, (3) tell about a specific song that connects to a particular memory or time from your life.

To get this project started, we dedicate an entire class period to guided freewriting. My students get out a favorite pen or pencil and plenty of paper. As my students begin to think about their papers, I ask them a series of questions related to their previous experiences with music.

Every two to three minutes I ask another question. Students are welcome to continue writing about the previous question or move on. Here are some of the questions I use for the guided freewrite:

1. What is your earliest memory of music? Did you have a favorite childhood song? Were you in a choir at school?
2. Who was your first favorite singer or band? Why did you like them so much?
3. Did you have songs you sang often as a kid?
4. Did you have a band or artist or song that was "yours" in junior high or high school? What was the connection to that song?
5. Do you have any CDs that you use to listen to on a regular basis but no longer enjoy? What changed?
6. If you were going to make a soundtrack of your life, what songs would be on the CD?

## Conclusion

Whether an instructor is looking for a fresh way to look at word choice or a new method for teaching tone, songs can easily be transferred from students' personal lives to the classroom. The bonus to this teaching technique is it allows for a connection to be made between the personal and the academic. As students start to understand the decisions behind songwriting, the songs they are already familiar with become models for developing their own writers' voices.

Any song can serve as a model in composition courses. The good, the bad, and the ugly all are examples of either effective or ineffective writing. Whether the songwriter creates a vivid picture of a specific moment or a songwriter fails to invite the listener into the song through vague and clichéd language, the students can learn a lesson that carries over to their own writing.

## Works Cited

Bareilles, Sara. "Love Song." *Little Voices*. Epic, 2007.

Bilyeu, Jody. "Jody Bilyeu Interview Questions." E-mail to Laurel Taylor. 20 January 2006.

Calkins, Lucy. *The Art of Teaching Writing*. Portsmouth, NH: Heinemann, 1994.

Carter, Stephen. "The Beatles and Freshman English." *College Composition and Communication* 20 (1969): 228-32.

Cates, Laurianne. Personal Interview. 17 December 2005.

Cobble, Tara Leigh. Personal interview. 11 September 2005.

Dixie Chicks. "Goodbye Earl." Written by Dennis Linde. *Fly*. Sony,1999.

Elbow, Peter. *Writing without Teachers*. 2nd ed. New York: Oxford UP, 1998.

Kroeger, Fred. "A Freshman Paper Based on the Words of Popular Songs." *College Composition and Communication*. 19 (1968): 337-340.

Paisley, Brad, and Allison Krauss. "Whiskey Lullaby." Written by Bill Anderson and Jon Randall. *Mud on the Tires*. Arista, 2003.

Smog. "Cold Blooded Old Times." Written by Bill Callahan. *High Fidelity Original Soundtrack.* Burbank, 2000.

Underwood, Carrie. "Jesus Take the Wheel." Written by Brett James, Hillary Lindsey, and Gordie Sampson. *Some Hearts.* Arista, 2005.

# Virtual Spaces: Building Communities in the Composition Classroom

## *Maria A. Clayton*

In "Do We Have to Talk the Talk?" David Starrett uses the term "digital immigrant" to distinguish a good number of educators from their "digital native" students—individuals "born in the last 30 years or so, who [have] always or mostly known a life with computers" (24). Diana G. Oblinger, Vice President for the EDUCAUSE teaching and learning initiatives,[19] reports that in a survey of college and university students today, 84% of them own their own computers, and 25% own more than one (39). In addition to their bond with computers, Starrett goes on to argue that these "digital learners [. . .] have different expectations of teachers, of the content, of the delivery, and of access to that content" (24). These "digital natives," also referred to as NetGeners or Millenials, comprise the great majority of students in the freshman composition courses I teach at Middle Tennessee State University (MTSU), and although I am certainly not a part of that generation—definitely a "digital immigrant"—I am keenly aware of their multi-tasking habits, of their impatience for results . . . yesterday . . . but more importantly (and happily), of their need to be connected. Be it through email, instant messaging, virtual chats, discussion boards, social networking sites[20] and the like, virtual spaces have become part of their popular culture, part of their daily lives. My students *want* contact with their peers. As their teacher, the first move I can make towards meeting some of their desires and expectations is to facilitate and encourage the need for contact, but how can I capitalize on it to improve their composition skills?

As I answer this question, I re-evaluate how pertinent the assigned rhetorical situations I construct are to my students, how I guide them through each one, and how I can integrate technology to meet desires and expectations, while ensuring the applications are pedagogically sound. Oblinger suggests this questioning and re-evaluation allow us to be able to serve the new generations of students well (42). To meet my students' desire/expectation to be connected, I've incorporated "academic versions" of the virtual spaces, personal and public, so prevalent in the digital aspect of popular culture today, through re-envisioned environments for composition peer

---

[19] EDUCAUSE is a nonprofit association; its mission focuses on advancing higher education by promoting the intelligent use of information technology (IT). One of its initiatives, the EDUCAUSE Learning Initiative (ELI) is a community of higher education institutions and organizations committed to advancing learning through IT innovation.

[20] Mostly out of curiosity, a recent venture into the world of Wikipedia—the free, online encyclopedia— left me in shock at discovering not only the ubiquitous FaceBook on the list of notable social networking websites, but no fewer than eighty-nine sites! While for me, Wikipedia is not a credible research source, I think this is one bit of information they are probably correct about.

groups that involve a student-centered approach.[21] My starting point, then, focuses on linking students and providing for them the contact they want through the use of student homepages for personal contact and through discussion boards (DBs) for both personal and academic contact. The use of these spaces contributes to promoting active engagement in the writing process by bringing them together in communities of student-centered learners and by fostering and promoting collaboration.

The learning management system currently used by my institution is WebCT, and, unfortunately, the personal spaces it provides are rather limited (student homepages); however, they do serve the purpose of providing a preliminary, community-building opportunity. One of the few options available in the homepages includes linking to favorite websites, but it was not until recently that I noticed students were including links to various social networking sites, primarily FaceBook and MySpace. I found it interesting that they had taken the initiative to invite their classmates to find out more about them. Since the invitation had been extended, I pondered the possibility of allowing our coursework, the writing, to spill out into these spaces. I saw this as a wonderful opportunity to capitalize on popular culture "icons" already established outside the classroom, where students dialogued with one another and with other audiences. Could the social networking spaces become a valid environment for student writers to invite classmates to offer input on pieces of writing? In this outside-the-classroom environment (extending even beyond the course's WebCT virtual space), writers could be more relaxed about finding their voices and also enjoy a more "real" sense of audience. If students felt the need or desire to expand that audience, other visitors with access to the writer's social network site could join that audience as well. This could provide enormous potential for feedback!

I soon discovered that this was not a unique idea, as others like Matt Villano had extolled the possibility of using these social networks "to improve communication and enhance instruction" (40). Villano also refers to Katie Livingston-Vale from MIT who suggests, "the challenge with social software lies in incorporating it seamlessly into the academic environment and utilizing it in an educational context to extend and amplify what students experience in the classroom" (qtd. in Villano 42). Although originality was thwarted, I was encouraged and felt validated by their ideas.

Thankfully, however, I had the wisdom to ask my social networking users to indicate through a show of hands whether they would like to improve their writing by really "going public" with it into these spaces. My digital immigrant enthusiasm (typical of any new convert) was dashed by their polite but firm response; the hands indicated clearly, although politely, that users preferred these spaces be maintained as distinct from academic activities. Their courteous reaction was reinforced at a recent EDUCAUSE Learning Initiative Meeting I attended, where graduate student Carrie Windham presented a session titled "Father Google and Mother IM:

---

[21] Because student-centered has come to have differing meanings in different contexts, let me clarify what it means for me. As part of our Academic Master Plan at Middle Tennessee State University in Murfreesboro, TN, a student-centered culture focuses on students by taking an approach to education that values the whole individual. This culture creates an environment that provides student-centered services through convenient, seamless, and high quality administrative programs. However, more importantly, this culture creates an environment that promotes student-centered learning through academic programs, classroom activities, and extracurricular activities, engaging students and allowing them to share in the responsibility for their own education.

Confessions of a Net Gen Learner." As part of fresh and eye-opening comments, she voiced the exact sentiment my students had conveyed: social networking sites are just that, social, not for academics. Even Michael Hirschorn in his highly complimentary article "About Facebook" focuses his praises on the "social media" aspect of this leading social networking giant but offers no mention of academic applications. Obviously, I was attempting to venture into an area of pop culture students prefer to keep personal.

In addition to my students' reluctance to use social networking spaces for academic purposes, there are a couple of tendencies prevalent in these sites that I've come to realize I'm not willing to let creep into my classroom: the creation of alternate personas and the potential for security lapses. Despite psychologist and sociologist Sherry Turkle's claims in "Who Am We?" about the benefits of alternate identities, I'm not convinced of their value, particularly in the writing classroom. I find most of my students struggle to find their actual voice without compounding the process by adding alternate ones. Turning to the issue of security, Windham emphasizes the need to make students more aware of the misconception of privacy in the social software tools (Windham, "Getting Past"). Similarly, in "Ensuring the Net Generation is Net Savvy," George Lorenzo and Charles Dziuban also highlight this key issue, among other valid concerns, about students' use of the internet. They see students not only as information gatherers, very inexperienced in assessing the quality of that information, but also as creators of information for public consumption (Lorenzo and Dziuban). Who can gain access to the information they share and for what purpose? From university administrators to individuals with criminal intentions, the answer is just about anybody, despite the safeguards in place and despite Hirschorn's assurances about Facebook's user control. Cornell's Tracy Mitrano suggests that "an individual not post online any information that they [sic] would not display in physical space." (24). She sees this awareness about personal safety as basic information for "the broader world of visibility in which they are living online" (24). Using course management programs, like WebCT's homepages, while not yet as versatile or as sophisticated as social networking sites, eliminates these two worrisome side-effects. These basic homepages are acceptable academic substitutes for their pop culture counterparts.

Still, there's the "call of the wild" beckoning, like the one sounded by Mitrano: "Higher education too should embrace these technologies, in pursuit of the academic mission. Social networking technologies speak to all that is fresh and innovative in research, teaching and learning, and outreach" (28). I've decided that modeling the strengths of social networking sites and expanding the use of in-course private and public virtual spaces is a good course of action to answer that call. For example, I'm going to investigate how I might expand WebCT's student homepages, linking them to a secure blog and allowing students to share feedback with each other, whether on personal issues or on issues that relate to course work. In this way, I can put into practice Derek Owens' suggestion about what writing classrooms should be: "a site within which writers can explore, devise, and articulate their own personalities and individualities" (162), a search for their writer's voice. This exploration can begin and be facilitated within the context of their in-class personal spaces.

However, virtual spaces for sharing personal information are just one dimension of the contact I want to provide for students. What I'm really interested in is giving them access to each other as writers. The most appropriate virtual space available through learning management systems suited for this purpose is the more public, topic-driven DB. Whether for use among peers in a single class or even better, by peers in multiple sections of the same course, DB's make possible the electronic exchange of ideas and text, facilitating the peer response process, and promoting active engagement and community building in the composition classroom. Providing a means for making files "public" and for receiving/giving feedback, these public spaces promote audience awareness, revision opportunities, and the all-critical active engagement. Additionally, because they can be conducted outside of class, DB peer groups extend the dialogue about writing beyond the constraints of time and space imposed by the physical classroom. As Peshe Kuriloff points out in "Breaking the Barriers of Time and Space: More Effective Teaching Using e-Pedagogy," "The opportunity to extend time and to reconfigure space [. . .], creates the potential to improve teaching and enhance learning in unique ways." Through this sharing, student writers become aware not only of their own process, but also of that followed by the other peers in the group. Virtual spaces in the composition classroom not only sidestep the limitation of time and space within the physical classroom, but also move students towards establishing communities of writers who help and learn from each other.

Beth Hewitt points out in "Characteristics of Interactive Oral and Computer-Mediated Peer Group Talk and Its Influence on Revision" that the use of DB's in the peer response process for composition courses is at once private and public in that the comments intended for one writer can be viewed by all members of the group (288). Members are invited to serve as first level audiences, coaches, support groups in assisting each writer to achieve his/her purpose in writing. Establishing such communities of writers puts collaboration into practice and reinforces student-centered learning, as students actively participate in their own learning. Katrina A. Meyer and Ruth E. Brown, among many contributors to the dialogue on pedagogically sound integration of technology, suggest that asynchronous dialogues, such as those conducted in DBs, offer a stage building process that affords "greater levels of interpersonal bonding or affiliation. The consequences for students of building community include improved confidence expressing oneself, learning from others, and feeling connected and accepted" (Meyer 22). Brown suggests three stages emerge in the process, culminating in increased engagement in "both the class and the dialogue" (18). The "public" nature of the dialogue promotes another key element in composition, audience awareness, and invites revision to meet that audience's needs. These are ideal conditions in the composition classroom.

The positive impact of using DB's for peer group can be further enhanced by expanding the peer communities to include members from other, similar composition sections.[22] This expansion of the peer feedback process contributes to giving even clearer presence—physical and/or

---

[22] The instructions for conducting the peer group process, both in-class and cross-class, are very detailed and include specific prompts to guide the feedback given each writer for each rhetorical situation assigned. Even in terms of the mechanics of the process, clear guidance is provided. For example, the steps in preparation to begin giving feedback include

- Groups should start as soon as all members are present.
- Class roll will be taken as groups work.
- Groups must sit at adjacent terminals.
- Groups must quickly come to order and get down to business.
- Groups must give equal time to all members' work.
- Everyone must participate.

virtual—to audience and to establishing communities of writers who help and learn from each other. During semesters when I'm assigned two sections of web-assisted English 1010, Expository Writing, at MTSU, I bring all students together for peer review purposes. Students' peer review teams cross each section's physical boundaries to include respondents from each of the two sections of the same course (the process need not be limited to two sections). When we begin the semester's work, the first essay relies only on in-class, face-to-face (f2f) peers for feedback on their essays' second draft (although part of the process is conducted virtually using WebCT's DB's). This gradual introduction to the specific technology and to the procedures to be used for peer work allows students to become competent before virtual communication among peers is the only type available. The in-class peers constitute a first-level audience with whom they become familiar over the three-time-a-week, f2f contact shared during the early weeks of the semester. The frequent contact establishes a comfort level and willingness to accept input—like that of siblings, friends, or roommates.

However, by the second essay, my students' audience expands to include peers from the other English 1010 section, an audience they have contact with only over email, personal homepages, and DBs. If convenient, when the two sections are scheduled back-to-back, a physical meeting can be arranged, although, I don't always arrange it. These two representations of their readership—physical and virtual—help each writer's developing understanding of what details are necessary/interesting, what level of formality/informality is called for, what tone is appropriate. While making these audience-based choices, the writer's role and purpose shape more clearly, and the writer's voice begins to emerge, leading the student closer and closer to developing his/her identity as a writer, to developing, improving, or honing writing skills. As Phillip Long and Stephen Ehrman argue in "Future of the Learning Space: Breaking out of the Box," in this way, the writing assignment helps the student by having him/her "doing what the student is learning to do" (44)—analyzing writing and learning from it. Long and Ehrman add that "Students can learn meaning in a discipline when teaching/learning activities are organized around the core process and tools of the discipline" (44). Nowhere is this more important than in the teaching of writing.

Moving one step further in capitalizing on the impact of virtual spaces in my composition classroom, I focused some of the details of the second essay to suggest an even broader audience than the cross-class aspect would provide. According to Linda Meyers-Breslin in "Technology, Distance, and Collaboration: Where are These Pedagogies Taking Composition," "As we move students from private to public audiences, it makes sense to place students into the Net. There we can ask them to write in a space where anyone and everyone can read their words, and students can exchange ideas in a more real world setting, with people situated in the real-world" (161-62). In addition to using the mix of in-class and cross-class peer members, my students' audience expands to include the university at large and beyond:

Your web-assisted composition class will participate in a collaborative peer group project for students from your instructor's two sections of 1010 Composition. This assignment will expand your writing communities and further develop your ability to analyze and to adapt your writing to specific, targeted audiences. There is a strong possibility that the resulting collection of essays will be made available to prospective MTSU students and their parents, incoming freshmen, and CUSTOMS Student Orientation Assistants. Possible inclusion of selected essays on the CUSTOMS' website implies a worldwide audience interested in reading about your University and the surrounding community.

> **TOPIC:**
>
> Now that you have had several weeks to adjust to your new role as a college student, it is time to explore what your college and the surrounding community have to offer its students. You will share that newfound knowledge with others in an informative essay of 1000 words minimum. You may choose one of two options:
>
> *   A profile of a campus program, publication, service, club, or place
>
> *   A profile of a place or activity in your campus's surrounding community
>
> **AUDIENCE/PURPOSE:**
>
> Since your essay could be published in a collection posted on the internet, anyone around the globe could read your essay, including future students for our institution. However, you will want to more specifically target readers at our University. The general purpose of your profile is to inform.

What is even more critical, as Myers-Breslin points out, is not just to bring students and their writing to these spaces, but to structure assignments that involve them in a conversation about the writing (162). Her views parallel my thinking. In-class members work as a team to respond to the writing from their cross-class peers. During this portion of the process, students dialogue about strengths and weaknesses they find in the writing in terms of audience, thesis, organization, detail, and a variety of other rhetorical elements specified in the assignment. The conversation strengthens peer response skills, builds confidence, and allows respondents to think about these very issues in their own writing—a very profitable exercise that I feel Kenneth Bruffee,[23] leading proponent of collaborative learning, would approve of. Kuriloff also agrees: "Collaboration improves student writing by giving writers insight into how an audience responds to their work in progress." This built-in element of collaboration is another beneficial aspect of these cross-class groups, collaboration which fosters conversation about writing.

Much like the information gathering that users accomplish through social networking spaces, the building of a repository of my students' writing is a significant side benefit of using DBs for the peer response process. Not only is this repository helpful in cases where canines develop an unexplainable appetite for work done for a composition class or when disks [or more up to date storing devices] are lost or stolen, but, more importantly, it also provides a record of the progress made in the writing process—from topic selection and tentative thesis to multiple drafts and "final" product, an invaluable record of their journey as writers.

---

[23] One of the leading early voices and strongest proponents of collaborative learning, Kenneth Bruffee was among the first to address the changing role of faculty as facilitators of well-structured assignments that bring students to active learning through collaboration. His *Collaborative Learning: Higher Education, Interdependence, and the Authority of Knowledge* (1999), provides solid ground for the theory and application of this pedagogy.

Another side benefit, minor but useful, is that my students practice other computer skills, yes, even the "digital natives," as they are sometimes not terribly literate in the area of document manipulation, use of attachments, and the like. When they complete the course, they have gained/increased their confidence in using "less popular" applications of technology, while capitalizing on the technology's facilitating of their work as writers. Some students even make a discovery not related to writing, seeing the advantages of posting writing and receiving virtual feedback as a paper-saving practice.

While I have not conducted formal data gathering of my students' reactions about the use of personal and public spaces in our composition class, from their participation in these spaces, I can see that my objectives for creating communities of writers are being reached, and, hopefully, I'm meeting some of their other desires and expectations. The majority of them show evidence of having actually established small communities of writers that define the primary goals as helping members improve their writing, fulfilling all requirements of the assigned rhetorical situation, and expanding their concept of audience. The positive attitude exhibited in their virtual and f2f discussions about writing and about the rhetorical situation's requirements support my expectation that these communities of writers have come together and worked as a team, giving feedback in whatever way they can. Although I'm glad that my students recognize that they are learning from each other, one small point about community which has yet to be mentioned by any is the fact that all my students in the class know each other by name. I wonder how many of their other classes they can say this about. This is a direct result from the virtual environments in the course and the community they help build.

Although thankful for the positive reception and attitude towards this aspect of their writing assignments, I must also acknowledge that some students have demonstrated a concerned attitude about everyone's commitment to the process. As is common in collaborative work, particularly among students, not all participants take on the same degree of responsibility, at times not putting any effort into their feedback or into their contributions. At these times, peers vested in the process have shown awareness of the importance of substantive comments required for feedback to actually be useful. In so doing, they have made me aware that additional modeling for effective peer process is called for. Even others have bemoaned the added effort expended, indicating that my goals of establishing a community of writers is simply too much to do just for writing a paper. I suspect this type of attitude is reflected by students who prefer writing as an activity conducted in isolation, or worse, by those who think of writing as a one-step process. So the questioning and re-evaluation begins anew. How do I need to revise my approach to draw them more satisfactorily into the community their dedicated classmates and I have established?

Despite having failed to meet the desires and expectations of *all* my students, I am encouraged by what I hear and read from the majority as they dialogue about writing. I am pleased to provide virtual environments like those prevalent in the pop culture all around them, where they can be wakened to rethinking about writing from a process carried out totally in isolation to one that not only considers audience, but also elicits feedback from it—a very public process, indeed. I also like that they discover they are not the only ones experiencing problems with the composition process. The benefits provided by our use of virtual personal and public spaces begin to materialize rather quickly as students form support groups for tech-related issues, but more importantly, for revision and editing needs, and for dialoguing about writing. Karen Frankola, in "The e-Learning Taboo: High Dropout Rates in Online courses," suggests that following best practices in interactivity "not only creates a sense of community for participants; it also stimulates learning through discussing ideas and practicing skills [. . . .] [Students] benefit from high interactivity with faculty and each other through exchanges like bulletin board discussions and e-mails" (16). Anytime we increase and deepen the dialogue about composition among our students, bring them together in communities of student-centered, active learners, and foster/promote collaboration, we move them towards clearer awareness of what constitutes good writing and towards improving their own. The "digital immigrant" in me rests a bit easier knowing I'm making strides in my quest to meet some of the desires and expectations of my "digital native" students, while providing a valid means of improving their composition skills.

## Works Cited

Brown, Ruth E. "The Process of Community-Building in Distance Learning Classes." *Journal of Asynchronous Learning Networks* 5 (2001): 18-35.

Frankola, Karen. "The e-Learning Taboo: High Dropout Rates in Online Courses." *Syllabus* June 2001: 14-16.

Hewitt, Beth L. "Characteristics of Interactive Oral and Computer-Mediated Peer Group Talk and Its Influence on Revision." *Computers and Composition* 17 (2000): 265-88.

Hirschorn, Michael. "About Facebook." *The Atlantic.com*. Oct. 2007. 9 Sept. 2007 <http://www.theatlantic.com /doc/200710/facebook>.

Kuriloff, Peshe. "Breaking the Barriers of Time and Space: More Effective Teaching Using e-Pedagogy." *Innovate* 2 (2005). 12 Nov. 2005 <http://www.innovateonline.info/index.php?view=article&id=64.>.

Long, Phillip D., and Stephen C. Ehrman. "Future of the Learning Space: Breaking out of the Box." *EDUCAUSE Review* July-Aug. 2005: 42-58.

Lorenzo, George, and Charles Dziuban. "Ensuring the Net Generation Is Net Savvy." Ed. Diana G. Oblinger. EDUCAUSE Learning Initiative White Paper. Sept. 2006 <http://www.educause.edu/ LibraryDetailPage/666?ID=ELI3006>.

Meyer, Katrina A. "The Web's Impact on Student Learning." *T.H.E. Journal* May 2003: 14-24.

Mitrano, Tracy. "A Wider World: Youth, Privacy, and Social Networking Technologies." EDUCAUSE Review Nov-Dec. 2006: 17-28.

Myers-Breslin, Linda. "Technology, Distance, and Collaboration: Where Are These Pedagogies Taking Composition?" *Reforming College Composition: Writing the Wrongs.* Ed. Ray Wallace, Alan Jackson, and Susan Lewis Wallace. Westport: Greenwood P, 2000. 161-77.

Oblinger, Diana G. "Boomer, Gen-Xers, and Millenials: Understanding the New Students." *EDUCAUSE Review* July-Aug. 2003: 37-47.

Owens, Derek. "Composition as the Voicing of Multiple Fictions." *Into the Field: Sites of Composition Studies*. Ed. Anne Ruggles Gere. New York: MLA, 1993. 159-75.

Starrett, David. "Do We Have to Talk the Talk?" *Campus Technology* Sept. 2005: 24-26.

Turkle, Sherry. "Who Am We?" *Life on the Screen: Identity in the Age of the Internet.* 1995. Rpt. In *Who Are We? Readings on Identity, Community, Work, and Career.* Ed. Rise B. Axelrod and Charles R. Cooper. New York: St. Martin's, 1997. 51-56.

Villano, Matt. "Social Revolution: Social Software Is Here to Stay, but What Is It Really, and Is It a Good Thing?" *Campus Technology* Jan. 2007: 40-45.

Windham, Carrie. "Father Google and Mother IM: Confessions of a Net Gen Learner." Paper presented at EDUCAUSE Learning Initiative Meeting. Atlanta, GA. 22-24 Jan. 2007.

---. "Getting Past Google: Perspectives on Information Literacy from the Millennial Mind." Ed. Diana G. Oblinger. EDUCAUSE Learning Initiative White Paper. Sept. 2006 <http://www.educause.edu/LibraryDetail Page/666?ID=ELI3007>.

# Writing Students Should Write about Advertisements

## *Claire Lutkewitte*

*Popular culture, despite its accessibility and familiarity, is an experience that we take for granted –why not reflect upon it?*

*Smelstor and Weiher, 1976*

Although studies tell us that "Advertisers spend more than $12 billion a year marketing to kids," and that the "average American child is exposed to 40,000 ads per year" (Report of the APA), presently, an onslaught of companies are opting to forgo traditional advertising practices to, instead, ask us to create, write, and star in our own advertisements. Suddenly, anyone who can put together a short clip for YouTube can also take on the role of ad exec. What's more, the consumers who create these Web ads have now been dubbed "Generation C," the 'C' standing for creative, and says Trendwatching.com director Reinier Evers, "they're part of the tsunami of consumer-generated 'content' on the Web" (qtd. in Kiley). Likewise, *TIME* magazine has also recognized an increase in creativity. Each year *TIME* selects a Person of the Year. In 2006, *TIME* selected you. Among the reasons for such a selection, *TIME* author Lev Grossman cites the revolution of Web 2.0 coupled with "an explosion of productivity and innovation." He says, "America loves its solitary geniuses--its Einsteins, its Edisons, its Jobses --but those lonely dreamers may have to learn to play with others," and by "learn to play with others," Grossman refers to those of us who are building "a new kind of international understanding, not politician to politician, great man to great man, but citizen to citizen, *person* to *person*" (38-41). Although Grossman's main point might not be to talk about the changing roles of consumers, he does observe that companies worldwide are now asking for our help in making key business decisions. Blurring the line between experts and novices, high and low cultures, observations, such as Evers and Grossman's, represent a current trend of addressing Smelstor and Weiher's call for a reflection on pop culture. Smelstor and Weiher's question, "Why not reflect upon it?" has, once again, been brought into the forefront, leaving those of us who teach writing to wonder, what can we learn from popular culture? And, how do we use what we learn about pop culture in the composition classroom?

Because we live in a pop culture, one which creates, writes, and stars in 40,000 yearly advertisements, a discussion of advertising in the composition classroom, then, becomes necessary to reflect upon the very pop culture that we often take for granted. Students who enter the writing classroom do so with pop culture experiences (such as the 40,000 advertisements' messages) already in mind and to ignore such thoughts would be a missed opportunity to critically examine the pop culture ways, or what Fitts calls "life practices," which influence what, how, and why we write in and out of the academy (91). Harkening back to Henry Giroux's 1992 call for pop culture to "become a serious object of study in the official curriculum," I would add that advertising analysis needs to become a serious object of study in the composition classroom since citizens are now working side by side with experts to create, write, and star in the advertisements of the very products they consume (31).

Therefore, in my first-year composition class, I teach a four-week advertisement analysis project as a way to not only heighten students' awareness of the advertisements they encounter and create on a daily basis but also to encourage students to actively engage in a discussion about critical analysis by examining rhetorical appeals in persuasive contexts. In other words, I ask students to pay closer attention to a part of the pop culture in which they live. I ask them to reflect.[24]

Although a quick scan of current handbooks and textbooks for first-year writing courses reveals similar approaches and attitudes of teaching advertisements, I feel a more in-depth advertisement analysis project is warranted. Taken as a whole, my ad analysis project calls for several writing opportunities in which students write essays, responses, reflections, and peer assessments. In the four weeks, we spend a great deal of time discussing the images and texts that make up advertisements, and through writing about them, students are able to heighten their awareness of the cultural "norms" and stereotypes which are represented and reproduced in this type of communication. After all, as Twitchell puts it, "Mass production means mass marketing, and mass marketing means the creation of mass stereotypes" (206).

## The Assignment

The assignment for the essay is as follows: compare and contrast a series of interrelated print ads and write an analysis that considers their persuasiveness in relation to their contexts. Also, in the assignment, I ask students to analyze the rhetorical appeals while thinking about the importance of time and place. In doing so, students are introduced to the rhetorical terms of ethos, pathos, and logos.

To select the series of interrelated ads, I advise my students to look for ads by companies they are interested in, then narrow their choice to one company and compare that company's different ad campaigns. As my students look for their series of interrelated ads, I tell them to search first through their favorite magazines, newspapers, and even websites. I feel that when students are interested in the advertisements, they are more willing to engage in a discussion about them. I also explain why students should find ads that not only feature one company but feature the same or very similar products or services. For instance, I explain to them that trying to compare an ad for a McDonald's hamburger with an ad for a Ronald McDonald House's children's charity might not be the best for an analysis project since the ads are for different products and services. Instead, I use McDonald's food ads as an example and share with them a comparison of their ad campaigns of 1997, 2000, and 2003. In each ad campaign, McDonald's attempts to sell their food products by using a different slogan each year. In those three years, McDonald's uses, "Did somebody say McDonald's?" "Put a smile on," and "i'm lovin' it." to sell

---

[24] This advertisement analysis project is the second project of the semester and follows my literacy narrative project because, as part of the literacy narrative project, I ask my students: how have your experiences (which cannot be separated from popular culture and advertisements) shaped your ongoing literacy development? Since it is through literacy that we come to know what we know and value, I believe that it is necessary then to address advertising literacy in the writing classroom since students are asked to write about their life experiences, life experiences which are not void of advertisements.

their products. To help students further their understanding of the assignment, I then ask students to consider why McDonalds's chose to change the slogan each year.

## Readings

As students embark on their search for a series of interrelated ads, I assign two readings. The first reading is an example of an advertisement analysis. For this reading, I try to find an analysis of a current advertisement, one featuring a familiar product or service. The internet is a great place to find such an example of an advertisement analysis. For instance, Seth Stevenson of *www.slate.com* writes a recurring column, called "Ad Report Card," which features his analysis of popular commercials. Recently, I chose his "Keep Soccer Beautiful!" analysis of a Nike soccer commercial and asked students to read and make notes about his analysis. Then, as a class, we watched the commercial and discussed the choices Stevenson made while writing his analysis.

The second reading is taken from Lester Faigley's *The Brief Penguin Handbook 2nd Ed.* Since chapters are short, I assign several for students to read at one time. I assign Chapter 1, "The Rhetorical Situation," because it introduces students to the rhetorical situation, the rhetorical appeals of ethos, pathos, and logos, and because it defines the immediate and broader contexts. I also assign Chapter 2, "Words, Images, and Graphics," and Chapter 7, "Analyzing Verbal and Visual Texts," so that students can familiarize themselves with approaches for critically analyzing texts and images.

Since the readings explain the rhetorical appeals in general and only briefly mention them in relation to advertisements, in a class discussion of the readings, I make sure to provide examples of my own that point to the rhetorical appeals specifically in the context of advertisements. For example, I ask my students to consider the appeal of ethos in a Snickers Marathon Energy Bar ad featuring a bike rider striving to reach the top of a hill. Below the bike rider, the ad reads: "FORTITUDE. If you have enough WHY, you can bear almost any HOW." As an example of an appeal to pathos, I use a Save the Children ad featuring a young child and the words "Making the world a better place for children." This ad demonstrates an appeal to the audience's emotions. And, finally, I show them the appeal of logos in a Dial Soap ad featuring soap that contains AT-7 which eliminates bacteria. I got these ads online, but magazines and newspapers also offer plenty of ads that appeal to ethos, pathos, and logos.

Following the examples, in a short reflection assignment, I invite my students to first describe the appeals of ethos, pathos, and logos in their own words and then to write about instances where they have seen advertisements use ethos, pathos, and logos both visually and textually. I assign this short homework assignment to get my students to start articulating their thoughts about how advertisements persuade their audiences into purchasing products and services. Then, in one class period, the students share what they wrote with each other and discuss why the appeals were or were not persuasive and effective in the advertisements.

## Classroom Activities

To go along with our discussion of ethos, pathos, and logos, I also ask students to consider contexts, both the immediate context and the larger, historical context so that they can make better informed judgments in their own essays. In another class exercise, I pass out several different print advertisements and have students work in groups to describe the advertisements' intended audiences. While the ads I passed out were all found in the same magazine, I do not tell my students where I found the ads. I want my students to consider just the ads and to formulate a description of the intended audience without the knowledge of the context. I advise them to consider what types of magazines the ads would most likely be found in. I ask them to consider what types of people these ads would mostly appeal to and ask them to explain their answers. Taking turns, each group shares its descriptions and its guesses as to which types of magazines carried the ads. I make a list on the board so that students can see how each group described the ads and to keep track of the guesses. Once every group has shared their thoughts, I reveal the name of the magazine, after which the groups discuss how their thoughts about their ad's intended audience changed. My goals for this exercise are 1) to help my students realize the importance of and complicated nature of contexts in determining the intended audience and 2) to begin to discuss their thoughts about how their world is represented in advertisements, that is, to question their culture's "norms" and stereotypes as portrayed in this form of communication. It is my hope that students will focus on the ideologies "that are maintained, challenged, or otherwise negotiated in language" and images in advertisements (Fitts 94).

To reiterate these two goals, the following day we spend another class period talking more about audiences and contexts. For the first half of the class, I invite students to write a description of the intended audience of the advertisements they chose specifically for their own writing projects. I first advise them to examine both the text and images. I prompt them with a few questions to get them started: Based on the clues the text and images give you, can you determine the age, gender, social class, race, ethnicity, culture, likes, or dislikes of the intended audience? I tell them to make specific references between their answers and the clues they found in the ads. Next, I ask them to examine the location of the ad, whether it was in a magazine or newspaper, in the front, middle, back, on the top of the page, bottom of the page, or near other advertisements. Then, I encourage them to think about the magazine or newspaper where they found their ads. I ask them: Who reads the magazine or newspaper? Did you buy the magazine? If so, where and who also shops there? When did you buy the magazine? Again, my goal is to get my students to make conscious connections between audiences and the smaller contexts as well as the larger, broader contexts. The last half of the class is spent discussing what the students wrote. Often this leads to a broader discussion about how they, as members of an advertising culture, are portrayed in advertisements. The students now feel more comfortable to ask their own questions, such as who is responsible for the images and messages that ads display? And, what can we learn from advertisements?

While they continue to work on their essays, the class spends a day in the library to get better acquainted with the resources the library has to offer and to help students further examine the contexts of advertisements. I encourage students to find out as much as they can about their particular ads, specifically telling them to find out the history of the ad campaign, the creators, and so forth. I also suggest that they research the company featured in the ad. The internet provides many resources for finding this information. But, of course, depending on the advertisements my students select, this is sometimes difficult and time consuming. On the other hand, the students who do make an effort to research their advertisements uncover interesting information that they include in their essays. For example, one first year composition student wrote about Old Spice and how Procter and Gamble bought the brand in 1990 and revamped the image of the brand from "grandpa's aftershave" to high-performance deodorant and body care products. The student then used this information to analyze a series of Old Spice advertisements.

Another student in the same class wrote an analysis of a Dr. Pepper ad featuring a logo with the numbers 10, 2, and 4. Since this logo was important to her visual analysis, she researched Dr. Pepper and found that the numbers actually referred to times of the day which the company believed were the best times of the day to drink Dr. Pepper. She also found information about a 1961 Dr. Pepper ad campaign and included this information in her analysis as well.

---

**Student Example**

Over the years, many of Dr. Pepper's ads have targeted their audience by challenging them to break away from the norm. In 1961, they released a series of ads with the phrase, "It's different…I like it!" Dr. Pepper wanted to appeal to the individual trying to break away from the mundane. The ad uses muted colors with a background of pale blue representing the dullness of everyday life. Then, the Dr. Pepper stands out in red, and the black letters show up very clearly, showing how good different can be. The font they chose to use for the phrase "Under every one of these [Dr. Pepper cap] is one of these [smile]" is a simpler font that looks like handwriting. This makes the ad more personal to its audience.

---

In her analysis, the student was able to connect what she found in her research to her critical analysis of the text and visuals.

In another class period, my students work together in groups to generate ideas for their essays. In the first part of this class period, my students share and discuss the advertisements that they specifically chose to write about in their essay. Then, they spend the second part of the class writing short responses to each of the members in their group. In the short responses, students address the other group members' ads and explain what they feel are the most important parts of the ad. I make sure to ask the students to describe their personal reaction/response/connection to their group members' ads. Then, each member offers suggestions on how to write the analysis. For instance, one student wrote to her group member who was writing about a jewelry company:

> The most interesting parts about your chosen ads is to me that while they [the ads] both stem from women's magazines according to your information, the two page ad stating 'with every step / with every stone / love grows' almost seems to be geared for a gift of diamonds. The other ad seems to favor independent women more, talking about a 'right-hand ring' and loving oneself—meaning, making the gift of a diamond to oneself. This is definitely an interesting contrast, and I would strive to try and find out whether these different campaigns for the same product originated in different years or from different advertising firms, and if so, why the approach to advertising has changed.

In her response, the student first pointed out what she thought was most interesting about her group member's ads for a jewelry company, but then also suggested how her group member might approach her analysis essay. I call these responses multiple perspectives because each student offers his/her perspective on each of the other group members' ads. Some students who are having trouble starting their essays have used their multiple perspectives responses as a way to generate ideas. For example, one student wrote in a reflection essay at the end of the project that she "had not thought about looking at her advertisements in that way" until her group member pointed it out in the multiple perspective response. I emphasize in this activity that it is sometimes good to hear others' opinions because sometimes we are not paying close attention.

Throughout the four weeks, I remind my students that an analysis is more than just describing what they see in the advertisements. An analysis requires a critical judgment in which students question the parts of the advertisement in relation to the whole. Every part of the advertisement's design (the text and the images) is there for a reason. Throughout the four weeks, I often ask them to free write about advertisements, prompting them with questions such as why do you remember some ads and not others? Do advertisements affect your purchasing decisions? Why or why not? Are you, as a member of the ad's intended audience, represented fairly? Why or why not? What stereotypes are reproduced in advertising? Sometimes, students then use their free writing to build their analysis essays.

As the end of the project approaches, I advise students to bring a draft to class for peer assessment. On the day of peer assessment, I invite students to exchange their drafts with two other students in the class. I advise them to read through the essay once without making any comments. Then, I tell them to reread the essay again and offer suggestions to the author. I prompt them with questions such as What connections, patterns, and relationships did the writer write about in his/her ad analysis? Did the writer take a stance or offer any judgments? If so, what are those judgments? If not, what suggestions could you give the writer to help them with their analysis? After the assessments, the students write their final drafts.

At the end of four weeks, the students come to class with their finished projects. They turn in an essay, their advertisements, their multiple perspectives responses, their peer assessments, and finally, an in-class reflection essay. For all my projects, students write these short reflection essays in class. For this ad analysis project, I ask my students to tell me what they like most about their essay, what they like least about their essay, and what they would do differently if they could do the entire project over again. The students reflect on these questions by making sure to cite specific examples in their answers. Overall, the reflections help students consider the whys behind their decisions when writing their essays. I find their reflective essays very informative in that they let me know what the students are feeling as well as what adjustments to make as I teach this project in the future.

## Summary

Giroux and Simon state that "Educators who refuse to acknowledge popular culture as a significant basis of knowledge often devalue students by refusing to work with the knowledge that students actually have" (182). I believe this ad analysis project can be used as a starting point for other projects that incorporate pop culture (and the necessary reflections of it) in the composition classroom. I teach this project prior to an argumentative project which includes analyzing persuasive images in pop culture. Any writing project that encourages students to engage/question/judge the experiences they have in pop culture can follow this ad analysis project, especially those which ask students to reflect upon the ways in which pop culture influences what, how, and why we write.

## Works Cited

1967 Dial Soap. Advertisement. 14 Apr. 2007 <http://adclassix.com/a3/67dialsoap.html>.

Dr. Pepper. Advertisement. 14 Apr. 2007 <http://www.gono.com/museum2003/ museum%20collect%20info/drpepper/drpepper.htm>.

Fitts, Karen. "Ideology, Life Practices, and Pop Culture: So Why Is this Called Writing Class?" *JGE* 54 (2005): 90-105.

Giroux, Henry. *Border Crossings: Cultural Workers and the Politics of Education*. New York: Routledge, 1992.

Grossman, Lev. "*TIME PERSON* OF THE *YEAR* You." *TIME*. 168 (2006): 38-41.

Kiley, David. "Advertising Of, By, and For the People." *Business Week* 6 (2005): 63-64.

Kunkel, Dale, Brian Wilcox, Joanne Cantor, Edward Palmer, Susan Linn, and Peter Dorwrick. "Report of the APA Task Force on Advertising and Children." 20 Feb. 2004. 14 Apr. 2007 <http://www.apa.org/releases/childrenads.pdf>.

Save the Children. Advertisement. 14 Apr. 2007 <http://www.savethechildren.org.nz/new_zealand/shopping/main.html>.

Smelstor, Majorie, and Carol Weiher. "Using Popular Culture to Teach Composition." *The English Journal* 65 (1976): 41-46.

Snickers Marathon Energy Bar. Advertisement. 5 Oct. 2007 <http://muse.jhu.edu/.../v007/images/7.2u07f36bike.jpg>.

Twitchell, James. "What We Are to Advertisers." *Signs of Life in the USA*. Ed. Sonia Maasik and Jack Solomon. Boston: Bedford/St. Martin's, 2003. 205-09.

# Contributors

**Rebecca Bobbitt** is pursuing a PhD in English at Middle Tennessee State University (MTSU) with a concentration in popular culture and composition. She earned an MA from Murray State University and a BA from the University of Tennessee at Martin. She is the author of the Instructor's Manual for *The Pop Culture Zone* (authored by Allison D. Smith, Trixie G. Smith, and Stacia Watkins), and she has a chapter on Patricia Bizzell in *COMPbiblio: Leaders and Influences in Composition Theory and Practice* (edited by Smith, Smith, and Karen Wright). Her pop culture obsessions include *Buffy the Vampire Slayer* (the TV series, not the movie), *Supernatural*, horror movies of varying quality, and online fandom. She is currently finishing her dissertation on *Buffy* and fairy tales.

**Maria A. Clayton**, an associate professor, has her MA in English from California University of Pennsylvania and a DA in English from MTSU, with an emphasis on rhetoric and composition. The focus of her research lies in this area, primarily in its intersection with popular culture's ubiquitous thirst for technology. She has presented in venues like the premier conference for IT integration into higher education, EDUCAUSE, its offshoot ELI (EDUCAUSE Learning Initiative), and Campus Technology (formerly Syllabus). Developer of the first online course for MTSU's English Department, Clayton is the recipient of several awards recognizing her contributions to the field, among them MTSU's Foundation Award for Outstanding Achievement in Instructional Technology and Tennessee Board of Regents Distance Education Committee's Innovations Award. Her work has been published in *Kairos: A Journal for Teachers of Writing in Webbed Environments, EDUCAUSE Quarterly,* and *Tennessee English Journal.*

**Kevin Haworth** is the author of *The Discontinuity of Small Things*, a novel that won the 2006 Samuel Goldberg Prize for Emerging Jewish Writers. It was also named runner-up for the 2006 Dayton Literary Peace Prize. His fiction and criticism have appeared in *Sentence, Another Chicago Magazine*, the *Jewish Literary Supplement, Poetica, Permafrost*, and other journals and magazines. He earned his BA from Vassar College and his MFA from Arizona State University. He teaches at Ohio University, where his classes include fiction writing, contemporary literature, and a first-year writing class focused on graphic novels. He has been writing about comic books for several years and reading them for much longer than that.

**Sarah Huffines** is assistant professor of English and director of the writing center at Covenant College in Lookout Mountain, Georgia. She has her BA from the University of Florida and her MFA from The Pennsylvania State University.

**Allison A. Hutira** teaches at Youngstown State University in Ohio, where she earned her BA and MA. She received her PhD from Kent State University. Popular culture is always incorporated into her undergraduate composition courses; in addition to researching and analyzing the significance of urban legends, she also uses aspects of music, film, advertising, and television. Her favorites include urban legends, Halloween, and the supernatural in American culture, an extension of her interest in Colonial American literature and culture, especially the Salem Witch Trials. Her teaching method uses popular culture to interest students in different aspects of literature, composition, and research by incorporating topics that students are familiar with, such as urban legends or Halloween, and then delving into the literary, historical, and fantastic elements surrounding these topics and their significance to local and American culture.

**Clifton Kaiser** is a full-time high-school English teacher at Battle Ground Academy, an independent K-12 school in Franklin, TN, and an adjunct instructor of English at MTSU. He holds his BA degree in English from the University of Evansville in Indiana and MA degree in English from Purdue University. In his classes he tries to use references to popular culture because the students tend to relate to them better. He strives to link canonical texts with pop culture to show the commonalities between them. As indicated by the subject of his article, he has great interest in using graphic novels in the classroom.

**Claire Lutkewitte** is a graduate assistant working on a PhD in Rhetoric and Composition at Ball State University, where she also teaches first year writing courses. She received her MA at Southern Illinois University, Edwardsville with an emphasis on the teaching of writing. She is also a first year writing instructor at Ivy Tech Community College. Her research interests include first year writing pedagogy, particularly pedagogy that asks students to write and critically think about their pop culture experiences. She is specifically interested in role advertisements play in our daily lives. Therefore, she has recently given a presentation on advertisements titled, "Transformation: The Rhetoric of Advertisements and the Meaning behind Products."

**Robert P. McParland**, PhD, is a composer and performer of music. His books include *Music and Literary Modernism* (2006), *Dickens and Melodrama* (2008), and the forthcoming *Charles Dickens's American Audience*. He has published widely on music and literature, book history, and nineteenth-century studies. Among his recently published essays on popular music and literature are "Jazz in James Baldwin's 'Sonny's Blues'," "The Geography of Bruce Springsteen: American Dreamscapes," and "Yesterday: Memory, Narrative, and The Beatles." He is currently assistant professor of English at Felician College in New Jersey.

**Stephanie Roach** has her PhD in English from the University of Connecticut, where she served as assistant director of freshman English for six years. Currently, Stephanie is writing program director and assistant professor of English at the University of Michigan-Flint. She teaches first-year and upper division writing courses and was awarded the 2006 Dr. Lois Matz Rosen Junior Faculty Excellence in Teaching Award for her work in the classroom. Stephanie researches and writes on issues of writing program administration and writing pedagogy. A subscriber of *Entertainment Weekly* for over 10 years, Stephanie reads each issue in order cover to cover— even when she falls behind a week, there is no skipping ahead. Stephanie is an avid movie fan and watches more television than most people can stand.

**Hillary Robson** is an adjunct faculty member in the departments of English and University Studies and is a full-time academic advisor for undeclared students in the Academic Support Center at MTSU. Her areas of scholastic interest are composition, pedagogy, fandom and fan culture, and popular culture studies. She has published essays in composition texts on using popular culture in the classroom; on composition leaders in the field of composition; and contributed essays on fandom and fan cultures for the television series *Alias, Lost,* and *Veronica Mars*. She is a co-author of the books *Saving the World: A Guide to* Heroes, Lost*'s Buried Treasures,* and *Unlocking* Battlestar Galactica*;* served as research assistant and contributor to *Unlocking the Meaning of* Lost*: An Unauthorized Guide*, and is co-program chair for the upcoming meeting of the Popular Culture and American Culture of the South Conference in 2008.

**Aaron Herschel Shapiro** is a poet, essayist, and teacher currently pursuing his MA in literature at MTSU. Before relocating to Murfreesboro, Aaron performed with the street poetry troupe the Guerrilla Poets and at poetry venues in Boston and New York. His poems have appeared in *The Mangrove Review*, *Speak These Words: A Guerrilla Poets' Anthology*, and *Collage*. He is a recipient of the Michael Hauptman Poetry Prize, a Vermont Studio Center Fellowship, a Paul Muldoon Poetry Fellowship, and the Tennessee Library Association's Freedom of Information Award. A long time pop junkie, Aaron is fascinated by the crossover between poetry and pop culture and has worked to develop workshops and discussion groups for the Murfreesboro community, as well as guest hosting the spoken word radio program *The Slow Education* at WMTS. He is currently writing a study of postmodern advertising tentatively titled: *I Hate Myself and Want a Soda*.

**Allison D. Smith** is professor of English and coordinator of graduate teaching assistants for English at MTSU. A long time ago, in a galaxy far, far away, she graduated from California State University, Long Beach (BA, MA), and the University of Illinois, Urbana-Champaign (PhD). Recent publications include *The Pop Culture Zone: Writing Critically about Popular Culture*, a freshman composition textbook (co-authored with Trixie G. Smith and Stacia Watkins); *COMPbiblio: Leaders and Influences in Composition Theory and Practice* (co-edited with Trixie G. Smith and Karen Wright); and a chapter in *More Ways to Handle the Paper Load: On Paper and Online*. She is also a series editor (with Trixie G. Smith) for the Fountainhead Press X Series for Professional Development. Allison is a fount of useless trivia related to film and television, and the pink (entertainment) and brown (arts and literature) categories in Trivial Pursuit are her favorites.

**Trixie G. Smith** is director of the writing center at Michigan State University, where she teaches courses in writing center theory and practice and works with the Tier II Writing Program (WID). Before arriving at MSU, she worked at MTSU in various positions, including director of the writing center, coordinator of TAs, and advisor for writing minors. Her publications include *COMPbiblio: Leaders and Influences in Composition Theory and Practice* (co-edited with Allison D. Smith and Karen Wright), "Collusion and Collaboration: Concealing Authority in the Writing Center" (co-authored with Brooke Rollins and Evelyn Westbrook) in *(E)Merging Identities: Graduate Students in the Writing Center*, and articles in Research Strategies and Southern Discourse. Her research interests in writing and gender studies often intersect with her love of popular culture. Trixie is addicted to her DVR, movies, and popular literature—not necessarily in that order.

**Laurel Taylor** received a BS in Education from Missouri State University and a MA in English at MTSU. While at MTSU, she taught FYC courses and worked in the University Writing Center as tutor, graduate student administrator, and peer mentor. Since completing her MA, she has been working in the high school setting, teaching freshman and sophomore English. She became interested in popular culture while developing her thesis entitled "'Beyond the Water and the Melody': Using Music and Song Lyrics to Build Bridges Between Students' Personal and Academic Lives." Since then, she has used music, movies, TV show clips, advertisements, and MySpace to help her students see connections between their daily lives and their writing experiences.

**Keri Mayes Tidwell** is a doctoral student and graduate teaching assistant in the English department at MTSU, where she teaches expository writing and research/argumentative writing. Her research interests are composition and rhetoric studies with an emphasis on second language writing and Old English language and literature. Her personal pop culture interests include *The Office*, *Lost*, and *Heroes* as well as cheesy 80s movies such as *The Goonies*, *Back to the Future*, and *Teen Wolf*.

**Stephanie Vie** is an assistant professor of composition and rhetoric at Fort Lewis College in Durango, Colorado, where she teaches "Monsters, Mayhem, and Machines: Popular Culture and Science Fiction." Her PhD from the University of Arizona is in Rhetoric, Composition, and the Teaching of English, and her dissertation, "Engaging Others in Online Social Networking Sites: Rhetorical Practices in MySpace and Facebook," examined the use of privacy settings in these sites within a Foucauldian framework. Each year, she looks forward to the national PCA/ACA conference, where she has presented in the past on popular culture topics like social networking sites, Japanese anime, and foreign travel. Her current research in popular culture looks at the use of computer and video games in the composition classroom to teach multimodal literacy, and her work on video game studies will be appearing soon in *The Review of Communication* and *Computers and Composition: An International Journal*.

**Jessica Ketcham Weber** is a doctoral candidate in Rhetoric, Writing, and Culture in the English Department of Louisiana State University. Her dissertation research explores new media's impact on activist literacy practices and the pedagogical possibilities of these textual, visual, and performative practices. Jessica also writes about the curricular intersections of media and environmental theory and consumption analysis. She has taught composition courses grounded in feminist theory and popular culture pedagogies, with emphases on media literacy, visual rhetoric, and digital media. She also enjoys teaching courses on representations of environmentalism in popular culture and women, gender, and media representation. Fascinated by both astronomy and philosophy, Jessica is also a diehard fan of *The Twilight Zone*, *The X-Files*, and *Lost*.

**Bronwyn T. Williams** is associate professor of English and director of composition at the University of Louisville. He writes and teaches about issues of literacy, popular culture, and identity. His books include *Tuned In: Television and the Teaching of Writing*, *Identity Papers: Literacy and Power in Higher Education*, and *Popular Culture and Representations of Literacy* (with Amy Zenger). In addition, he has published articles in *College Composition and Communication*, *College English*, and numerous other journals and edited collections. He also writes a regular column on issues of literacy and identity for the *Journal of Adolescent & Adult Literacy*. He is currently studying the intersections of literacy and popular culture in online settings and how such connections are shaping reading, writing, and the performance of identity.

**Karen Wright** holds the MA degree in English with an emphasis in composition and rhetoric from MTSU where she taught first-year composition and served as the assistant director of the University Writing Center. Karen combines her research interests, including technology, composition, and tutoring, by working as an online tutor and developing course themes about humor and art for future composition classes. An avid fan of popular literature, Karen's favorite television shows include *The Colbert Report*, *The Daily Show with Jon Stewart*, and *Battlestar Galactica*, and she is addicted to The Food Network. Karen has incorporated various aspects of popular culture in each of her classes with great success. Her dream project would be a Food

Network show held in the green room of *The Colbert Report* in which Karen offers tasty snacks to the guests while discussing the grammatically correct way to serve dinner to a Cylon.

# For Further Reading

*Adbusters.* 28 Apr. 2008 <http://www.adbusters.org>.

*Advertising Age.* 28 Apr. 2008. 28 Apr. 2008 <http://www.adage.com>.

*The* Advertising Age *Encyclopedia of Advertising*. Ed. John McDonough and Karen Egolf. New York: Fitzroy Dearborn, 2003.

*AFI.com*. 2008. American Film Institute. 29 Apr. 2008 <http://www.afi.com>.

Alexander, Jonathan. *Digital Youth: Emerging Literacies on the World Wide Web*. Cresskill, NJ: Hampton, 2006.

*Alfred Hitchcock: Centenary Essays*. Ed. Richard Allen and S. Ishii-Gonzalès. London: BFI, 1999.

Allen, Robert C., and Annette Hill, eds. *The Television Studies Reader*. London: Routledge, 2004.

Alvermann, Donna E., Jennifer S. Moon, and Margaret C. Hagood. *Popular Culture in the Classroom: Teaching and Researching Critical Media Literacy*. Chicago: National Reading Conference, 1999.

Atwan, Robert, Donald McQuade, and John W. Wright. *Edsels, Luckies, and Frigidaires: Advertising the American Way*. New York: Dell, 1979.

Azerrad, Michael. *Our Band Could Be Your Life: Scenes from the American Indie Underground 1981– 1991*. London: Little, 2001.

Barnet, Sylvan. *A Short Guide to Writing about Art*. 7th ed. New York: Longman, 2003.

Beacham, Sally, and Lori J. Davis. *Digital Scrapbooking*. Boston: Course Technology PTR, 2004.

Bear, John. *The #1 New York Times Bestseller: Intriguing Facts about the 484 Books That Have Been #1 New York Times Bestsellers Since the First List in 1942*. Berkeley, CA: Ten Speed, 1992.

Belton, John, ed. *Movies and Mass Culture.* New Brunswick, NJ: Rutgers UP, 1996.

Berlin, James, and Michael Vivion. *Cultural Studies in the English Classroom.* Portsmouth, NH: Boynton/Cook, 1992.

Best Travel Writing.com. 2007. 19 Feb. 2008 <http://www.besttravelwriting.com/>.

*BFI.org*. 2008. British Film Institute. 29 Apr. 2008 <http://www.bfi.org.uk/>.

*Billboard.com*. 29 Apr. 2008. *Billboard*. 29 Apr. 2008 <http://www.billboard.com>.

*The Blues Foundation*. 2008. 29 Apr. 2008 <http://www.blues.org>.

Bogle, Donald. *Blacks in American Films and Television: An Encyclopedia.* New York: Garland, 1988.

Boorstin, Daniel. *The Image: A Guide to Pseudo-Events in America.* 1961. New York: Vintage, 1992.

Bright, Brenda Jo, and Liza Bakewell, eds. *Looking High and Low: Art and Cultural Identity.* Tucson: U of Arizona P, 1995.

Browne, Ray B., ed. *Mission Underway: The History of the Popular Culture Association/American Culture Association and the Popular Culture Movement, 1967–2001.* Bowling Green, OH: PCA/APA, 2002.

---. *Profiles of Popular Culture: A Reader*. Madison, WI: U of Wisconsin Popular P, 2005.

Browning, Dominique, ed. *House of Worship: Sacred Spaces in America*. New York: Assouline, 2006.

Brunvand, Jan Harold. *The Study of American Folklore: An Introduction*. New York: Norton, 1998.

Buckingham, David. *Media Education: Literacy, Learning, and Contemporary Culture*. Cambridge: Polity, 2003.

Bulman, Robert C. *Hollywood Goes to High School: Cinema, Schools, and American Culture*. New York: Worth, 2005.

Butler, Jeremy G. *Television: Critical Methods and Applications*. Mahwah, NJ: Routledge, 2006.

Calmes, Anne M., ed. *Community Association Leadership: A Guide for Volunteers*. Alexandria, VA: CAI, 1997.

Carr, Jay. *The A List: The National Society of Film Critics' 100 Essential Films.* New York: Da Capo, 2002.

Carter, James Bucky, ed. *Building Literacy Connections with Graphic Novels: Page by Page, Panel by Panel*. Urbana, IL: NCTE, 2007.

Caudron, Shari. *Who Are You People? A Personal Journey into the Heart of Fanatical Passion in America.*
Fort Lee, NJ: Barricade: 2006.

Cawelti, John. *Adventure, Mystery, and Romance: Formula Stories as Art and Popular Culture.*
Chicago: U of Chicago P, 1976.

*Cinema-(to)-Graphy: Film and Writing in Contemporary Composition Courses.* Ed. Ellen Bishop.
Portsmouth, NH: Boynton/Cook, 1999.

Clover, Carol J. *Men, Women, and Chain Saws: Gender in the Modern Horror Film.* Princeton: Princeton
UP, 1992.

*CLWG: The Children's Literature Web Guide.* University of Calgary. 15 Apr. 2008
<http://www.ucalgary.ca/~dKbrown/>.

Corrigan, Timothy. *A Short Guide to Writing about Film.* 5th ed. New York: Pearson, 2004.

Costanzo, William V. *Great Films and How to Teach Them.* Urbana, IL: NCTE, 2004.

---. *Reading the Movies: Twelve Great Films on Video and How to Teach Them.* Urbana, IL: NCTE, 1992.

Counihan, Carole, and Penny Van Esterik, eds. *Food and Culture: A Reader.* New York: Routledge, 1997.

*Country Music Hall of Fame.* 29 Apr. 2008. Country Music Hall of Fame and Museum: Nashville. 29 Apr.
2008 <http://www.countrymusichalloffame.com>.

Cronin, Anne M. *Advertising Myths: The Strange Half-Lives of Images and Commodities.* London:
Routledge, 2004.

Crusie, Jennifer, ed. *Flirting with Pride & Prejudice: Fresh Perspectives on the Original Chick-Lit
Masterpiece.* Dallas: Benbella, 2005.

---. Smart Pop Series. Dallas: Benbella.

Dethier, Brock. *From Dylan to Donne: Bridging English and Music.* Portsmouth, NH: Boynton/Cook,
2003.

Dick, Bernard F. *Anatomy of Film.* 5th ed. Boston: Bedford/St. Martin's, 2005.

Dines, Gail, and Jean M. Humez, eds. *Gender, Race, and Class in Media: A Text-Reader.* 2nd ed. Thousand
Oaks, CA: Sage, 2002.

Dunne, Michael. *Metapop: Self-Referentiality in Contemporary American Popular Culture.*
Jackson: UP of Mississippi, 1992.

Edgerton, Gary R., and Brian G. Rose, eds. *Thinking Outside the Box: A Contemporary Television Genre
Reader.* Lexington, KY: UP of Kentucky, 2005.

Ellis, Jack C., and Virginia Wright Wexman. *A History of Film.* 5th ed. Boston: Allyn, 2002.

*Emmys.org.* 2008. Academy of Television Arts and Sciences. 29 Apr. 2008 <http://emmys.org>.

*Encyclopedia of Major Marketing Campaigns.* Ed. Thomas Riggs. Detroit: Gale, 2000.

*Entertainment Weekly.* 2008. 29 Apr. 2008 <http://www.ew.com>.

Escott, Collin. *Good Rockin' Tonight: Sun Records and the Birth of Rock 'n' Roll.* New York: St. Martin's,
1992.

*ESPN.com.* 2008. 29 Apr. 2008 <http://espn.go.com>.

Ewen, Stuart. *All Consuming Images: The Politics of Style in Contemporary Culture.* New
York: Basic, 1988.

Fiske, John. *Television Culture.* London: Routledge, 1987.

---. *Understanding Popular Culture.* Boston: Unwin Hyman, 1989.

*Film Analysis: A Norton Reader.* Ed. Jeffrey Geiger and R. L. Rutsky. New York: Norton, 2005.

*FlowTV: A Critical Forum on Television and Media Culture.* 2008. 29 Apr. 2008 <http://flowtv.org>.

Freccero, Carla. *Popular Culture: An Introduction.* New York: New York UP, 1999.

Gabler, Neil. *Life the Movie: How Entertainment Conquered Reality.* New York: Knopf, 1998.

*Game Studies: The International Journal of Computer Game Research.* 2007. 28 Apr. 2008
<http://gamestudies.org/>.

Gee, James Paul. *What Video Games Have to Teach Us about Learning and Literacy.* Rev. ed. New York:
Palgrave Macmillan, 2007.

Gelder, Ken. *Popular Fiction: The Logics and Practices of a Literary Field.* New York: Routledge, 2005.

George, Diana, and John Trimbur. "Cultural Studies and Composition." *A Guide to Composition Pedagogies*. Eds. Gary Tate, Amy Rupiper, and Kurt Schick. New York: Oxford, 2001. 71-91.

---. *Reading Culture: Contexts for Critical Reading and Writing*. New York: Pearson, 2007.

Giroux, Henry A. *Disturbing Pleasures: Learning Popular Culture*. New York: Routledge, 1994.

Golden, John. *Reading in the Dark: Using Film as a Tool in the English Classroom*. Urbana, IL: NCTE, 2001.

*Grammy.com*. 2008. The Recording Academy. 29 Apr. 2008 <http://www.grammy.com>.

Gray, Herman. *Watching Race: Television and the Struggle for "Blackness."* Minneapolis: U of Minnesota P, 1995.

Gray, Jonathan, and Cornel Sandvoss. *Fandom: Identities and Communities in a Mediated World*. New York: New York UP, 2007.

Hague, Angela, and David Lavery, eds. *Teleparody: Predicting/Preventing the TV Discourse of Tomorrow*. New York: Wallflower, 2002.

Halberstam, David, ed. *The Best American Sports Writing of the Century*. Boston: Houghton, 1999.

Harris, Joseph, Jay Rosen, and Gary Calpas. *Media Journal: Reading and Writing about Popular Culture*. 2nd ed. New York: Longman, 1998.

Hebdige, Dick. *Subculture: The Meaning of Style*. New York: Routledge, 1979.

Hellekson, Karen, and Kristina Busse. *Fan Fiction and Fan Communities in the Age of the Internet*. Jefferson, NC: McFarland, 2006.

Hills, Matt. *Fan Cultures*. London: Routledge, 2002.

Hyde, Stuart. *Idea to Script: Storytelling for Today's Media*. Boston: Allyn, 2003.

*Internet Movie Database (IMDb)*. 2008. 29 Apr. 2008 <http://www.imdb.com>.

Kilbourne, Jean. *Killing Us Softly* (1, 2, and 3). Video Series. Northampton, MA: Media Education Foundation, 1979, 1987, 2000.

Jackson, Blair. *Garcia: An American Life*. Boston: Penguin, 2000.

Jenkins, Henry. *Convergence Culture: Where Old and New Media Collide*. New York: New York UP, 2006.

---. *Fans, Bloggers, and Gamers: Media Consumers in a Digital Age*. New York: New York UP, 2006.

---. *Textual Poachers: Television Fans and Participatory Culture*. New York: Routledge, 1992.

Johnson, Steven. *Everything Bad Is Good for You: How Today's Popular Culture Is Actually Making Us Smarter*. New York: Penguin, 2005.

Jones, Gerard. *Killing Monsters: Why Children Need Fantasy, Super Heroes, and Make-Believe Violence*. New York: Basic, 2002.

Joyrich, Lynne. *Re-Viewing Reception: Television, Gender, and Postmodern Culture*. Bloomington: Indiana UP, 1996.

*The Journal of Popular Culture*. 2008. PCA. 29 Apr. 2008 <http://www.blackwellpublishing.com/journal.asp?ref=0022-3840>.

*Journal of Popular Film & Television*. 2008. 29 Apr. 2008 <http://www.heldref.org/jpft.php>.

Kaplan, E. Ann. *Rocking Around the Clock: Music Television, Postmodernism, and Consumer Culture*. New York: Methuen, 1987.

Kaveney, Roz. *Teen Dreams: Reading Teen Films and Television from* Heathers *to* Veronica Mars. London: I. B. Tauris, 2006.

King, Stephen. *On Writing*. New York: Pocket, 2002.

Korda, Michael. *Making the List: A Cultural History of the American Bestseller, 1990–1999*. New York: Barnes and Noble, 2001.

Krueger, Ellen, and Mary T. Christel. *Seeing & Believing: How to Teach Media Literacy in the English Classroom*. Portsmouth, NH: Boynton/Cook Heinemann, 2001.

Lamott, Anne. *Bird by Bird: Some Instructions on Writing and Life*. New York: Anchor, 1995.

Lavery, David, ed. *This Thing of Ours: Investigating* The Sopranos. New York: Columbia UP, 2002.

Lee, Kylie. "My Life as an *Enterprise* Slash Writer." *Youth Subcultures: Exploring Underground America.* Ed. Arielle Greenberg. New York: Pearson/Longman, 2007. 86-97.

*Left Margins: Cultural Studies and Composition Pedagogy.* Ed. Karen Fitts and Alan W. France. Albany: State U of New York P, 1995.

*Lonely Planet Guide to Travel Writing.* Los Angeles: Lonely Planet, 2005.

Low, Setha M., and Denise Lawrence-Zuaniga. *The Anthropology of Space and Place: Locating Culture.* Boston: Blackwell, 2003.

MacDonald, Ian. *Revolution in the Head: The Beatles' Records and the Sixties.* New York: Holt, 1995.

Mandell, Judy. *Magazine Editors Talk to Writers.* Hoboken, NJ: John Wiley, 1996.

Marc, David. *Comic Visions: Television Comedy and American Culture.* Malden, MA: Blackwell, 1997.

Markowitz, Robin. *Cultural Studies Central.* 28 Apr. 2008 <http://www.culturalstudies.net/ index.html>.

Mast, Gerald, and Bruce F. Kawin. *A Short History of the Movies.* 8th ed. New York: Longman, 2003.

Mazzarella, Sharon R. *Girl Wide Web: Girls, the Internet, and the Negotiation of Identity.* New York: Peter Lang, 2005.

McAllister, Matthew, Ian Gordon, and Mark Jancovich. "Blockbuster Meets Superhero Comic, or Art House Meets Graphic Novel?: The Contradictory Relationship Between Film and Comic Art." *Journal of Popular Film & Television* 34 (2006): 108-15.

McHugh, Patrick. "Is Student Resistance Futile? Teaching Popular Culture in Composition Classes." *Journal for the Psychoanalysis of Culture and Society* 6.2 (2001) 305.

McLuhan, Marshall, and Quentin Fiore. *The Medium Is the Message: An Inventory of Effects.* 1967. New York: Genko, 2005.

McNeil, Alex. *Total Television: The Comprehensive Guide to Programming from 1948 to the Present.* 4th ed. New York: Penguin, 1996.

McNeil, Legs. *Please Kill Me: The Uncensored Oral History of Punk.* London: Grove, 2006.

*mental_floss* 29 Apr. 2008. 29 Apr. 2008 <http://mentalfloss.com>.

Miller, Toby, ed. *Television Studies.* London: BFI, 2002.

Milner, Murray, Jr. *Freaks, Geeks, and Cool Kids: American Teenagers, Schools, and the Culture of Consumption.* New York: Routledge, 2006.

Modleski, Tania. *Loving with a Vengeance: Mass Produced Fantasies for Women.* Archon, 1982.

---. *Studies in Entertainment: Critical Approaches to Mass Culture.* Bloomington: Indiana UP, 1986.

Morrell, Ernest. *Linking Literacy and Popular Culture: Finding Connections for Lifelong Learning.* Norwood, MA: Chrisopher-Gordon, 2004.

Moscowitz, John E. *Critical Approaches to Writing about Film.* 2nd ed. Pearson, 2006.

Mukerji, Chandra, and Michael Schudson, eds. *Rethinking Popular Culture: Contemporary Perspectives in Cultural Studies.* Berkeley: U of California P, 1991.

Muller, Gilbert H., and John A. Williams. *Ways In: Approaches to Reading and Writing about Literature and Film.* 2nd ed. Boston: McGraw, 2003.

*Museum of Broadcast Communications (MBC).* 2008. 29 Apr. 2008 <http//www.museum.tv>.

*The NCAA News.* 29 Apr. 2008. National Collegiate Athletic Association (NCAA). 29 Apr. 2008 <http://www.ncaa.org>.

Nye, Russel. *The Unembarrassed Muse: The Popular Arts in America.* New York: Dial, 1970.

Palmer, Robert. *Deep Blues: A Musical and Cultural History of the Mississippi Delta.* New York: Penguin, 1982.

Penrod, Diane, ed. *Miss Grundy Doesn't Teach Here Anymore: Popular Culture and the Composition Classroom.* Portsmouth, NH: Boynton/Cook, 1997.

Phinney, Kevin. *Souled American: How Black Music Transformed White Culture.* New York: Billboard, 2005.

*Popular Culture: A Reader.* Ed. Raiford Guins and Omayra Zaragoza Cruz. London: Sage, 2005.

*Popular Culture Association/American Culture Association (PCA/ACA).* 2008. 29 Apr. 2008 <http://pcaaca.org>.

*Popular Culture: Opposing Viewpoints.* Ed. John Woodward. Detroit: Greenhaven, 2005.

Pratt, Mary Louise. "Arts of the Contact Zone." *Profession* (1991): 33-40.

Radner, Hilary. *Shopping Around: Feminine Culture and the Pursuit of Pleasure.* New York: Routledge, 1995.

*Rock and Roll Hall of Fame + Museum.* 2008. The Rock and Roll Hall of Fame and Museum. 29 Apr. 2008 <http://rockhall.com>.

*Rolling Stone.com.* 2008. *Rolling Stone.* 29 Apr. 2008 <http://www.rollingstone.com>.

Rosen, Wendy. *Crafting as a Business.* New York: Sterling, 1998.

*Rotten Tomatoes.* 2008. 29 Apr. 2008 <http://www.rottentomatoes.com>.

*Salon.com.* 29 Apr. 2008. *Salon.* 29 Apr. 2008 <http://www.salon.com>.

Sauls, Samuel J. *The Culture of American College Radio.* Ames, IA: Iowa State UP, 2000.

*Saving the World: A Guide to* Heroes. Ed. Lynnette Porter, David Lavery, and Hillary Robson. Toronto: ECW, 2007.

Selfe, Cynthia L., and Gail E. Hawisher, eds. *Gaming Lives in the Twenty-First Century: Literate Connections.* New York: Palgrave Macmillan, 2007.

Simon, Richard Keller. *Trash Culture: Popular Culture and the Great Tradition.* Berkeley: U of California P, 1999.

Simon, Ron, Robert J. Thompson, Louise Spence, and Jane Feuer. *Worlds Without End: The Art and History of the Soap Opera.* New York: Abrams, 1997.

Simpson, Paul, Helen Rodiss, and Michaela Bushell. *The Rough Guide to Cult Movies.* 2nd edition. London: Rough Guide, 2004.

---. *The Rough Guide to Superheroes.* London: Rough Guide, 2004.

*Slate.com.* 29 Apr. 2008. *Slate.* 29 Apr. 2008 <http://www.slate.com>.

Smith, Richard D. *Can't You Hear Me Callin': The Life of Bill Monroe, Father of Bluegrass.* London: Little, 2000.

*Soundtrack.net: The Art of Film and Television Music.* Ed. David A. Koran. 29 Apr. 2008. 29 Apr. 2008 <http://www.soundtrack.net>.

Spigel, Lynn. *Make Room for TV: Television and the Family Ideal in Postwar America.* Chicago: U of Chicago P, 1992.

*Sports Illustrated.com.* 2008. *Sports Illustrated.* 29 Apr. 2008 <http://sportsillustrated.cnn.com/>.

Stark, Steven D. *Glued to the Set: The 60 Television Shows and Events That Made Us Who We Are Today.* New York: Free, 1997.

Stewart, Jon, Ben Karlin, and David Javerbaum. *America (The Book): A Citizen's Guide to Democracy Inaction.* New York: Warner, 2004.

Stoller, Debbie. *Stitch 'N Bitch: The Knitter's Handbook.* New York: Workman, 2004.

Storey, John. *An Introduction to Cultural Theory and Popular Culture.* Athens: U of Georgia P, 1998.

---. *Inventing Popular Culture.* Malden, MA: Blackwell, 2003.

*Television: The Critical View.* 7th ed. Ed. Horace Newcomb. New York: Oxford UP, 2007.

Thorburn, David, and Henry Jenkins, eds. *Rethinking Media Change: The Aesthetics of Transition.* Cambridge: MIT, 2003.

Unterberger, Richie. *Music USA: The Rough Guide.* London: Rough Guides, 1999.

Walker, Nancy. *Shaping Our Mothers' World: American Women's Magazines.* Studies in Popular Culture. Jackson: UP of Mississippi, 2000.

Weaver, John A. *Popular Culture: A Primer.* New York: Peter Lang, 2005.

Werner, Craig. *A Change Is Gonna Come: Music, Race, and the Soul of America.* New York: Penguin, 1999.

Williams, Bronwyn T. *Tuned In: Television and the Teaching of Writing.* Portsmouth, NH: Boynton/Cook, 2002.

Williams, Bronwyn T., and Amy Zenger. *Popular Culture and Representations of Literacy.* London: Routledge, 2007.

Wilstein, Steve. *Associated Press Sports Writing Handbook*. London: Schaum, 2001.

*The Wired Campus*. *The Chronicle of Higher Education*. 20 Mar. 2008 <http://chronicle.com/wiredcampus/>.

Wolf, Naomi. *The Beauty Myth: How Images of Beauty Are Used Against Women*. New York: Anchor, 1992.

Wolff, Janice. *Professing in the Contact Zone: Bringing Theory and Practice Together*. Urbana, IL: NCTE, 2002.

Zachary, Lois J. *Creating a Mentoring Culture: An Organization's Guide*. San Francisco: Jossey-Bass, 2005.

Zook, Kristal Brent. *The Fox Network and the Revolution in Black Television*. New York: Oxford UP, 1999.